ADVENTURES iN SCRiPTURE
FOR KiDS
SERiES COLLECTiON

6 Engaging Books on Fruit of the Spirit, Armor of God, Bible Heroes, and Jesus' Life —Building a Strong, Faith-Filled Foundation for Your Child

Lorie Eubank

GTO PUBLISHING

Contents

Adventures in Scripture for Kids: Exploring The Great Men of the Bible

Adventures in Scripture for Kids: Exploring The Great Women of the Bible

Adventures in Scripture for Kids: Exploring the Fruit of the Spirit

Lorie Eubank

Dedication

To my children, Thadyn, Geordyn, and Oslyne thank you for your support and encouragement while I worked on this series. I couldn't have done it without you. I am so honored to be your mom and walk this life journey with you.

To my Sunday school students, especially those who were with me in the early days of 2002 when I began my journey teaching and helping in the Children's Ministry. Jonathan, there will never be a time that I don't think of you when discussing the Red Sea. Aaron, Sean, Tiffany, Lauren, Joshua, Wesley, Emily, Jack, Luke, Bryant, Sharon and Shirley, and so many more of you, thank you for inspiring me to learn more and grow in a deeper relationship with the Lord so that I could be a better teacher.

To all of those children who grew with me through the years to love the Lord, I pray the seeds sown in the classes will continue to grow and bear fruit in your lives. May your children walk in the fellowship and relationship with the Lord and be a light just as you have been.

Setting Off on a Fruitful Adventure

Greetings, young adventurers!

You might wonder where we're heading as we begin this new journey. No, it's not a trek through a dense forest or a hike up the steepest mountain. This is a unique adventure that focuses on developing heart character and exploring the treasures that exist within us. These treasures, called the Fruit of the Spirit, are wonderful qualities we can all nurture and grow.

What are the Fruit of the Spirit?

Perhaps you've heard of them, or maybe they're entirely new to you. Either way, you're in for a treat! The Fruit of the Spirit isn't like the fruit we eat—apples, oranges, or bananas. Instead, they're like inner qualities or virtues that we can cultivate in our lives.

They are:

1. Love

2. Joy

3. Peace

4. Patience

5. Kindness

6. Goodness

7. Faithfulness

8. Gentleness

9. Self-control

Each of these is like a badge of honor, a sign that we are growing and becoming better people. They are mentioned in the Bible, in Galatians, where the Apostle Paul lists these nine virtues to guide and inspire us.

Why are they important?

Now, think about a garden for a moment. Imagine it filled with blooming flowers, tall trees, and fluttering butterflies. But if the gardener doesn't tend to the plants or water them regularly, they might wither away. Similarly, our hearts are like that garden, and the Fruit of the Spirit are the vibrant flowers and trees within. When we nurture and care for these virtues, our lives become more fulfilling, more joyful, and more harmonious.

But why, you ask? Why are these nine virtues so crucial?

For starters, they shape our character. Character is like our identity, the very essence of who we are. The more we embrace and practice these virtues, the more we become individuals others look up to and admire.

For instance, when we practice patience, we learn to wait our turn, to listen more than we speak, and to understand others. We spread warmth and light with kindness, making someone's day brighter. Joy allows us to celebrate the little things in life, and love lets us care for others deeply.

How they help us in our daily lives

In our everyday life, we encounter numerous challenges, from difficult math problems to disagreements with friends. Sometimes, things don't go as planned, and we feel upset or frustrated. It's natural. But this is where the Fruit of the Spirit can come to our aid!

1. **Love**: When we act with love, we show others we care about their feelings. This means listening to them, supporting them, and being there when they need us.

2. **Joy**: Life is filled with ups and downs, but by embracing joy, we can find happiness in the smallest of things, like a beautiful sunset or a kind gesture from a friend.

3. **Peace**: In moments of chaos or disagreement, seeking peace helps us calm down, think clearly, and find solutions without getting upset.

4. **Patience**: Whether waiting for our turn in a game or trying to understand a tricky subject in school, patience reminds us that everything has its time.

5. **Kindness**: A simple act of kindness, like sharing our toys or helping someone, can brighten someone's day and make us feel good too.

6. **Goodness**: By choosing to do what's right, even when no one is watching, we develop integrity.

7. **Faithfulness**: Sticking to our promises, honoring our word when we say we will do something, and being reliable makes us trustworthy.

8. **Gentleness**: Instead of getting angry or raising our voices, gentleness teaches us to handle situations softly and kindly.

9. **Self-control**: From not eating all the cookies at once to staying calm when we're upset, self-control guides us to make balanced decisions.

By understanding and practicing the Fruit of the Spirit, our daily life becomes smoother. We can handle challenges better, build stronger friendships, and, most importantly, grow internally, becoming wiser and more understanding with each passing day.

So, are you ready to take a leap of faith into this journey? As we explore each fruit in the chapters ahead, we'll discover stories, examples, and fun activities to help you understand and nurture these virtues in your life. It promises to be a rewarding expedition where we learn, grow, and change for the better together.

Let's set off on this fruitful adventure and explore the treasures that lie within our hearts!

Love

"And now these three remain: faith, hope, and love. But the greatest of these is love." - 1 Corinthians 13:13

Discovering Love

What is love? It's a simple word, but it holds so much power. Love isn't just a feeling; it's an action, a decision, and a way of living. Love is when Mom or Dad tucks you into bed at night with a sweet story or your sibling shares their favorite toy with you. It's the warmth you feel when surrounded by your family and friends, laughing, playing, and making memories together.

What does love look and feel like?

Imagine a warm, comforting blanket wrapped around you on a chilly day. That's love. It's the feeling you get when Grandma bakes your favorite cookies just because she knows they make you smile. Love is in the tiny moments, like a smile from a friend, a hug from Mom, or a high-five from Dad after you've done something amazing. Love can be seen in the way your teacher patiently explains something until you understand or when a friend helps you when you're feeling down.

Bible stories about love

The Bible is filled with stories that shine a light on love in its purest form. Remember the story of Ruth and Naomi? Ruth's unwavering love for her mother-in-law, Naomi, is a beautiful example of dedication and loyalty.

Ruth and Naomi: Ruth's determination to stay with Naomi, her mother-in-law, after the death of her husband is a picture of steadfast love. She told Naomi, "Where you go, I will go; where you stay, I will stay." (Ruth 1:16)

Another powerful story is of David and Jonathan, whose friendship was so strong that they were like brothers. Their bond showed that love could be found not only in family ties but also in profound friendships.

David and Jonathan: Their friendship transcended family ties, politics, and even threats to David's life. It's said in the scriptures, "Jonathan loved David as he loved himself." (1 Samuel 18:3)

My personal favorite, probably because it was the first scripture I ever learned, was the love God had for each of us. No matter who you are or what mistake you have made, God loves you.

God gave His Son: Perhaps the most profound expression of love is noted in John 3:16-17 (NLT), "For God so loved the world that He gave His one and only Son, that whoever believes in him shall not perish but have eternal life. God sent his Son into the world not to condemn the world, but to save the world through him." This embodies the essence of sacrificial love.

How Jesus showed love

Jesus is the ultimate example of love. He healed the sick, fed the hungry, and spent time with those society had cast aside. He welcomed children, taught lessons of kindness, and even washed the feet of His disciples. But His most significant act of love is laying down His life for all of us so we might have eternal life. Jesus once said, *"Greater love has no one than this: to lay down one's life for one's friends."* And He did exactly that for us.

Jesus's life is a testament to unwavering love. Here are some of the ways He showed His great love:

1. **Healing the Sick:** Jesus did not differentiate based on status. Whether it was a leper or a leader's daughter, He showed love by healing them.

2. **Feeding Thousands:** With just five loaves and two fishes, Jesus fed a crowd of five thousand, showing love and compassion for the hungry masses.

3. **Embracing Children:** When the disciples tried to shoo away mothers bringing their children for blessings, Jesus said, "Let the little children come to me, and do not hinder them." (Matthew 19:14)

4. **The Last Supper:** In one of His final acts before His

crucifixion, Jesus washed the feet of His disciples, a task typically reserved for servants. This humble act was a demonstration of servant leadership and profound love. He was living out the example that He wanted them to follow, not the washing of feet, but the act of serving others.

5. **Sacrifice on the Cross:** Jesus's crucifixion is the ultimate act or example of His love. By sacrificing Himself, He paved the way for humanity's salvation. No other sacrifice would ever be required to atone or forgive sin. He was the perfect Lamb, provided by God to forgive us of our sins forever. All we have to do now is ASK God to forgive us of our sins, and He is faithful to forgive us.

Other Expressions of Love

Love isn't limited to serious moments; it's also in play! Think about the times you are playing with your friends. Sharing toys, taking turns, and being there for one another all stem from love. When you create games that everyone can enjoy or make sure no one feels left out, you're showcasing love in the purest childlike manner.

Here are three ways you can show love to one another, drawing inspiration from the way Jesus shows love:

1. **Unconditional Acceptance and Kindness**

- **What Jesus Did:** Jesus associated with and showed kindness to people society rejected or looked down upon, such as tax collectors, lepers, and sinners. He taught that everyone deserves love and understanding.

- **What You Can Do:** You can demonstrate this type of love by being inclusive and welcoming to all peers, regardless of their differences or backgrounds. For instance, if you notice a classmate sitting alone during lunchtime, you might invite that classmate to join your group, ensuring no one feels left out or isolated.

2. Forgiveness and Reconciliation

- **What Jesus Did:** Jesus emphasized the importance of forgiveness on multiple occasions. One of the most powerful examples is when He forgave those who crucified Him, saying, "Father, forgive them, for they do not know what they are doing" (Luke 23:34).

- **What You Can Do:** If another child inadvertently hurts you, whether through words or actions, you can choose to forgive, emphasizing the importance of your relationship over holding onto grudges. For instance, if two friends disagree about a toy, rather than holding a grudge, one could say, "It's okay, I forgive you. Let's find a way to share."

3. Selfless Service and Generosity

- **What Jesus Did:** Jesus washed the feet of His disciples (John 13:1-17), an act of humble service, signifying that no task is beneath us when done out of love for others.

- **What You Can Do:** You can put others' needs ahead of your own. For example, if you see a peer struggling with their homework or an art project, you might offer help or share your materials. Another instance might be when someone willingly gives up their turn on the swing so another child can have a chance to enjoy it.

Following these examples not only helps you grow stronger bonds of friendship but also lays the foundation for cultivating Christ-like love as you grow.

Fun activities: making love-filled crafts

Craft time can be a fun way to express love. Think about the joy of creating a handmade card for Mom on Mother's Day or a special drawing for Dad's office. Every stroke of the brush, every color you choose, and every glittery sticker you add is an expression of your love. These crafts are special because they come straight from the heart.

Another delightful activity is creating a "Love Jar." You only need an empty jar, some colored paper, and pens. Write down little notes of things you love about your family members, fold them, and place them in the jar. On days when someone needs a bit of cheering up, they can pull out a note and be reminded of the love surrounding them.

These are just a small example of how you can show love to others. Flip the switch and use your creative imagination to think of a few ways that your love for them might bless others. Sometimes, for a family, it might be as simple as telling them you love them. For a friend, it may just be you playing with them or saying an encouraging word. For others, it could be as simple as recognizing they are there and including them in what you are doing.

Heartwarming moments with family and friends

Recall a time when you felt incredibly loved. Maybe it was your birthday, and everyone came together to celebrate you. Or perhaps it was a quiet moment with your family, watching a movie or reading a book together. Love is present in both grand gestures and silent moments. It's in how your friend listens to you, how your pet curls up beside you, or when your family comes together to celebrate special occasions.

Spreading Love Every Day

Love isn't just a one-time thing; it's a daily choice. Each day presents opportunities to showcase love in all we do.

Small Acts of Love

Simple acts, like helping set the dinner table, holding the door open for someone, or sharing your snack, are ways we can show love daily. It's about putting others before ourselves and making the world a little brighter with our actions.

Loving our pets and toys

Our pets, whether fluffy, scaly, or feathery, bring so much joy to our lives. We can express our love by caring for them, feeding them, playing with them, and giving them cuddles.

Similarly, taking care of our toys, treating them gently, and even occasionally giving them a "spa day" (read: cleaning day) are ways we love the inanimate yet cherished members of our playroom.

Saying kind words to our friends

"Thank you," "You're awesome," "I appreciate you"—words have power. When we use kind words, we're spreading love in the most vocal way. It takes only a moment to compliment a friend or thank someone.

As we venture into the next chapter on the Fruit of Joy, we must remember that Love leads. If we let love lead our every action and decision, we will reflect the love of Christ in all we do. Like love, if we choose Joy, even when we are not happy about everything going on around us, it will help us get through to the other side.

Joy

"Though you have not seen Him, you love Him, and even though you do not see Him now, you believe in Him and are filled with an inexpressible and glorious joy." - 1 Peter 1:8

Finding Joy

Have you ever watched the sunrise, painting the sky with shades of pink and gold, and felt a warm glow inside? Or heard a joke so funny you couldn't stop laughing? That's the feeling of joy. It's more than just being happy because something good happened. Joy is a deep-rooted emotion, like a bubbling spring in our hearts, that can always be present, even during challenging times.

Joy vs. just being happy

Happiness is a wonderful feeling, but it often comes from external events. Maybe you're happy because you got a new toy or because it's your birthday. Joy, on the other hand, goes deeper. It's an inner feeling that doesn't always depend on what's happening around us. While happiness might be like a gentle stream, joy is like a powerful, ever-present ocean wave. You can

have joy even on days when things don't go as planned, reminding you that every cloud has a silver lining.

Bible Stories of Celebration and Joy

The Bible, our guidebook for life, is filled with stories that teach us about joy. These stories teach us that joy can be found in unexpected places and moments.

The Birth of Jesus (Luke 2:1-20): The story of the Birth of Jesus, often referred to as the Nativity begins with Mary and Joseph traveling from Nazareth to Bethlehem due to a decree from Caesar Augustus that required everyone to return to their ancestral towns to be registered. With Bethlehem crowded and accommodations scarce, they found shelter in a stable. There, Mary gave birth to Jesus, wrapping Him in swaddling cloths and laying Him in a manger. This humble beginning contrasts sharply with the significance of Jesus' birth, symbolizing the approachability and humility of Christ coming into the world.

On the night of Jesus' birth, an angel of the Lord appeared to shepherds in the nearby fields, illuminating the darkness with the glory of God. The angel announced the joyous news of the Savior's birth, a message of great joy for all people, indicating that Jesus came not just for the elite or the religious, but for every-one, from the humble shepherds to future generations across the world. Suddenly, a multitude of heavenly hosts joined the angel, praising God and saying, "Glory to God in the highest, and on earth peace, goodwill toward men!" Moved by this divine revelation, the shepherds went to Bethlehem to see the newborn Jesus, confirming the angel's message. They left glorifying and praising God, spreading the word about what they had witnessed. The joy in this story emanates from the fulfillment of ancient prophecies and the incarnation of God's love in human form, offering hope, redemption, and a deep, abiding joy to all humankind.

Paul and Silas in Prison (Acts 16:25-34): The account of Paul and Silas where they find themselves imprisoned in Philippi after being severely beaten for casting a spirit out of a slave girl, leading to a loss of income for her masters. Instead of succumbing to despair, Paul and Silas choose to engage in prayer and sing hymns to God, even in the depths of the night, their bodies wounded and confined in the innermost part of the prison. This act of worship in the face of dire circumstances demonstrates an extraordinary depth of faith and an unshakable joy in their belief in God's sovereignty, regardless of their physical conditions.

Remarkably, their joy and faith set the stage for a miraculous event: a sudden earthquake shakes the prison, opening the doors and loosening the chains that bind the prisoners. This supernatural occurrence catches the attention of the jailer, who, fearing that the prisoners had escaped, was about to take his own life. Paul intervenes, assuring him that all the prisoners were present. This leads to the pivotal moment where the jailer, moved by the integrity and the unwavering faith of Paul and Silas, seeks salvation, asking, "Sirs, what must I do to be saved?" They respond with the simple yet profound truth, "Believe in the Lord Jesus, and you will be saved, you and your household." The story culminates in the jailer washing their wounds and being baptized along with his entire household, rejoicing in his newfound faith.

This story beautifully illustrates how joy, rooted in faith, can transcend the most challenging circumstances, leading not only to personal freedom but also impacting the lives of others. The joy Paul and Silas exhibited in their darkest hour became a powerful testimony, leading to the transformation and salvation of the jailer and his family. It serves as a compelling reminder of the powerful impact that a joyous faith in God can have, capable of bringing light to the darkest places and turning despair into hope.

The Healing of the Lame Man by Peter and John (Acts 3:1-10): Peter and John encounter a man lame from birth at the Beautiful Gate of the temple in Jerusalem, where he was placed daily to beg for alms or money. When he sees Peter and John about to enter the temple, he asks them for money. Instead of offering silver or gold, Peter, filled with the Holy Spirit, offers something far more powerful. He commands the man in the name of Jesus Christ of Nazareth to rise up and walk. Peter then takes the man by the right hand and helps him up. Instantly, the man's feet and ankles become strong, enabling him to stand, walk, and even leap for the first time in his life. The man enters the temple courts with them, walking, jumping, and praising God.

This miraculous healing serves not only as a testament to the power of faith in Jesus Christ but also illustrates the transformative joy that comes with experiencing God's work firsthand. The lame man's joy is spontaneous and unrestrained, drawing the attention of all those present in the temple. His reaction to the miracle—leaping and praising God—captures the essence of joy that cannot be contained. This scene creates a ripple effect among the witnesses, leading to awe and wonder about the power and compassion of God.

The story of the healing of the lame man underscores the theme that true joy and fulfillment come not from material possessions but from the presence and power of God in one's life. The man's leap is not just a physical action but a symbol of the spiritual liberation and joy that comes with faith and healing in Jesus' name. It highlights how the acts of faith by believers can lead to miraculous outcomes, bringing joy not only to the recipients of God's grace but also to the broader community, inspiring faith and praise to God.

As we discussed in the last chapter on Love, God loves us so much that He gave His Son as a final sacrifice so we no longer had to live under judgment or condemnation.   When we repent, God is faithful to forgive. Not only does His forgiveness restore us to Him, but because we are restored to His presence, His Joy becomes our strength to be strong and not sin again. Or at least the Holy Spirit tries to encourage us to make the right choices.

Sharing Joy Daily

Every day presents countless opportunities to experience and spread joy. But what's powerful about the Fruit of Joy is its ability to magnify and reverberate, especially when shared.

The adage "A joy shared is a joy doubled" underscores a fundamental human experience. Emotions, especially positive ones like joy, have a contagious quality. Consider the simple act of smiling at a stranger on the street. While it might seem insignificant to you, it can light up someone else's day, prompting them to carry that warmth forward. This ripple effect can turn a single act of joy into a cascade of happiness, affecting countless individuals.

But why does sharing joy amplify it? Well, humans are inherently social beings. We thrive on connection, understanding, and shared experiences. When we are in a state of joy and choose to share it, we not only validate our own feelings but also invite others to partake in that emotional state. It's like lighting candles – one flame can ignite countless others without diminishing its own brightness.

Walking in the Fruit of Joy also means recognizing that joy isn't just in grand gestures or significant life events. It's in the daily, often overlooked moments. It's in a child's laughter, the aroma of a freshly baked pie, a favorite song playing on the radio, or even the feeling of the sun's rays on a cold day. When we acknowledge these moments and share them – be it through a story, a gesture, or an act of kindness – we create avenues for others to recognize and cherish their joy-filled moments too.

Moreover, sharing joy serves as a reminder that happiness isn't finite. There isn't a set amount of joy in the world that gets depleted with sharing. On the contrary, it's an ever-growing, boundless resource. The more we tap into it and distribute it, the richer and more widespread it becomes. Joy is a choice; you can choose joy to overcome other emotions. It finding something good in the mundane.

So, in the journey of life, as we strive to walk daily in the Fruit of Joy, it's essential to remember its intrinsic communal nature. Our individual joy can become a collective experience, reinforcing connections, building communities, and reminding everyone of the beauty that life holds, one joyful moment at a time.

Something as simple as a smile can spread joy. When you smile at someone, more often than not, they'll smile back. And that simple exchange can brighten someone's day. The same goes for laughter. Sharing a funny story or joke can bring joy to a whole group, making the moment memorable.

Finding joy in simple things

Sometimes, the simplest things can bring the most joy. The fluttering of a butterfly, the aroma of freshly baked cookies, the feel of soft grass beneath your feet—these are all moments of joy waiting to be discovered. Every day is an opportunity to create joy-filled memories. Whether it's a family picnic, a day at the park, or just sitting together reading a book, these moments become treasures of joy that we can revisit time and again.

As we journey through life, let's remember to seek out and spread joy in every corner. Because, in the end, it's these joy-filled days that make our lives truly rich and meaningful. As we continue our journey in learning more about the Fruit of the Spirit, leading with Love, and sharing Joy, take us to walk in Peace.

Peace

*"Peace I leave with you; my peace I give you. I do not give to you as the world gives. Do not let your hearts be troubled and do not be afraid." - *John 14:27

Understanding Peace

What does "peace" mean to you? Some might think of a serene landscape, a calm lake with birds chirping, or maybe a quiet evening with family. Peace isn't just the absence of noise or trouble; it's a deep sense of calm and contentment, regardless of what's happening around us.

What it feels like to be peaceful

Close your eyes for a moment and imagine you're in your favorite place, perhaps a garden or your cozy bed. There's no loud noise, no rush, just you feeling safe and relaxed. That's peace. It's a feeling that everything is alright, even if it's just for that moment. When we're peaceful, our hearts feel light, our thoughts are clear, and we feel secure.

Bible stories about finding calm

The Bible has many stories that teach us about finding calm amidst chaos.

Elijah and the Still Small Voice (1 Kings 19:11-13): It unfolds after Elijah's dramatic victory over the prophets of Baal on Mount Carmel, where he demonstrated the power of the one true God. Following this triumph, Queen Jezebel threatened Elijah's life, driving him into the wilderness, where he fell into despair, even asking God to take his life. God led Elijah to Mount Horeb, also known as Mount Sinai, to seek God's presence.

While on the mountain, Elijah experienced a series of powerful natural events. God instructed him to stand on the mountain as the Lord was about to pass by. A great and strong wind tore through the mountains, shattering rocks, but God was not in the wind. After the wind, there was an earthquake, but God was not in the earthquake. Following the earthquake came a fire, but God was not in the fire. After the fire, there was a gentle whisper, a still small voice, where Elijah found God's presence. In response, Elijah covered his face with his cloak and stood at the cave entrance, ready to listen to God.

This story emphasizes the contrast between God's dramatic manifestations and His quiet, subtle ways of communication. It teaches the importance of seeking God not only in extraordinary events but also in the calm, still moments of life. The "still small voice" symbolizes God's gentle, reassuring presence that guides and comforts us in times of trouble and uncertainty. It reminds us that God's guidance often comes in quiet, unexpected ways, encouraging us to listen attentively for His direction amidst the noise and distractions of life. In listening and waiting on God, He will fill you with His peace.

Daniel in the Lion's Den (Daniel 6): Daniel, a devout servant of God, was among the Jewish captives in Babylon. Due to his exceptional wisdom and integrity, Daniel gained favor with King Darius, which led to jealousy among other officials. They conspired against Daniel, manipulating the king into issuing a decree that, for thirty days, no one could pray to any god or human except to the king himself. Daniel, unwavering in his faith, continued to pray openly to God three times a day.

The conspirators reported Daniel to King Darius, who, bound by his own decree, was forced to order Daniel's punishment: being thrown into a den of lions. Despite his anguish, the king hoped Daniel's God would rescue him. The next morning, Darius hurried to the den and was overjoyed to find Daniel unharmed. Daniel declared that God had sent an angel to shut the lions' mouths because he was found innocent in God's sight. Astonished by the miraculous deliverance, King Darius then issued a new decree, proclaiming that all his people should tremble and fear before the God of Daniel, who is the living God, enduring forever.

The story reminds us of the triumph of faith and integrity over deceit and envy. It teaches that unwavering trust in God can lead to His divine protection and deliverance from seemingly unbeatable challenges. Daniel's story is a testament to the power of steadfast faith and the peace that comes from knowing God is always in control, even in the most difficult situations.

Jesus Calms the Storm (Mark 4:35-41): It begins with Jesus suggesting to His disciples that they cross to the other side of the Sea of Galilee. As they sailed, a fierce storm unexpectedly arose, with high winds and waves so intense they began filling the boat with water. Despite the chaos and fear of the disciples, Jesus remained asleep on a cushion in the stern of the ship, undisturbed by the tumult around Him.

Fearing for their lives, the disciples woke Jesus, asking Him if He cared that they were about to perish. Jesus stood up, rebuked the wind, and said to the sea, "Peace! Be still!" The storm immediately ceased, and there was a great calm. He then turned to His disciples and questioned their faith, asking why they were so afraid and if they still had no faith. The disciples were left in awe, marveling at Jesus' power and questioning among themselves who He was, that even the wind and the sea obeyed Him.

This story highlights several important points. Firstly, it demonstrates Jesus' authority over nature, affirming His divine nature and power. Secondly, it addresses the theme of faith, challenging the disciples (and the readers) to trust in Jesus even in the most terrifying circumstances. The calming of the storm serves as a metaphor for the peace Jesus brings amid life's metaphorical storms. It reassures us that, with faith in Jesus, we can find peace and security regardless of the chaos and challenges we might face in the world.

Jesus and peace

Our Savior, Jesus Christ, is often called the "Prince of Peace." Throughout his life, Jesus exemplified what it means to have inner peace. When a furious storm rocked the boat he was in, Jesus remained calm, even asleep, amidst the panic. Upon waking, he commanded the winds and waves to be still, bringing peace to the scared disciples and the turbulent sea.

His teachings, too, emphasize the importance of peace. He taught us to love our enemies, to turn the other cheek, and to live in harmony with everyone. Through His teachings and actions, Jesus showed that true peace comes from trusting God and loving others.

Peaceful Playtime

While peace often feels like quietness, there are many activities and games that can help us understand and cherish this wonderful feeling better.

Relaxing activities and crafts

Crafts have a special way of focusing our energies and helping us find calm. Consider creating a "Peaceful Place" collage: gather magazines, colored papers, and glue. Cut out images that represent peace to you, then stick them on a larger piece of paper. This collage can be a daily reminder of what peace looks like.

Another calming activity is drawing or coloring. There are many coloring books available with intricate designs and patterns. Coloring can be therapeutic, helping our minds focus and relax.

Talking about peaceful moments

Remember the last time you felt completely at peace? Maybe it was after listening to a beautiful song or spending a day with family. Sharing these moments helps us recognize the value of peace in our lives. It's also an opportunity to learn from others about what brings them peace and tranquility.

Keeping Calm Every Day

Every day might not be peaceful, but we can find peace every day. Let's explore some practical ways to maintain calm in our daily lives.

Breathing exercises for kids

Breathing deeply and slowly can be a great way to find calm quickly. Try this exercise:

1. Sit or lie down comfortably.

2. Close your eyes and take a deep breath in through your nose, counting to four.

3. Hold your breath for a count of four.

4. Slowly exhale through your mouth for a count of four.

Repeating this a few times can help clear your mind and calm your heartbeat.

Peaceful bedtime routines

A calm evening can set the stage for a peaceful night. Consider these steps for a tranquil bedtime routine:

1. Dim the lights an hour before sleep.

2. Listen to calming music or read a gentle story.

3. Share with your family one good thing that happened during the day.

4. Say a prayer, thanking God for His protection and asking for a peaceful night.

Handling disagreements with friends

Conflicts can disrupt our peace but are also opportunities to practice maintaining calm. When disagreements arise:

1. Listen to your friend without interrupting.

2. Speak calmly, expressing how you feel.

3. Look for a solution together; remember, disagreements are okay, but arguing is not.

In the end, peace is a gift from God. By understanding it, experiencing it in different ways, and practicing it daily, we can truly appreciate this precious fruit of the Spirit. As we grow, remember to seek peace, share it with others, and treasure those calm skies and quiet nights. As we continue learning more about the Fruit of the Spirit, leading with Love, sharing Joy, walking in Peace, and persevering in Patience.

Patience

"But those who wait on the Lord shall renew their strength; they shall mount up with wings like eagles, they shall run and not be weary, they shall walk and not faint." - Isaiah 40:31

Learning About Patience

When you hear the word "patience," what comes to mind? Perhaps sitting and waiting for your turn at a game or looking at the sky, waiting for the rain to stop so you can play outside. While all these moments require patience, it's more than just waiting. Patience is a quiet strength, a gentle perseverance, and the ability to remain hopeful even when things don't go as planned. It's like patience is a superpower.

Why patience is more than just waiting

So, think about that seed you plant in a garden. Planting it is just the beginning. Once it's in the ground, your job isn't just to sit on a chair and stare at it, hoping it'll turn into a beautiful flower overnight. Nope, that's not how it works!

Instead, you give that little seed some TLC – tender loving care. You make sure it gets a drink of water when it's thirsty. You shield it from those sneaky bugs that might want a nibble. And you always ensure it gets plenty of sunshine.

Now, here's the cool part. While you're doing all these things, you also have this amazing trust deep inside you. Even if you can't see anything happening right away, you believe that one day, that tiny seed will sprout and grow into something beautiful.

That belief and care you put in and the time you wait all mixed together? That's what we call patience. It's not just about waiting; it's about believing, caring, and hoping all at the same time. Remember, great things take time, just like how it takes time for that seed to blossom. So, the next time you're getting a little antsy waiting for something, think about that seed and remember that patience is so much more than just waiting. It's a journey filled with care and hope.

Bible stories of waiting and rewards

Have you ever had to wait for something so long that it felt like forever? Well, some of the heroes in the Bible waited for many, many years, and their stories teach us a thing or two about patience.

Noah Builds the Ark (Genesis 6:9-22; 7-8): The story of Noah and the Ark, found in the book of Genesis, is a powerful narrative of unwavering faith and patience. God, grieved by the wickedness of humanity, decides to cleanse the earth with a great flood. However, Noah finds favor in the eyes of the Lord due to his righteousness amidst a corrupt world. God instructs Noah to build an ark, a massive vessel capable of holding his family and representatives of all animal species. Despite the monumental nature of this task and the absence of any visible sign of a flood (as it had never rained on the earth before), Noah embarks on this daunting project with steadfast obedience and patience.

For approximately 120 years, Noah diligently worked on the ark, enduring what can be imagined as widespread doubt and ridicule from those around him. This period of building is not just a testament to Noah's patience but also his profound trust in God's promise and timing. When the floodwaters finally come, Noah's faith and patience are vindicated. The ark serves as the vessel of salvation for his family and the animal kingdom, preserving life to repopulate the earth post-flood. Noah's story emphasizes the virtues of patience and obedience to God's will, teaching us the value of trusting in God's plan, even when it unfolds over long periods and in ways that might be difficult to understand or accept.

Can you imagine being told to build a gigantic boat, even when there was no sign of rain? Now, here's the kicker: Noah spent *120 years* building that ark and waiting for the flood. That's longer than the oldest person you probably know! But he trusted God, stayed patient, and in the end, he and his family were safe. Plus, as a cherry on top, God gave him a beautiful promise in the sky—a vibrant rainbow.

Abraham and Sarah Await Isaac (Genesis 12-21): When God first called Abram (later named Abraham), He promised not only to make him a great nation but also that through his offspring, all the nations of the earth would be blessed. However, this promise seemed impossible from a human perspective, as Abraham was 75 years old and Sarah was barren. Despite the improbability, Abraham chose to believe in God's promise, a decision credited to him as righteousness.

As years passed, the fulfillment of God's promise seemed increasingly remote. Sarah, growing impatient, offered her maidservant Hagar to Abraham, resulting in the birth of Ishmael. Yet, this was not the fulfillment of God's promise. When Abraham was 99 years old, God reaffirmed His covenant, specifically promising that Sarah would bear a son named Isaac. Sarah, overhearing this, laughed in disbelief due to her and Abraham's advanced age. Despite the laughter, the skepticism, and the decades of waiting, God's promise came to fruition when Sarah bore Isaac, embodying the joy and fulfillment of long-awaited promises.

The story of Abraham and Sarah waiting for Isaac teaches us lessons on the virtue of patience and the importance of faith in God's timing and promises. It demonstrates that even when circumstances seem utterly contrary to the fulfillment of a promise, God's plans are not bound by human limitations or expectations. Abraham's and Sarah's journey from doubt to fulfillment illustrates the transformative power of faith and patience, encouraging believers to trust in God's timing, even when it stretches far beyond our own understanding or expectations.

So, whenever you feel impatient or think that things are taking too long, remember Noah with his ark and Abraham and Sarah with their long-awaited son. Their stories remind us that with trust, patience, and a sprinkle of faith, we're all on a journey to something wonderful. Keep that chin up and keep on waiting; good things are on the horizon!

The benefits of being patient

You know, sometimes waiting can feel like the hardest thing, especially when you're super excited about something. As mentioned before, patience is like having a secret superpower. Here's why:

1. **Growth and Maturity:** Imagine a tiny caterpillar all wrapped up in its cocoon. It doesn't just pop out as a butterfly overnight. It takes time, waiting, and lots of transformation inside that cocoon. Similarly, when we patiently wait, we're also transforming. Those moments when we feel like nothing's happening. We're actually learning, growing, and getting stronger, just like that caterpillar. So, the next time you're waiting for something, think of it as your "cocoon time" - a special time to grow and get ready to spread your wings.

2. **Understanding and Empathy:** Have you ever noticed when someone lets you finish your story, even when you're speaking slowly or searching for words? That's them being patient. And it feels good, right? When

we're patient with others, we show them that we care about how they feel. It helps us really "walk in their shoes" and understand what they're going through. So, by being patient, not only are you being a rockstar listener, but you're also becoming a kinder and more caring friend.

3. **Reduced Stress:** Imagine you're trying to build the tallest tower with your blocks, but it keeps falling. If you rush and get frustrated, it feels stressful, right? But when you take a deep breath, stay patient, and try again calmly, it's way more fun! Being patient helps keep the stormy clouds of stress away, leaving you with a sunny, peaceful day.

So, the next time you find yourself tapping your feet or feeling restless, just remember that patience is your superpower. It helps you grow, understand others, and keep you calm and happy. Keep rocking that patience cape, and watch how it makes you and everyone around you smile!

Being Patient Every Day

In our daily lives, there are countless opportunities to practice patience.

You know, Jesus has this amazing way of showing patience to all of us. Wouldn't it be cool if we could show patience just like Him? Here are three ways you can do just that with your friends:

1. **Wait Your Turn:** You know how sometimes you're so eager to go on the swing or slide during recess? Well, just like Jesus waits for us, even when we take a little while to understand things, you can do the same. Next time you're at the playground, and everyone wants a turn, try saying, "Hey, you can go first. I'll wait." Trust me, waiting can be a game-changer and makes playtime fun for everyone.

2. **Listen Up:** Jesus is the best listener ever. He hears all our stories, big or small. So, when one of your friends is super excited to share something with you, give them your full attention. Even if their story is long or they're taking time to find the right words, stay with them. Show them you care by nodding, asking questions, or just being there. It's like giving them a mini-hug with your ears!

3. **Lend a Hand:** You're smart and super talented! But sometimes, just like all of us, your friends might need a bit of help. Jesus is always there to guide us, and you can do the same for your buddies. If you see someone stuck on a math problem or confused about something in class, offer to help. You could say, "Wanna see how I figured it out?" By sharing what you know, you're not just being patient, but you're also being a rockstar friend. (however, this would not be appropriate when

you are taking a test! ;o})

Remember, every time you show patience, it's like you're shining a little light, making the world a brighter place. You've got this!

Techniques for waiting nicely

1. **Deep Breathing**: When waiting gets tough, take a deep breath. Inhale slowly and exhale even slower. It'll calm your mind and body.

2. **Distraction**: If waiting is making you restless, divert your attention to something else. Maybe count the number of blue items in the room or sing a song in your mind.

3. **Positive Self-talk**: Remind yourself of the rewards of being patient. Think to yourself, "I can wait a bit longer, and it'll be worth it."

Praising moments of patience

Whenever you or someone around you displays patience, please take a moment to praise it. It can be as simple as saying, "I appreciate you for waiting so calmly," or "Thank you for being so patient." Such positive reinforcement will encourage even more patient behaviors in the future.

In conclusion, patience is a beautiful virtue that offers us growth, understanding, and peace. As we journey through life, remember that sometimes the best things come to those who wait. Just like after a rainy day, with a little patience, we can always look forward to a beautiful rainbow.

Kindness

"Therefore, as God's chosen people, holy and dearly loved, clothe yourselves with compassion, kindness, humility, gentleness and patience." - Colossians 3:12

Uncovering Kindness

Kindness. It's a simple word, but it has a profound impact. At the heart of it, kindness means genuinely caring for others, wanting the best for them, and taking action to make a positive difference in their lives. It's like planting a seed of love wherever you go, knowing that each small act can grow into something beautiful.

Acts that show kindness

There are countless ways to show kindness, from a simple smile to a neighbor, to helping someone in need. Think of those times when you shared your snack with a friend who forgot theirs or when you cheered up a sibling who was feeling down. Those are all acts of kindness. The great thing about kindness is that it doesn't have to be big to be meaningful. Sometimes, the smallest gestures have the most significant impact.

Bible stories of compassion and care

The Bible is filled with stories of kindness and compassion.

The Widow's Offering (Mark 12:41-44): In the Gospel of Mark, the story of the widow's offering unfolds as Jesus sits opposite the temple treasury, observing people putting money into the offering box. Many rich individuals contribute large sums, making a show of their generosity. Amidst this, a poor widow approaches quietly and deposits two small copper coins, which together are worth only a fraction of a penny. This act might have gone unnoticed by most, given the modesty of the amount and the humble status of the woman, but it captures Jesus' attention.

Jesus calls his disciples to him and points out the widow's act as an extraordinary example of true giving. He explains that while the wealthy gave out of their abundance, contributing only a small portion of their surplus wealth, the widow, in her poverty, has given everything she had to live on. Her contribution, though financially minimal, is of immense value in the eyes of Jesus because it represents a profound act of faith, trust, and self-sacrifice. This story highlights the principle that the value of a gift is not measured by its size but by the spirit in which it is given. The widow's offering serves as a powerful lesson on the true nature of generosity and kindness, emphasizing the importance of the heart's intention over the magnitude of the gift.

The Feeding of the 5,000 (John 6:1-14): The Feeding of the 5,000 is one of the most well-known miracles of Jesus, recorded in all four Gospels, with the account in John providing specific details that highlight the theme of kindness and compassion. In this story, a large crowd has followed Jesus to a remote place because of the signs he was performing on the sick. As the day wears on, Jesus sees the multitude and, moved by compassion, recognizes their need for food. Instead of sending them away hungry, Jesus decides to feed them. He inquires about available food, and the disciples bring forward a young boy who has five barley loaves and two small fish. While this seems insufficient for such a large crowd, Jesus takes the loaves and fish, gives thanks, and distributes them to the people.

The act of feeding the 5,000 goes beyond merely satisfying physical hunger; it is a powerful demonstration of Jesus' kindness and concern for the well-being of the people. The miracle reveals Jesus' power over nature and His ability to provide abundantly for the needs of His followers. Furthermore, the involvement of the young boy with his modest offering underscores the theme that no act of kindness or contribution is too small in the hands of Jesus. It can be transformed and multiplied to achieve great things. This story teaches that kindness, coupled with faith, can lead to extraordinary outcomes, encouraging believers to trust in God's provision and to share what they have, no matter how little it might seem, to meet the needs of others.

Jesus Heals the Leper (Mark 1:40-45): In the narrative of Jesus healing the leper found in Mark, a leper approaches Jesus with a plea for cleansing, fully confident in Jesus' ability to heal him if He is willing. Leprosy at the time was not just a physical ailment but a condition that rendered individuals ritually unclean and socially ostracized, forcing them to live apart from the community and announce their impurity. Jesus moved with compassion, does something remarkable and culturally shocking: He reaches out and touches the man. This act alone was significant, as touching a leper would make one ritually unclean according to Jewish law. However, Jesus' touch conveys acceptance, dignity, and healing. He affirms His willingness to heal the man, saying, "I am willing; be clean," and immediately, the leprosy leaves the man.

This story goes beyond the physical healing of a dreadful disease; it illustrates a profound act of kindness that challenges social norms and stigma. Jesus' willingness to touch the leper breaks down the barriers of fear and prejudice, showcasing a model of inclusivity and compassion. The healing restores not only the man's physical health but also his social and relational standing, enabling him to rejoin the community and reconnect with those from whom he had been estranged. This act of kindness by Jesus emphasizes the value of every individual, regardless of their social status or condition, and teaches the transformative power of compassion and the importance of reaching out to those marginalized by society.

How Jesus was kind to everyone

Jesus, our ultimate role model, showcased kindness at every turn. He healed the sick, dined with those whom society had cast aside, and consistently put others before Himself. His actions were driven by pure love and compassion, making Him the epitome of kindness. The way He treated children, the stories He shared, and His ultimate sacrifice for us all are enduring examples of His boundless kindness.

Being Kind Every Day - Talking about kind acts we've seen or done

Discussing acts of kindness reinforces their importance. Maybe you saw someone help an elderly person cross the road or witnessed a friend stand up against bullying. Sharing these stories allows us to appreciate and learn from them. Kindness isn't a one-time act; it's a lifestyle. It's choosing to be gentle, understanding, and caring every day, in every situation.

Helping out at home

Simple acts like setting the table, assisting with chores, or making a bed can be acts of kindness towards your family. It shows respect and love for those you live with.

Being nice to classmates

School offers numerous opportunities for kindness. Sharing study notes, including someone in a game, or simply offering a listening ear when a classmate is upset can create a more loving environment.

Random acts of kindness ideas

1. Leaving Notes: Write kind note cards and leave them in library books for others to find.

2. Donating Old Toys: Give away toys you no longer play with to those in need.

3. Nature Cleanup: Spend an afternoon picking up litter in a park.

4. Baking for Neighbors: Bake some cookies and share them with neighbors just to make them smile.

In conclusion, kindness is a gift everyone can afford to give. It doesn't cost a thing but has immeasurable value. As we journey through life, let's remember that the world becomes a better place with each act of kindness. Whether we're sharing, caring, or simply being there for someone, our acts of kindness create ripples of love and positivity. And just as rain nourishes the earth, our kindness can nurture the souls of those around us.

Goodness

"Do not be overcome by evil, but overcome evil with good." - Romans 12:21

Exploring Goodness

In a world filled with choices, standing firmly by what is right and good can sometimes feel like a challenge. From the playground to home, from school to the neighborhood, every day we're presented with numerous decisions. The quality of 'goodness' is all about choosing actions that reflect a good heart, even when no one is watching.

What does it mean to be good?

At first glance, 'being good' might sound like simply following rules or doing what you're told. But in truth, goodness goes much deeper. It's about the intentions of our hearts and the impact of our actions. To be good means to act with compassion, fairness, and honesty, especially in situations when it would be easier not to.

Bible examples of choosing the right path

The Good Samaritan (Luke 10:25-37): It begins with a lawyer testing Jesus, asking what he must do to inherit eternal life. Jesus responds with the question back to the lawyer, who answers with the commandment to love God and one's neighbor as oneself. Seeking to justify himself, the lawyer then asks, "And who is my neighbor?" In response, Jesus tells the story of The Good Samaritan.

The story unfolds with a man traveling from Jerusalem to Jericho who is attacked by robbers, beaten, stripped, and left half-dead by the roadside. A priest and then a Levite, both respected figures in Jewish society, pass by the injured man, choosing to avoid him and continue on their way. In contrast, a Samaritan, considered an outcast and enemy by the Jews of the time, stops to help the injured man. He bandages his wounds, transports him on his own animal to an inn, and pays for his care, promising to cover any additional expenses upon his return.

The parable of The Good Samaritan teaches just how big the term "neighbor" really is. It emphasizes that kindness and compassion should extend beyond the limits of social, ethnic, or religious boundaries. The Samaritan's actions embody the essence of true neighborly love and the principle of treating others as one would wish to be treated, regardless of their background or status. This story challenges us to show mercy and act with goodness towards all people, illustrating that the practice of genuine compassion is a fundamental aspect of living a life aligned with God's will.

David and Mephibosheth (2 Samuel 9): The story of David and Mephibosheth presents a moving example of kindness, loyalty, and the restoration of dignity to the less fortunate. Mephibosheth was the son of Jonathan and the grandson of Saul, the king of Israel before David. After Saul and Jonathan were killed in battle, Mephibosheth, then a young child, was crippled in both feet during an accident that occurred as his nurse fled with him in panic.

Years later, King David, remembering his covenant of friendship with Jonathan, sought out any remaining members of Saul's family to show them kindness. He discovered Mephibosheth, who was living in obscurity and likely expecting retribution, as was customary when new dynasties took power. Instead of seeking revenge, David restored to Mephibosheth all the lands that had belonged to Saul and invited him to eat regularly at the king's table, effectively treating him as one of his own sons.

This story illustrates several important themes. Firstly, it underscores the value of kindness and loyalty that transcend familial and political boundaries. David's actions towards Mephibosheth demonstrate a commitment to honor his promise to Jonathan, showing that true friendship and loyalty outlive even death. Secondly, the narrative highlights the theme of restoration and grace. Despite Mephibosheth's lineage and his disability, David restores his fortune and dignity, integrating him into the royal household. This act of generosity reflects the broader biblical themes of redemption and the inclusive nature of God's kingdom, where mercy and kindness are extended to all, irrespective of their past or their physical condition.

Dorcas' Acts of Kindness (Acts 9:36-42): Dorcas was a disciple who lived in Joppa, and she was well-known for her good deeds and acts of charity, particularly for making clothes for the widows and the needy in her community. Her life was a testament to her faith, expressed through her selfless service to others.

Tragically, Dorcas fell ill and died, leaving the community in mourning. Her body was washed and placed in an upper room. When the disciples heard that Peter was nearby in Lydda, they sent two men to urgently request his presence, hoping for a miracle. Upon his arrival, Peter was taken to the room where Dorcas' body lay, surrounded by grieving widows who showed him the tunics and garments Dorcas had made for them. Peter sent everyone out of the room, knelt down to pray, and then, turning to her body, said, "Tabitha, get up." Miraculously, she opened her eyes, saw Peter, and sat up. He took her by the hand, helped her to her feet, and presented her alive to the saints and widows. The news of this miracle spread throughout Joppa, leading many to believe in the Lord.

The story of Dorcas highlights the profound impact of kindness and charitable acts in a community. Dorcas' legacy was not just in the clothes she made but in the love and care she poured into her community, embodying the Christian call to serve and love one another. Her resurrection by God through Peter not only underscores the power of God working through the apostles but also serves to amplify the importance of Dorcas' life and deeds. Her story teaches children and adults alike the value of compassion and generosity, illustrating that acts of goodness can leave a lasting imprint on the hearts of those around us and, in some cases, can lead to extraordinary outcomes that reaffirm faith and inspire entire communities.

Times when it's tough to be good

It's not always easy to be good. Peer pressure, wanting to fit in, or even just a tempting situation can sometimes make it challenging to choose the right path. Remembering the story of Joseph and his brothers can be helpful here. Even when sold into slavery by his siblings, Joseph maintained his integrity and trusted in God. Eventually, he rose to great power and was in a position to save his family during a famine. His journey wasn't easy, but he always leaned towards goodness.

Goodness Through Play

Believe it or not, playtime can be a brilliant way to understand and explore the concept of goodness. Playtime isn't just about having fun; it's like a colorful, open book that teaches us so many things without us even realizing it. And one of those things is goodness. Yes, you heard that right! Through play, we can learn and show what it means to be good, just like the heroes in those Bible stories.

1. **Team Games and Sportsmanship:** When you're playing a team game, whether it's soccer, basketball, or even a board game, there's a golden opportunity to practice goodness. Being a good sport means playing fair, following the rules, and respecting everyone - even the other team. It's not just about winning; it's about how you play the game. Cheering for your teammates, giving a high five to the opposing team, or even helping someone up when they fall – that's showing goodness in action.

2. **Sharing and Taking Turns:** Whether you're at the park or in your backyard, sharing your toys or taking turns on the swing demonstrates goodness. It's like saying, "I care about your happiness as much as mine." This simple act of sharing brings smiles and spreads joy, just like the warmth and forgiveness in the story of the Prodigal Son.

3. **Role-Playing Games:** Ever pretended to be a superhero, a teacher, or maybe a doctor? Role-playing games are amazing for sparking imagination, but they also let you walk in someone else's shoes for a bit. This helps you understand others better, showing empathy and compassion, which are big parts of being good. You learn to solve problems, help others, and make fair de-

cisions in your imaginative play world.

4. **Building and Creating Together:** When you build something with someone else, like a giant LEGO castle or a cool sandcastle, you're working together, sharing ideas, and respecting each other's creativity. It teaches you that by cooperating and being kind, you can create something beautiful and have lots of fun doing it!

So, you see, playtime is like a mini-world where you can practice being good in so many ways. Each game, each shared laugh, and every high five is a step towards understanding what goodness truly means. And just like Daniel, Joseph, and the father of the Prodigal Son, you learn that goodness might not always be the easiest path, but it's definitely the most rewarding and fun one when you're playing!

The Power of Sharing Good Choices:

Sharing our moments of goodness is not just about recounting our good deeds; it's about building a foundation of moral understanding and empathy. When we take the time to sit together and share the instances when we chose the path of goodness, it becomes an enriching experience for everyone involved.

Imagine this: your family is gathered around, maybe after dinner or during a weekend hangout, and you start to share stories. Not just any stories, but personal anecdotes about times when you were faced with a choice and opted for goodness. These stories don't have to be grand or dramatic; even the simplest acts of kindness, fairness, and honesty shine brightly.

For others, hearing about the time you returned a lost wallet, stood up for a friend, or even chose to be patient in a frustrating situation, is incredibly impactful. It shows them that goodness isn't just a concept in fairy tales or ancient stories; it's alive and thriving in the everyday actions of the people they know and look up to.

Reflection and Discussion:

This sharing session becomes a treasure trove of life lessons. But it's not just about listening; it's also about engaging. Ask others what they think about each story shared. Would they have done the same? What would they have found difficult? This isn't about judging choices but understanding the layers of thought and emotion behind each act of goodness.

Balancing the Narrative:

And here's something equally important: discussing the times we've stumbled. Yes, everyone makes mistakes or faces moments of weakness. Sharing these moments with the same openness as the good choices is crucial. It lets others know that it's okay to not always get it right, as long as we learn, grow, and strive to do better next time.

This balanced narrative helps us understand that the journey of goodness is ongoing. It's not about being perfect but about continually choosing to act with compassion, fairness, and integrity, even when it's challenging.

Celebrating Goodness:

Finally, let's celebrate these moments of goodness, no matter how small. Recognition and appreciation go a long way in reinforcing and developing positive behavior. It's a gentle reminder that goodness is valued, celebrated, and an integral part of who we are as a family.

By sharing and discussing our good choices, we not only highlight the beauty of doing right by others but also instill a deep-seated sense of morality and empathy.

Reflecting on our choices

At the end of each day, taking a moment to reflect on our actions can be incredibly beneficial. It's an opportunity to consider the choices made, appreciate the good ones, and think about how to improve on any not-so-great decisions.

In conclusion, goodness is a path that might sometimes be challenging but is always rewarding. It's a journey of the heart, one where every step, every choice, molds us into better versions of ourselves. In the end, choosing good over bad isn't just about doing the right thing; it's about shaping a world filled with love, compassion, and goodness.

Faithfulness

"Let love and faithfulness never leave you; bind them around your neck, write them on the tablet of your heart." - Proverbs 3:3

Discovering Faithfulness

Imagine your favorite blanket - the one that keeps you warm, snug, and feels oh-so-comfortable. No matter how many times you've used it, it always remains the same: cozy and reliable. That's a bit like faithfulness. Faithfulness is all about being dependable, trustworthy, and steadfast. When someone is faithful, you can count on them no matter what.

Loyalty and Trust in the Bible

The Story of Abraham's Test Genesis 22:1-13

The Bible is full of examples that shine a light on loyalty and trust. Abraham is one of my favorite Old Testament examples. Abraham wasn't just any ordinary man; he was a friend of God, known for his unwavering faith and trust in God. But one day, Abraham faced the greatest test of his life, a test that would show just how deep his trust in God really was.

God had blessed Abraham with a son named Isaac. Isaac was not just a son to Abraham; he was a precious gift, especially because Abraham and his wife, Sarah, had waited many, many years for him. Abraham loved Isaac more than anything in the world.

Then, one day, God asked Abraham to do something that seemed beyond understanding. God wanted Abraham to take Isaac to a mountain and offer him as a sacrifice. Now, to us, this request might seem confusing and even scary. But back in those times, such tests were ways to show deep trust and faithfulness.

Abraham was faced with a choice that would make anyone's heart ache. Imagine being asked to give up something or someone you love dearly. It's not easy, right? But Abraham, even with his heart heavy, chose to trust God completely. He believed that God's plans were good, even if they didn't make sense to him.

So, Abraham and Isaac set off on a journey to the mountain that God had told them about. Isaac, who was a smart and observant boy, noticed that they were carrying everything needed for a sacrifice, like wood and fire, but there was no lamb to offer.

"Father," Isaac asked, "where is the lamb for the burnt offering?"

Abraham replied with gentle assurance, "God Himself will provide the lamb for the burnt offering, my son." Abraham's words were a beacon of faith, shining with trust in God's goodness.

When they reached the place God had told him about, Abraham built an altar and arranged the wood on it. As Abraham prepared to follow through with God's difficult request, his heart was undoubtedly racing, his mind swirling with thoughts, yet his trust in God never wavered.

But just as Abraham was about to make the ultimate sacrifice, an angel called out to him from heaven, "Abraham! Abraham!"

"Here I am," he replied.

The angel said, "Do not lay a hand on the boy. Do not do anything to him. Now I know that you fear God because you have not withheld from me your son, your only son."

At that moment, Abraham looked up and saw a ram caught by its horns in a thicket. He understood that God had provided a sacrifice. The ram was offered in Isaac's place, and Isaac was safe. This moment was a powerful reminder of Abraham's faith and trust in God.

Through this story, we learn that faithfulness means trusting God, even when His plans seem mysterious or challenging. Abraham's trust in God was rewarded, and as promised, he became the father of many nations. His descendants were as numerous as the stars in the sky he once gazed upon, a beautiful testament to the strength of faithfulness and trust.

So, whenever we're faced with tough situations or decisions that don't make sense, let's remember Abraham's story. Let's be brave like Abraham, holding onto our trust in God, believing in

His promises, and knowing that He always has a plan for us, just as He did for Abraham and Isaac.

The Story of Ruth -Ruth 1-4

Ruth's story is one of true loyalty and faithfulness. Ruth was married to Naomi's son, but tragedy struck when Naomi lost not only her husband but both of her sons as well, including Ruth's husband. In those times, for a woman to lose her husband and sons meant more than just losing loved ones; it meant losing her security and place in society.

Naomi, heartbroken and defeated, decided to return to her homeland of Bethlehem. She urged her daughters-in-law, Ruth and Orpah, to stay in Moab and remarry, as she had nothing left to offer them. Orpah, tearfully, decided to stay behind, but Ruth's response was different.

With a heart full of love and determination, Ruth spoke words that would echo through the ages, "Where you go, I will go, and where you stay, I will stay. Your people will be my people and your God my God." These weren't just words; they were a solemn vow, a commitment that Ruth made not only to Naomi but to God as well.

So, Ruth left everything she knew behind—her family, her land, her people—to accompany Naomi to Bethlehem. Imagine how difficult that must have been. Ruth stepped into a world unknown, with only her faithfulness to guide her.

In Bethlehem, Ruth faced the reality of her and Naomi's situation. They needed food and support, so Ruth took it upon herself to work and provide for them both. She went to the fields to glean leftover grains, a practice allowed for the poor and the widows. The field she happened to work in belonged to a man named Boaz, who was not only wealthy but also a relative of Naomi's late husband.

Boaz noticed Ruth from the very start, not just because of her hard work but also because of the loyalty and kindness she showed Naomi. Word of Ruth's faithfulness had spread, and Boaz was moved by her dedication. He ensured that Ruth was protected in his fields and had enough to glean, showing favor towards her.

Ruth's unwavering dedication to Naomi led not only to their survival but to a new beginning. Boaz, struck by Ruth's loyalty and character, took her as his wife. This union blessed Naomi with a family once again and Ruth with a new, secure life. Moreover, Ruth and Boaz's lineage would become one of great significance, leading to King David and, eventually, to Jesus Christ himself.

Ruth's story teaches us that faithfulness isn't just about sticking by someone in easy times; it's about holding on and walking together through the storms of life. It's about making sacrifices for the sake of others and trusting that God has a plan through it all.

So, whenever we face tough choices or when loyalty is tested, let's remember Ruth. Let's remember that sometimes, faithfulness means taking the harder road, not for our gain but for the love and care of others. And in this journey, we're never alone; just as Ruth had Naomi and Boaz came to support Ruth, God is with us, guiding our steps toward a future filled with hope and blessing.

The Story of Shadrach, Meshach, and Abednego Daniel 3

These three were not just ordinary young men; they were captives from Judah, living in Babylon, yet they had risen to positions of trust because of their wisdom and integrity. However, their greatest challenge was yet to come, a challenge that would test their faithfulness to the utmost.

King Nebuchadnezzar, in his pride, made a colossal golden statue and decreed that everyone must bow down and worship this image when music played. The penalty for defying this order was a terrifying one: to be thrown into a blazing furnace. The king's command put everyone in the kingdom to the test, but for Shadrach, Meshach, and Abednego, the choice was clear.

Their faith in God was unwavering, their principles unshakeable. They knew they could not bow to any god but the one true God they worshiped. When the music sounded, signaling the time to bow, everyone in the kingdom fell to their knees except for these three courageous young men.

Word of their defiance reached the king, and in his fury, he summoned them. Nebuchadnezzar, in disbelief, offered them one more chance to bow down to his golden statue. But Shadrach, Meshach, and Abednego remained resolute. They responded to the king with words that echoed their unbreakable faith, "O Nebuchadnezzar, we do not need to defend ourselves before you in this matter. If we are thrown into the blazing furnace, the God we serve is able to save us from it, and He will rescue us from your hand, O king. But even if He does not, we want you to know, O king, that we will not serve your gods or worship the image of gold you have set up."

Enraged, King Nebuchadnezzar ordered the furnace to be heated seven times hotter than usual. The flames were so intense that the soldiers who threw Shadrach, Meshach, and Abednego into the furnace were consumed by the fire. But when the king looked into the furnace, his anger turned to astonishment. Instead of three men consumed by the flames, he saw four men walking unharmed in the fire, and the fourth looked like "the Son of God."

Realizing the miraculous nature of their deliverance, Nebuchadnezzar called them out of the furnace. To everyone's amazement, not a hair on their heads was singed, their clothes were unharmed, and they didn't even smell of smoke. This miraculous event showed not only their faithfulness but the power and faithfulness of their God.

The courage and trust of Shadrach, Meshach, and Abednego led to a remarkable outcome. King Nebuchadnezzar, who had once ordered everyone to worship his golden image, now praised their God, proclaiming, "Praise be to the God of Shadrach, Meshach, and Abednego, who has sent his angel and rescued his servants! They trusted in him and defied the king's command and were willing to give up their lives rather than serve or worship any god except their own God."

Furthermore, the king made a decree that no one, anywhere, should speak against the God of Shadrach, Meshach, and Abednego, acknowledging the might and sovereignty of their God.

This story of Shadrach, Meshach, and Abednego teaches us about the power of steadfast faith and the importance of being faithful to our beliefs in God, even in the face of the fiercest trials. Their story is a testament to the fact that when we stand firm in our faith, trusting in God's plans and protection, extraordinary things can happen, not only for us but also influencing those around us, just as it did with King Nebuchadnezzar.

How Being Faithful Helps Us

Have you ever had a friend who you could trust with anything? The kind of friend who would be there when you needed them, and never let you down? That's the beauty of faithfulness. Being a faithful friend ensures stronger bonds and deeper connections. When we're reliable, it builds trust, and this trust serves as the foundation for lasting relationships.

Faithfulness teaches us resilience and commitment, qualities that deepen our relationships. It's like planting a tree; the more we nurture it with trust and reliability, the deeper its roots grow, making it unshakable even in the fiercest winds. This staying power in friendship not only strengthens our bonds but also shapes us into more dependable, compassionate individuals, creating a ripple effect that enriches our entire community.

Being Loyal Every Day

Every day presents opportunities to practice faithfulness. Whether it's by keeping a promise, being there for a friend, or simply being honest, everyday acts of loyalty can have a lasting impact. Incorporating faithfulness into our daily routines might seem small, like holding the door open for someone or remembering to call a friend who's going through a tough time, but these acts of kindness echo the depth of our loyalty.

Over time, these consistent gestures build a picture of trust, showing those around us that we value integrity and commitment. It's in these moments, often unnoticed, where the true essence of loyalty shines brightest, transforming ordinary days into a testament of our steadfastness and love.

Trust Exercises with Friends

Building trust is a vital aspect of any relationship. Try these simple exercises, like blindfolded obstacle courses where one friend guides another or two-person artwork where one describes and the other draws. It will not only be fun, but it will help you see how trust plays a vital role in friendships. If you really think about it, you wouldn't want to do this with someone who you didn't trust. You trust the person who has been a faithful friend.

Keeping Promises

Promises are not just words; they're commitments. Whenever we make a promise, whether it's to finish our homework or help out with chores, it's essential to follow through. By doing so, we show that we're reliable and trustworthy.

In conclusion, faithfulness is a beautiful and essential fruit of the spirit. In a world that's constantly changing, being someone that others can rely on is invaluable. Whether it's through stories, songs, games, or everyday acts, cultivating and celebrating faithfulness enriches our lives and the lives of those around us.

Gentleness

"Let your gentleness be evident to all. The Lord is near." - Philippians 4:5

Embracing Gentleness

Imagine a butterfly landing on a delicate flower, or the soft rustle of leaves in a gentle breeze. There's a beauty and strength in such softness and delicacy. In life, there are moments that call for power and might, but there are many more instances where gentleness and kindness shine the brightest.

Understanding the Strength in Softness

Being gentle doesn't mean being weak. Think about water – it's soft and flowing, but over time, it can shape mountains and carve valleys. In the same way, a gentle heart can make a significant impact on the world around us. It's the strength to respond with softness even when faced with challenges, and it's choosing kindness over anger.

Bible Stories about Handling Situations Gently

The Bible gives us many examples of gentleness in action.

Jesus and the woman caught in adultery (John 8:1-11)

This testimony is a profound example of gentleness in the face of potential condemnation. The narrative begins with Jesus teaching in the temple when the scribes and Pharisees bring before Him a woman caught in the act of adultery, a crime punishable by stoning according to Mosaic Law. They question Jesus, attempting to trap Him into saying something they could use against Him. If Jesus were to dismiss the charges, He would appear to condone sin, but if He urged them to execute her, He would be in conflict with Roman law, which reserved capital punishment for itself.

Instead of reacting impulsively or harshly, Jesus responds with remarkable gentleness and wisdom. He stoops down and writes in the dirt with His finger, not immediately addressing their question. As they continue to press Him, He stands and delivers the famous line, "Let any one of you who is without sin be the first to throw a stone at her." One by one, beginning with the oldest, the accusers leave until only Jesus and the woman remain. Jesus then stands up again, and seeing no one but the woman, He asks her where her accusers have gone and if no one has condemned her. When she replies that no one has, Jesus responds with gentle grace, "Neither do I condemn you; go now and leave your life of sin."

This story highlights the power of gentleness and compassion over judgment and condemnation. Jesus defuses a volatile situation with calmness and wisdom, protecting the woman's life and offering her a chance for redemption. The narrative teaches that while sin is to be acknowledged, the approach to dealing with it should be characterized by understanding and the opportunity for repentance, rather than harsh judgment. Jesus exemplifies a gentle response that preserves dignity and encourages transformation, reminding us of the importance of compassion and forgiveness in our interactions with others, especially when they are at their most vulnerable.

David Spares Saul's Life (1 Samuel 24): The story of David sparing Saul's life unfolds as a dramatic encounter between the future king of Israel and the reigning monarch. Saul, consumed by jealousy and fear of David's rising popularity and God's favor towards him, sets out to kill David. David, along with his men, finds refuge in the caves of En Gedi. Unbeknownst to Saul, while he enters one of these caves to relieve himself, David and his men are hiding deeper within the same cave.

In this vulnerable moment for Saul, David's men see an opportunity for David to kill Saul, interpreting the situation as God delivering Saul into David's hands. However, David chooses a path of remarkable restraint and gentleness. Instead of killing Saul, he secretly cuts off a corner of Saul's robe. Even this act causes David to feel remorseful for having "cut off a corner of [the king's] robe" as he respects Saul's anointed status by God. After Saul leaves the cave, David emerges to reveal his action, demonstrating to Saul that he had the opportunity to kill him but chose not to. David's words and actions convey a message of respect, loyalty, and the refusal to harm the Lord's anointed, despite Saul's intentions against him.

This story is a powerful testament to the strength inherent in gentleness and the choice of mercy over vengeance. David's decision to spare Saul's life, even when it seemed justifiable to take revenge, showcases the virtue of respecting God's plan and the dignity of every individual, even one's enemies. It highlights the principle that true leadership and honor are rooted in the ability to respond with gentleness and integrity, even in the face of aggression and hostility. Through this act of mercy, David not only preserves his moral integrity but also sets an example for his men and for future generations about the power of a gentle spirit over might or vengeance.

Joseph Reassures His Brothers (Genesis 50:15-21): After the death of their father Jacob, Joseph's brothers feared retribution for their past actions of selling Joseph into slavery. They were concerned that Joseph had been restraining his vengeance out of respect for their father and that, with Jacob gone, Joseph might now seek revenge. In their anxiety, they sent a message to Joseph, claiming it was their father's wish for Joseph to forgive his brothers. When they met, the brothers even offered themselves as slaves to Joseph, demonstrating their guilt and fear of possible retaliation.

Joseph's response to his brothers was one of profound gentleness and compassion. He was moved to tears by their plea and reassured them that he had no intention of harming them. Joseph told his brothers not to be afraid, for he was not in the place of God to exact vengeance. He acknowledged the evil of their actions but chose to focus on the positive outcome, stating that God had used their deeds to save many lives during the famine. Instead of seeking vengeance, Joseph promised to provide for them and their children, ensuring their safety and well-being.

This story exemplifies the power of gentleness and forgiveness. Joseph's gentle reassurance to his brothers not only calmed their fears but also healed a family torn apart by jealousy and wrong-doing. It highlights the importance of seeing beyond personal hurt to the broader picture of God's plan and the potential for good even in adverse circumstances. Joseph's actions teach that gentleness, forgiveness, and trust in God's sovereignty can transform relationships and bring about healing and reconciliation.

The Grace of Being Kind and Soft

Being gentle means treating others the way you'd want to be treated. It's realizing that every person has feelings and that our actions and words can impact them deeply. Jesus embodied this throughout his life, teaching his followers the value of being meek and gentle-hearted.

Being Gentle Every Day

Life is filled with moments that test our patience and gentleness. But each day also brings countless opportunities to showcase our gentleness, both in action and words.

Handling Things with Care

For instance, consider the way we treat a pet. Pets are living creatures that rely on us for care and affection. We use gentle hands to pet them, careful not to be too rough, which shows our respect and love for them. Just like pets, other things in our world need to be treated with kindness and care too.

Think about the simple act of turning the pages of a book. Books are gateways to adventure, learning, and imagination, but they are also delicate objects that can be damaged if we're not careful. By turning the pages gently, we show respect for the stories and knowledge held within, and we ensure that others can enjoy the book after us. This same idea applies to toys, belongings, and even the environment—like picking up a flower or handling a bug. When we treat everything around us with gentleness, we're not only taking care of our things and nature, but we're also learning an important value: respect. This respect for our belongings, for others, and for the world around us helps make the world a kinder, gentler place for everyone to live in.

Speaking Softly and Kindly

Words have power, and the way we use them can make a big difference. A gentle word can calm a crying friend, and a soft voice can soothe a scared heart. When I was growing up, there was an old saying, "If you don't have anything nice to say, don't say anything at all." We need to encourage one another to use our words for comfort, praise, and kindness so that we can cultivate a lifetime of gentle speech.

In conclusion, gentleness is one of the most powerful qualities a person can possess. It's the choice to act with kindness, to speak with softness, and to handle everything with care. The world can sometimes be a challenging and noisy place, but with gentleness, we can bring a touch of calm and serenity to it. By embedding this quality into our hearts, we ensure a future filled with compassion, understanding, and grace.

Self-Control

"Like a city whose walls are broken through is a person who lacks self-control." - Proverbs 25:28

Learning Self-Control - Taming the Inner Wild Horse

Imagine a wild horse, galloping freely across the plains, its mane flowing with the wind, and nothing holding it back. While the sight is magnificent, a tamed horse can offer much to the community: it can carry heavy loads, help plow the fields, and even become a loyal companion. Just like the wild horse, our emotions and impulses can sometimes run free, but with self-control, we can harness them for better purposes.

Why it's sometimes hard to control ourselves

Each one of us has a range of feelings, from bubbling excitement to deep disappointment. These emotions can be quite powerful, pushing us to act without thinking. Maybe you've felt the urge to shout when you're upset, or perhaps you've wanted to grab a third piece of cake even though you're full. This is entirely natural! However, self-control is about recognizing these impulses and deciding how to act on them.

Bible Examples of Resisting Temptations

The Bible is rich with stories that teach us about the value of self-control.

Joseph Resists Temptation (Genesis 39): Joseph, sold into slavery by his brothers, finds himself in Egypt, serving in the household of Potiphar, an officer of Pharaoh. Joseph excels in his duties, earning Potiphar's trust and becoming overseer of his house. However, Potiphar's wife repeatedly attempts to tempt Joseph. Despite the potential benefits of yielding to her advances—possibly gaining favor or avoiding conflict—Joseph steadfastly refuses. He recognizes the moral and ethical implications, emphasizing that giving in would be a sin against God and a betrayal of Potiphar's trust. When she makes a final attempt, grabbing his cloak, Joseph flees, leaving his garment behind.

This moment leads to Joseph being falsely accused by Potiphar's wife, who presents the cloak as evidence of Joseph's supposed advances. Despite his innocence and the unjust consequences, Joseph is imprisoned. This story highlights Joseph's remarkable self-control and his commitment to righteousness, even in the face of severe temptation and subsequent hardship. Joseph's ability to prioritize his integrity and his faithfulness to God over immediate personal gain is a powerful lesson in the value of self-control. It teaches that true strength lies not in succumbing to momentary desires but in adhering to one's principles, even when the right choice leads to challenging outcomes. Joseph's story reassures us that maintaining integrity and trusting in God's plan despite unfair circumstances can lead to greater fulfillment and divine favor in the long run.

Jesus' Temptation in the Wilderness (Matthew 4:1-11): The story of Jesus' temptation in the wilderness unfolds immediately after Jesus' baptism, marking the beginning of His public ministry. Led by the Spirit into the desert, Jesus fasts for 40 days and nights, a period of preparation and spiritual fortitude. It is in this state of physical vulnerability that Satan approaches Him with a series of temptations, each designed to exploit human weakness and challenge Jesus' obedience to God's will.

The first temptation involves turning stones into bread, appealing to Jesus' physical hunger. The second temptation is to test God's protection by throwing Himself down from the temple's pinnacle, challenging the trust in divine care. The third and final temptation Satan offers Jesus is all the kingdoms of the world in exchange for worshiping him, targeting the desire for power and authority. In each case, Jesus responds with quotations from Scripture, not only resisting temptation but also affirming His complete reliance on God's word and authority. Jesus' refusals emphasize the principles of living by every word that comes from God, not testing God, and worshiping only the Lord.

This story highlights the importance of self-control and the power of God's word as a tool for resisting temptation. Jesus demonstrates that physical needs, pride, and the allure of power should not dictate our actions when they conflict with God's will. For children, this story serves as an example of using wisdom and self-control in difficult situations, and it underscores the importance of knowing and relying on God's word for guidance and strength in times of challenge.

Benefits of mastering our impulses

Imagine being able to handle disappointments without tears or facing a challenging task without giving up. Self-control equips us to manage our reactions, leading to better relationships, more accomplishments, and a greater sense of well-being. When we pause and think before we act, we make choices that are more in line with who we want to be.

Using Self-Control Every Day

Practicing self-control is like strengthening a muscle; the more we use it, the stronger it becomes. By incorporating techniques and reminders into our daily lives, we can enhance our ability to remain calm, thoughtful, and in control.

Techniques for managing excitement or disappointment

- **Deep Breathing:** Whenever feelings become too intense, take a moment to breathe deeply. Count to four while inhaling, hold for four counts, then exhale for another four counts.

- **Counting to Ten:** If something upsets you, before reacting, count to ten slowly. This gives you a chance to calm down and think about your response.

Creating a Self-Control Reward Chart

Create a chart with various self-control challenges, like "I spoke kindly even when I was upset" or "I waited patiently without complaining." Every time you accomplishes one of these challenges, you can place a sticker or draw a star on the chart. After a certain number of stickers or stars, you can receive a reward that you work out with your parents or caregiver. This visual representation can be motivating and make the journey of mastering self-control even more rewarding.

In conclusion, self-control is one of the most essential skills we can nurture when we are young. It prepares us to handle the ups and downs of life gracefully, make thoughtful decisions, and develop into responsible, mature individuals. Like taming the wild horse within, with patience and perseverance, we can harness our emotions and impulses, channeling them into positive actions that benefit not only ourselves but also those around us.

Becoming a Fruitful Explorer

"But the fruit of the Spirit is love, joy, peace, patience, kindness, goodness, faithfulness, gentleness, and self-control." - Galatians 5:22-23

Mixing the Fruits - Blending All the Fruits Together

Imagine a delicious fruit basket filled with a variety of colorful and tasty fruits. Each fruit has its unique flavor and texture, but when they are combined, they create a delightful and harmonious medley. Similarly, the Fruit of the Spirit, though distinct in their characteristics, come together to shape a complete and balanced Christian life. Each "fruit" enhances and complements the others, helping us develop a well-rounded character.

How all the Fruit of the Spirit work together

- **Love** provides the foundation, as it's the root from which all other virtues sprout. It motivates our actions and deepens our compassion.

- **Joy** and **Peace** nourish our inner well-being, ensuring we remain content and grounded.

- **Patience, Kindness,** and **Goodness** guide our interactions, ensuring we treat others with respect and understanding.

- **Faithfulness** strengthens our bond with God, while **Gentleness** and **Self-Control** teach us to approach situations with a calm and considerate demeanor.

All these virtues intertwine, helping us face life's challenges with grace and wisdom.

Bible characters who showed multiple fruits

- **Joseph** displayed **Patience** during his years in prison, **Faithfulness** to God's plan, and **Kindness** when he forgave his brothers.

- **Ruth** showcased her **Loyalty** and **Goodness** by staying with Naomi, her **Love** was evident in her commitment, and her **Joy** blossomed when she found a new family with Boaz.

- **Daniel** exhibited **Faithfulness** by praying to God despite the king's decree, **Self-Control** when he opted for vegetables over the king's feast, and **Peace** in the lion's den.

Each of these characters, through their trials and tribulations, demonstrated a blend of the Fruit of the Spirit, reminding us of the beauty of a pure spiritual life.

The beauty of a balanced spirit

Just as a balanced diet helps our physical health, a balanced spirit nurtures our soul. Embracing all the Fruit of the Spirit ensures we are not just kind but also patient, not just joyful but also peaceful. This biblical approach to spirituality enriches our relationship with God, with others, and with ourselves.

Celebrating All We've Learned

Our spiritual voyage through the Fruit of the Spirit is drawing to a close, and it's a heartwarming moment to reflect on the profound insights we've gathered. Each chapter, each lesson, has been a unique revelation, unveiling the essence of a life that mirrors God's boundless love and wisdom. Like the branches of a fruit-bearing tree, our understanding has grown, sprouted leaves, and now bears the sweet fruit of spiritual enlightenment.

Navigating the intricate realms of **Love, Joy, Peace, Patience, Kindness, Goodness, Faithfulness, Gentleness,** and **Self-Control,** we have journeyed across an expansive spiritual terrain. Let's recap the essence of these cherished learnings:

- **Love:** It manifested as an innate, unwavering affection, reminding us that true love flows unconditionally, demanding nothing in return.

- **Joy:** More than a fleeting emotion, it is a profound inner contentment anchored in our faith, revealing that genuine joy radiates even in trials.

- **Peace:** We recognized the tranquil depths of true peace, realizing it's not about the absence of turmoil but the presence of trust in God.

- **Patience:** This taught us that waiting is an act of hope, showcasing our trust in God's timing and the unfolding of His plans.

- **Kindness & Goodness:** We learned the power of benevolence, understanding that true goodness arises from a place of compassion and seeking the well-being of others.

- **Faithfulness:** It showcased unwavering loyalty, emphasizing the beauty of standing firm in our beliefs and commitments.

- **Gentleness:** Here, we grasped the might of softness, realizing that sometimes the most profound strength is displayed not in dominance but in understanding and kindness.

- **Self-Control:** We looked at the mastery of our impulses, recognizing the empowerment that comes from reigning in our desires and reactions.

Our metaphorical basket, brimming with these fruits, is now a testament to the transformative power of the scriptures and God's guiding hand.

The Lifelong Journey of the Fruit of the Spirit

While the pages of this book might end, the journey of growing in the knowledge of the Fruit of the Spirit is continual. Each day presents a lot of opportunities to live these virtues, to choose love over indifference, patience over haste, and gentleness over harshness.

Life will, of course, throw its challenges. We will encounter crossroads where our values will be tested. Yet, fortified with the wisdom of the Fruit of the Spirit, we possess the tools to navigate these situations with grace.

A tree doesn't bear fruit just once; it's a recurring miracle, reflecting the seasons of growth, nurturing, and eventual fruition. Similarly, our relationship with the Fruit of the Spirit is a continual journey nurtured by our experiences and choices.

Encouraging Continuous Growth and Exploration

Now, as we step out and truly walk in the fruit of the spirit, it's important to nurture this newfound wisdom. Here are some ways to continually grow in the light of the Fruit of the Spirit:

- **Daily Wonder Time:** Let's make some time every day to think quietly. Remember when you were super kind or patient today? And if there were times when you

could have been a little nicer or more patient, that's okay
too! It's all about learning and doing better next time.

- **Bible Adventure:** The Bible is like a treasure map, filled
  with stories and inspirations that can help us be our best
  selves. Whenever you're feeling puzzled or just want a
  boost of encouragement, open up your Bible and start
  exploring!

- **Chat and Share:** Talking with your family and friends
  about the cool things you're learning about kindness,
  patience, and all the other awesome ways we can act is
  really fun. It's like passing around a basket of goodies
  where everyone can take a piece and share one too!

- **High-Five Moments:** Whenever you notice someone
  being extra kind or patient, or maybe when you've done
  something really nice, give them(or yourself) a big
  high-five! It's like saying, "Hey, you're doing great!" and
  it makes everyone feel super special.

- **Always Curious Club:** Remember, even though we're
  learning a lot and getting really good at walking in love,
  joy, and the peace of God, as well as being patient,
  kind, good, faithful, gentle, and walking in self-control,
  there's always more to discover. Being curious and ready
  to learn more is what makes this adventure so exciting!

In wrapping up our "Adventures in Scriptures for Kids: Exploring the Fruit of the Spirit," remember that this isn't an end but a beginning. We are now ambassadors of these God-given virtues, entrusted with the mission to make our surroundings a little more loving, a tad more peaceful, and significantly more joyful.

May your days ahead be filled with the sweet aroma of these fruits, and may every step you take resonate with the love, wisdom, and grace of God. Our adventure may have concluded within these pages, but outside, in the vast expanse of life, a new, enriching chapter awaits. Here's to becoming the most fruitful explorers of our time!

Adventures in Scripture for Kids: Exploring The Full Armor of God

Lorie Eubank

"Armor Up!": Discovering God's Protection

Hello, young champions of faith! We're about to embark on an incredible journey that will lead us through the pages of the Bible to discover the amazing Armor of God. This isn't just any armor; it's a special set of tools that God gives us to stay strong and courageous in our daily lives.

The significance of the Armor of God:
Imagine wearing a belt of truth that helps you tell right from wrong or carrying a shield of faith that can protect you from fears and doubts. These aren't just pieces of metal and leather; they're symbols of God's love and strength that are always with us, even though we can't see them with our natural eyes.

In our expedition through the Scriptures, we'll engage in a remarkable exploration of the Armor of God. Each piece of the armor represents a core principle that empowers us to live as God intends, strong and full of hope. Let's put on the shoes of peace!

As we walk the paths of our daily lives, these shoes remind us to step gently and peacefully, spreading kindness and the good news that God loves us and wants us to live in peace with one another. Next, let's envision fastening the belt of truth around our waists. This isn't any ordinary belt; it's the foundation that holds everything together. Just as a belt secures the clothes of a warrior, truth secures our spiritual lives, ensuring the snares of deception do not trip us up.

Then, we have the breastplate of righteousness guarding our hearts. Righteousness, my young friends, is about being right with God—living in a way that pleases Him. This breastplate defends us against the wrongs that try to pierce our hearts, teaching us to choose actions that shine with God's goodness.

The helmet of salvation is crucial, too. It's not just a piece of headgear but a symbol of what Jesus has done for us. By accepting God's salvation through Jesus, we protect our minds from thoughts that can lead us astray. It's like having an invisible helmet that whispers, "You are loved and saved."

The sword of the Spirit, God's word, is unique. It's not for hurting but for healing, defeating the principalities of darkness by using the Word of God, and triumphing over temptation. Knowing and speaking God's word can cut through confusion and stand firm in truth.

Lastly, the shield of faith—what a wondrous defense it is! Our faith in God's promises can extinguish the flaming arrows of fear, worry, and doubt. Nothing can shake us when we lift our shields high, believing in God's power and love.

These symbols are powerful reminders of God's love and strength, ever-present, guiding, and protecting us in a world that often feels like a battleground. Remember, dear ones, our physical eyes do not see the Armor of God, but it is felt and witnessed in our actions, choices, and the unwavering spirit within us. As we journey together, we'll learn to wear this armor not just in our imaginations but in our everyday lives.

You might ask, "How can this armor help me today?" That's a fantastic question! Together, we will learn how the truth can defend us against lies, how righteousness can keep our hearts right, and how the good news of peace can guide our steps. We will see how faith can block out worries, how salvation keeps our thoughts safe, and how God's word is better than any sword in battle. This armor is real and powerful, and God gives it to us to use every single day.

Laying the foundation for the adventures ahead:
As we dive into the Bible and the stories of God's people, we'll see how they used this armor in their lives. And just like them, we can use it too! You'll learn how to put on each piece of God's Armor through thoughtful questions and exciting stories. So, let's open our hearts and minds as we step into the Bible's truths, ready to "Armor Up!" and learn how to stand strong in God's

mighty power. It's time to explore one of the greatest adventures of all, walking in the full Armor of God every day!

The Shoes of Peace

"You will keep in perfect peace all who trust in you, all whose thoughts are fixed on you!" Isaiah 26:3

Stepping Out in Faith

When we talk about stepping out in faith while wearing the Shoes of Peace, we are discussing a very special kind of trust in God. Imagine you're getting ready for a big adventure, but instead of packing a bag, you slip on the shoes God gave you. These aren't ordinary shoes; they carry you forward, even when you're unsure of the path ahead. Just as the Lord said to Joshua, "I will be with you; I will never leave you nor forsake you" (Joshua 1:5, NIV), we know that wearing these shoes means God is with us on our journey.

Understanding that we have the peace of God with us gives us the courage to take steps we might otherwise be too scared to take. Remember David, the young shepherd who faced Goliath? He didn't wear the king's armor; he stepped out with just a sling and his faith in God (1 Samuel 17:38-50). His trust wasn't in protective gear or even in his strength—it was in the Lord's power. So when we wear our Shoes of Peace, we can step out in faith, knowing that God's peace is a sign that He is with us, guiding our steps.

Understanding the Gospel of Peace

The "gospel of peace" sounds like a beautiful phrase, but what does it mean? The word "gospel" means good news, and this good news is about peace—peace between us and God and peace between each other. This is the message that Jesus brought to Earth, which heals and brings together, like in Ephesians 2:14, where Jesus is called "our peace," the one who breaks down the walls that separate us.

Wearing the Shoes of Peace means we understand this message deeply and want to live it out. It's like walking a path that has been smoothed out by Jesus' love and sacrifice, making it possible for us to go and share this peace with others. When Jesus sent out His disciples, He told them, "Peace be with you! As the Father has sent me, I am sending you" (John 20:21, NIV). He was giving them—and us—the mission to walk in His peace and spread it everywhere we go.

Importance of Being Prepared and Ready

Just like a scout packs their bag with the essentials before a hike, we must be prepared for the journey God calls us on. The Shoes of Peace are part of that preparation. They remind us to be ready to move when God says it's time—being prepared means knowing the good news of Jesus so well that it's like a song in our hearts, ready to be sung at any moment.

The apostle Peter tells us, "Always be prepared to give an answer to everyone who asks you to give the reason for the hope that you have" (1 Peter 3:15, NIV). This doesn't mean we need to have all the answers, but we should be ready to share the love and peace of Jesus with anyone we meet. The Shoes of Peace help us to stand firm in what we believe and to walk confidently, sharing God's word just as the disciples did on their many travels, bringing the message of peace to new places and new faces.

Biblical Instances of Those Ready to Share God's Word

Throughout the Bible, there are many examples of individuals who were ready and eager to share God's word. Take Philip, for example. In Acts 8:26-40, the Spirit told Philip to go to a desert road, where he met an Ethiopian official reading about the prophet Isaiah. Philip ran up to his chariot and was ready to explain the scriptures, leading the official to faith in Jesus. Philip was prepared, with his Shoes of Peace on, ready to walk wherever God led him to spread the good news.

Another example is the apostle Paul. In Acts 16:9-10, Paul had a vision of a man in Macedonia begging him, "Come over to Macedonia and help us." After the vision, Paul and his companions got ready to leave for Macedonia, concluding that God had called them to preach the gospel to them. They were always prepared to share the word of God, understanding that the Shoes of Peace are not just for standing but for going out into the world to spread the peace of Christ.

Adventures of Evangelism

Evangelism is a big word that means telling others the good news about Jesus. It's a bit like being a messenger in a royal court, sent out with an important announcement for the entire kingdom. But instead of a king or queen sending us, it's God who gives us the message, and our kingdom is the whole wide world!

Jonah is sent to Nineveh

When we think of someone sent on an adventure to share God's message, we can't forget Jonah. God told him to go to Nineveh, a big city with many people who were not living the way God wanted them to. At first, Jonah was scared and ran away! But

God showed him that when He sends us on a mission, it's important to listen because He has a plan. After spending three days in the belly of a big fish, Jonah went to Nineveh and told the people what God wanted him to say. And guess what? They listened! They changed their ways, and God had mercy on them (see the Book of Jonah). Jonah's story teaches us that even when we're scared to share God's word, He is with us, and He can do amazing things through us when we listen to Him.

Spreading the Word in Our Communities

You don't have to be a grown-up to spread God's word; you can do it right where you are, in your own community! Just like Jesus' disciples walked around telling people about Jesus, we can share His love with our friends, our family, and even with people we meet while playing at the park or during a day at school. It can be as simple as being kind to someone who is sad, talking about why you love going to church, or even inviting a friend to come to Sunday school with you.

Activities and Reflections

Engaging in activities and reflections can help you better understand how to live out your faith and share God's love with others.

Let's explore some ways you can do this, whether on your own, with friends, or with your family.

Map: Planning Your Journey of Sharing

Create a map of your world—it can be a drawing of your neighborhood, school, or anywhere you spend time. On this map, mark places where you can share God's love. Maybe it's a friend's house, the local park, or a family member's kitchen table. Next to each place, write down how you might share God's love there. Will you tell a friend about Jesus? Will you show kindness to a new kid at school? This map will help you plan your journey of sharing the good news.

As you look at your map, think about Jesus' Great Commission: "Go therefore and make disciples of all nations" (Matthew 28:19). Although you might not be traveling to distant countries, your community is a great place to start fulfilling this mission!

Team Challenge: Sharing God's Love in Fun Ways

Form a team with your friends, Sunday school class, or family, and come up with creative ways to share God's love. Maybe you'll organize a community cleanup, make cards for people in a nursing home, or put on a play about a Bible story for your neighbors. Each act of kindness is a way to share God's love.

After completing each activity, gather your team to talk about the experience. What did you learn? How did it feel to work together and share God's love? Reflect on Galatians 5:13, which says, "Serve one another humbly in love." Each time you serve others, you are sharing God's love.

Family Discussion: Being Ambassadors of Peace

As a family, you can discuss what it means to be ambassadors of peace. An ambassador is someone who represents a country or a leader. Just like ambassadors, we are called to represent Jesus wherever we go. Read 2 Corinthians 5:20, which talks about being Christ's ambassadors, and discuss what this looks like in your family's daily life.

Questions for your family discussion might include: How can we show God's peace at home, at work, at school, or with our friends? Can you think of a time when you made peace in a difficult situation? What can we do to better represent Jesus to those around us?

These activities and reflections can help you put your faith into action and share Jesus's peace in practical, tangible ways. Remember, even the smallest pebble creates ripples in the water—so, too, your actions and words can have a big impact in sharing God's love and peace.

As we tie the laces of our Shoes of Peace, ready to step out and spread harmony wherever we go, let's remember that our journey with God is both sure-footed and purposeful. Now, with our feet firmly grounded in His peace, let's gird ourselves with the Belt of Truth, preparing our hearts and minds to embrace and live out the ultimate truth found in God's Word. Onward we march, from walking in peace to standing strong in truth!

The Belt of Truth

"And you know the truth, and the truth will set you free."
John 8:32

Securing our Foundations

The Belt of Truth is like the part of our spiritual armor that holds everything else in place. In ancient times, soldiers would wear a belt around their waist to keep their armor secure and carry their weapons. It was essential for being ready for battle. In the same way, the Bible teaches us that truth is the foundation for everything we do as followers of Jesus. Ephesians 6:14 says, "Stand firm then, with the belt of truth buckled around your waist," which tells us that truth is what holds us up and keeps us ready for whatever comes our way.

Having the Belt of Truth means we are secure in knowing who God is, who we are in Him, and what He promises us in His Word. It's the truth of the Bible that keeps us from believing lies and getting confused. Jesus said in John 17:17, "Sanctify them by the truth; your word is truth." This means that God's

Word makes us pure and sets us apart for Him, and it's the truth that makes us different from the world. When we know God's truth, we can stand firm like a house built on solid rock, not shifting with the winds or washing away with the rain (Matthew 7:24-25).

Understanding the Meaning of Truth

Truth isn't just about facts; it's about being real and reliable. It's something that stays the same, no matter what else changes. For Christians, the meaning of truth starts with God because He is the source of all truth. The Bible says in John 14:6 that Jesus declared, "I am the way and the truth and the life." This means that everything about Jesus—His life, His words, His love—is the truth we can always trust.

Putting on the Belt of Truth means we try to live like Jesus, who was always true in what He said and did. We use the Bible as our guidebook for truth, helping us understand right from wrong. When we tell the truth and live by it, we reflect Jesus' character to the world. It's like a bright light that guides us and shows others the way (Psalm 119:105). In a world that sometimes doesn't value truth, choosing to be truthful is a powerful way to show we belong to Jesus.

The Significance of Honesty in Our Daily Life

Being honest in our daily lives is like walking in bright daylight where everyone can see clearly. It builds trust and shows that we are followers of Jesus, who is the truth. When we tell the truth, we don't have to remember what we said to whom; we can be at peace, knowing that our words match our actions. Colossians 3:9-10 (NLT) tells us, "Do not lie to each other, for you have stripped off your old sinful nature and all it's wicked deeds. Put on your new nature, and be renewed as you learn to know your Creator and become like Him." This means that being honest is part of becoming more like God, who made us.

Honesty is not just about not telling lies; it's also about living in a way that's true to God's teachings. When we make good and right choices, even when it's hard or when no one else is looking, we are wearing our Belt of Truth tightly. These daily choices build a life of honesty and integrity, which is like a shining light that guides us and those around us to God (Proverbs 12:22).

Bible Stories Exemplifying Truthfulness

There are many stories in the Bible about people who chose to be truthful. One such person was Nathanael. When Jesus saw Nathanael approaching, He said, "Here truly is an Israelite in whom there is no deceit" (John 1:47, NIV). Jesus praised

Nathanael for being honest and truthful, without trickery or lies.

Another example of truthfulness is the story of Queen Esther. She revealed her true identity and stood up for her people, even though it was risky. Her honesty and bravery saved her people from great danger (Book of Esther). By telling the truth, Esther showed great faith and courage. These stories encourage us to wear our Belt of Truth proudly and to be honest like Nathanael and brave like Esther, knowing that God values and works through those who live in truth.

Adventures of Honesty

Honesty is like a bright light that guides us through the dark, showing us the way and keeping us safe from stumbling. When we wear the Belt of Truth, we wrap ourselves in this light, ensuring that every step we take aligns with God's truth. But what happens when we choose to ignore this vital piece of armor?

Story of Ananias and Sapphira

In the Book of Acts, we find a cautionary tale about Ananias and Sapphira, a husband and wife who decided to be dishonest with their community and, more importantly, with God. They sold a piece of property and, wanting to appear more generous than they were, they lied about the amount of money they received, keeping part of it for themselves. They thought they could deceive the apostles and the early Christian community, but God saw their hearts.

Peter confronted Ananias, asking, "Ananias, how is it that Satan has so filled your heart that you have lied to the Holy Spirit and have kept for yourself some of the money you received for the land?" (Acts 5:3, NIV). When Ananias heard this, he fell down and died, and the same fate met Sapphira when she also lied. This shocking event was a powerful reminder to the early church of the seriousness of honesty and the consequences of deceit.

Consequences of Not Wearing the Belt of Truth

Ananias and Sapphira's story isn't just a tale from long ago; it's a lesson for us about the importance of truth in our lives. When we choose not to wear the Belt of Truth, we open ourselves up to small compromises that can lead to big consequences. Just like a tiny crack in a dam can eventually cause it to break, a small lie can lead to more dishonesty, hurting us and those around us.

Not wearing the Belt of Truth can also separate us from God. God is truth, and when we live in dishonesty, we move away from Him. Like Ananias and Sapphira, we might think we're only deceiving people, but in reality, we're also trying to hide from God, which is impossible. Psalm 51:6 says, "Yet you desired faithfulness even in the womb; you taught me wisdom in that secret place." This verse reminds us that God values truth deep within us, in the secret places of our hearts where only He can see.

Wearing the Belt of Truth isn't always easy, but the story of Ananias and Sapphira teaches us that honesty is not optional for those who follow Christ. It's a crucial part of our armor, protecting us from the inside out and keeping us close to God, who is the source of all truth.

Activities and Reflections

Integrating the Belt of Truth into our daily lives can be enlightening and fun. Through activities like games, journaling, and family discussions, we can explore the value of honesty in a tangible and memorable way. Ephesians 4:25 urges, "Therefore each of you must put off falsehood and speak truthfully to your neighbor, for we are all members of one body."

Journaling: A Day of Complete Honesty

Encourage yourself and a friend to keep a journal for a day, recording every time they are faced with a choice, to be honest or not. At the end of the day, reflect on how being honest made them feel, what challenges they faced, and what they learned about the value of truth.

This reflective practice can help deepen our understanding of Proverbs 12:22, which says, "The Lord detests lying lips, but he delights in people who are trustworthy." Journaling about our experiences with honesty can help us see more clearly how truth impacts our relationship with God and others, and how, like the Belt of Truth, it holds together the integrity of our character.

Family Discussion: The Importance of Truth at Home

Set aside time for a family discussion about the importance of truth in your household. Talk about why being honest is crucial and how it affects the trust and respect between family members. You can share stories from the Bible, like the story of Ananias and Sapphira, to illustrate the consequences of dishonesty and the blessings of living truthfully.

This conversation can be anchored in scriptures like Zechariah 8:16, which advises, "Speak the truth to each other, and render true and sound judgment in your courts." Discussing the role of truth at home reinforces the idea that honesty strengthens the family unit, builds trust, and creates a safe space where every member feels valued and understood. It's a practical way to weave the Belt of Truth into the fabric of everyday life, ensuring that the principles of God's Word are lived out not just in words but in actions and interactions within the home.

The Breastplate of Righteousness

"I walk in righteousness, in paths of justice." Proverbs 8:20

Welcome to another chapter in our Adventures in Scriptures! We're diving into an essential piece of the Armor of God: the Breastplate of Righteousness. Just like a knight wears a breastplate to protect his heart in battle, God gives us righteousness to guard our hearts from things that might try to hurt us.

Protecting the Heart -What Righteousness Means

Righteousness is indeed a big word with an even bigger meaning, especially when we think about how it fits into our lives as followers of Jesus. You see, righteousness is all about living in a way that is right and good, just like you learned. But here's an amazing secret: the righteousness we wear as part of our spiritual armor doesn't actually come from the good things we do. It comes from Jesus Christ Himself!

When Jesus came to Earth, lived a perfect life, and chose to die on the cross for us, He did something extraordinary. He took all the wrong things we've ever done or will do and said, "I've got this. I'll take your sin on Me." And in exchange, He gives us His righteousness. It's like if you had a really messy, scribbled-on piece of paper and Jesus said, "Here, take My clean, perfect piece of paper instead." 2 Corinthians 5:21 explains this beautifully: "God made him who had no sin to be sin for us, so that in him we might become the righteousness of God."

This means that when God looks at us, He doesn't see our mistakes or the times we haven't been perfect. Instead, He sees us as right and good because He sees Jesus' goodness covering us. This is why we can wear the Breastplate of Righteousness and protect our hearts. It's not about being perfect on our own; it's about trusting that Jesus has made us right with God.

Knowing that our righteousness comes from Jesus helps us make choices that please God and show love and respect to others. We do this not because we're trying to earn God's love but because we're so grateful for what Jesus has done for us. It's like wearing a thank-you note close to our hearts, reminding us to live in a way that honors Him. So, when you think about righteousness, remember it's a gift from Jesus. We wear it to protect our hearts, to remind us of His love, and to help us live in a way that reflects His goodness and love to the world around us.

Why Our Heart Needs Protection

Our heart is like a treasure chest that holds everything we care about the most. It's where our feelings, like love and joy, come from, but it's also where we feel sadness and fear. Just like a treasure chest must be kept safe from pirates, our hearts need protection from things that could hurt or lead us astray.

Sometimes, we might see something we want, even if it's not good for us, like maybe taking a toy that isn't ours or saying something unkind to get a laugh from others. These moments are like tests, challenging what's in our hearts and what we truly believe is important. The Breastplate of Righteousness, given to us by God, acts like a strong, shiny armor over our treasure chest, helping us remember what's truly valuable—being kind, honest, and loving like Jesus.

This breastplate doesn't just keep the bad stuff out; it also keeps the good things in, like peace, joy, and love. When we choose to follow Jesus and let His righteousness protect us, our hearts become like well-guarded treasure chests full of God's goodness. This means even when things get tough or we're tempted to make wrong choices, we can remember the love of Jesus that guards our hearts and choose to do what's right.

Biblical Figures Who Wore Their Breastplate Well

Many people in the Bible showed us how to wear the Breastplate of Righteousness.

Daniel in the Lion's Den

Daniel is a shining example of someone who wore his Breastplate of Righteousness exceptionally well. In the face of laws that forbade praying to anyone other than the king, Daniel continued to pray to God, not hiding his faith even when it meant facing deadly consequences. His commitment to righteousness and his unwavering faith in God protected him when he was thrown into a den of lions, a situation where any physical armor would have been useless. God sent an angel to shut the lions' mouths, and Daniel emerged unharmed, demonstrating the protective power of spiritual integrity (Daniel 6).

Esther's Courage and Wisdom

Esther, a young Jewish girl who became queen, also displayed remarkable righteousness. When her people were threatened with being destroyed, Esther had to make a choice. She could stay silent and protect herself or risk her life to save her people. Esther chose righteousness, fasting, praying, and then bravely approaching the king to plead for her people. Her righteous actions, guided by faith and love, led to the salvation of the Jews in Persia (Esther 4-8).

Job's Enduring Faith

Job's story is a powerful testament to the strength of the Breast-plate of Righteousness in withstanding personal loss and suffering. Despite losing everything he held dear, Job refused to curse God or turn away from his righteousness. His faith was tested through extreme trials, yet he maintained his integrity, not understanding why he suffered but refusing to compromise his righteousness before God. In the end, God restored Job's fortunes, doubling what he had lost, and blessed his latter days more than his beginning (Job 1-42).

Mary's Humble Submission

Mary, the mother of Jesus, exemplified righteousness through her humble obedience and faith. When told by the angel Gabriel that she would conceive the Son of God, Mary responded with faith, despite the potential for social scorn and misunderstanding. Her response, "I am the Lord's servant, may everything you have said about me come true." reflects a heart fully committed to God's will, protected by righteousness even in the face of uncertainty and potential danger (Luke 1:26-38).

Righteousness, like a sturdy breastplate, keeps us safe when we're faced with choices. Daniel could have decided not to pray and avoid trouble, but his commitment to doing right kept him safe, even in a den of hungry lions. It shows us that when we're faced with tough decisions, choosing what's right according to God's way can protect us from harm.

Activities and Reflections – Craft: Design Your Breastplate

Grab some craft supplies, and let's make our own breastplates! You can use cardboard as the base and decorate it with symbols that represent righteousness to you. It could be a heart to show love, a cross to remind us of Jesus, or anything that helps you remember to choose what's right.

Role-playing: Tough Choices Scenarios

Act out different scenarios with your friends or family where you have to make a tough choice. Maybe you find money and have to decide whether to keep it or find the owner, or someone asks you to cheat on a test. Discuss what the righteous choice would be in each situation.

Family Discussion: Daily Acts of Righteousness

Gather your family and talk about small ways to practice righteousness daily. It could be sharing with a sibling, doing your chores without being asked, or standing up for someone who's being treated unfairly. Together, you can make a plan to help each other remember and choose righteousness every day.

Remember, our righteousness comes from Jesus as a gift. Wearing the Breastplate of Righteousness is about making choices that protect our hearts and show love to God and others. Just like Daniel and many others in the Bible, we can face any challenge bravely when we choose what's right. Remember, righteousness isn't just for the big moments; it's for every choice we make, big or small. So, let's put on our breastplates and set out on today's adventure, ready to do what's right!

The Helmet of Salvation

"Restore to me the joy of your salvation, and make me willing to obey you." Psalm 51:12

Just as a helmet protects a soldier's head in battle, the Helmet of Salvation guards our minds, keeping our thoughts focused on God's great love and the salvation He offers us through Jesus. If you look at the picture on the cover, you will notice that the helmet covers the head, including the ears and mouth. You need the guard over your ears and mouth to protect the gates to your heart. When we give our hearts to God and accept Jesus as Our Savior, He lives in our hearts. It changes you from the inside out. Having Jesus in your heart makes you change your words; you want to be kinder to others. You want to listen to different and better things that encourage and lift you up. It changes the way you think and feel about things.

Guarding the Mind – Understanding Salvation's Significance

Salvation is a beautiful gift from God. Jesus was on a rescue mission, not to judge mankind but to save us from sin and its consequences. By believing in Jesus and what He did for us on the cross, we are saved and become part of God's family forever. This amazing truth is something we keep in our minds, just like wearing a helmet on our heads. When our enemy Satan comes to tell us we are in trouble with God or that God is mad at us, we can remember that if we repent, God will forgive us. Through forgiveness, we are restored to God's family.

How Our Thoughts Guide Our Actions

What we think about really matters because our thoughts often turn into actions. If we fill our minds with the truth about God's love and salvation, we're more likely to live in a way that shows we belong to Jesus. The Bible says in Philippians 4:8 to think about things that are true, noble, right, pure, lovely, and admirable. Keeping our minds on these things is like keeping our helmets strapped on tight. When we spend time reading our Bibles, we learn what good and pleasing behavior is in the eyes of God. As we think about these things, they become our actions, and people watching us can see how salvation through Jesus has changed us from the inside out.

In 2 Corinthians 3:2, "You yourselves are our letter, written on our hearts, known and read by everyone." People watch and see how your heart and mind have changed, followed by how you behave and the powerful impact Jesus has made in your life. You probably feel pretty powerful when you consider the other armor you are also wearing, the Shoes of Peace, the Belt of Truth, and the Breastplate of Righteousness.

Bible Heroes Who Remained Mentally Strong

Paul and Silas kept their minds focused on God, even when things got tough. Think about when they were thrown into prison for telling people about Jesus. Even there, they prayed and sang hymns to God (Acts 16:25). Their minds were guarded by the Helmet of Salvation, keeping them strong in faith despite their circumstances.

Paul and Silas are not the only Bible heroes who demonstrated incredible mental strength and resilience, safeguarded by what we can liken to the Helmet of Salvation. Their ability to maintain focus on God and express joy through singing and prayer, even in dire circumstances, is a powerful testament to the strength that comes from a deep-rooted faith in God. This same kind of mental fortitude, anchored in faith, is evident in the lives of several other biblical figures.

David's Confidence in God

David, before he became king, faced numerous life-threatening challenges that tested not only his physical strength but also his mental and emotional resilience. Facing Goliath, a giant warrior, David's confidence wasn't in his strength but in the power of God, who had delivered him from the paw of the lion and the bear. This trust in God's deliverance was David's mental armor, enabling him to confront and defeat Goliath against all odds (1 Samuel 17). Throughout his life, despite various trials, including being pursued by King Saul, David continually sought God's guidance. He expressed his fears, hopes, and gratitude through the Psalms, demonstrating his mental strength rooted in his relationship with God.

Elijah's Recovery and Renewal

After a significant victory on Mount Carmel, where he triumphed over the prophets of Baal, Elijah found himself fleeing for his life from Queen Jezebel's threats. In a moment of fear and exhaustion, he prayed for death. However, God met Elijah in his despair, providing food, rest, and a gentle whisper to strengthen and reassure him. This encounter shows the importance of spiritual and mental restoration, where God's gentle presence and provision can renew our minds and spirits, helping us to stand firm again (1 Kings 19).

Jesus in the Wilderness

Jesus Himself, after being baptized, faced a significant mental and spiritual test in the wilderness for forty days. During this time, He was tempted by Satan but countered every temptation with Scripture, demonstrating the power of God's Word to protect and strengthen the mind. Jesus' use of Scripture as a defense showcases the ultimate example of the Helmet of Salvation and the Sword of the Spirit at work, ensuring mental and spiritual integrity in the face of temptation (Matthew 4:1-11).

These stories illustrate that mental strength in the face of trials, rooted in faith, is a key aspect of spiritual resilience. Just as Paul and Silas worshipped in prison, Job held onto his integrity, David trusted in God's deliverance, God's gentle care restored Elijah, and Jesus wielded the Word of God in the wilderness, we too are called to guard our minds with the truth and hope of salvation, standing firm in our faith no matter the circumstances.

Adventures of Redemption

The story of Paul, formerly known as Saul, is a powerful testament to the transformative power of the Helmet of Salvation. Initially, Saul was a fervent persecutor of Christians, dedicated to eradicating the followers of Jesus. However, on his way to Damascus, a blinding light from heaven and the voice of Jesus stopped him in his tracks, leading to a profound personal trans-formation. Blinded and humbled, Saul was led into Damascus, where Ananias, a disciple of Jesus, healed him in the name of the Lord. This moment marked Saul's conversion, and he was baptized as Paul, dedicating his life to spreading the gospel of Christ. Paul's story, found in Acts 9:1-19, illustrates how the truth of salvation can dramatically change one's life and set them on a new path of righteousness and service to God.

Modern-day Distractions from Our Salvation

In the hustle and bustle of our modern lives, distractions are everywhere, vying for our attention and often pulling our focus away from the things that truly matter. For young minds especially, the allure of video games, the endless scroll of social media, and the constant bombardment of entertainment can make it challenging to keep our thoughts centered on Jesus and the incredible gift of salvation He offers.

The Allure of the Screen

Video games and social media aren't inherently bad. Still, they can become significant distractions when they consume too much of our time and energy—time and energy that could be spent building our relationship with God. These platforms are designed to keep us engaged, often making us crave the next level in a game or the next batch of "likes" on a post. This continuous loop of instant gratification can shift our focus from the eternal joy found in Jesus to temporary pleasures.

The Noise of the World

Beyond screens, the world around us is full of noise that can drown out God's still, small voice. From peer pressure at school to the latest trends and gadgets, getting caught up in wanting to fit in and have the newest, coolest things is easy. This pursuit can lead us away from the contentment and peace that come from knowing we are saved and loved by God, no matter what we have or what others think of us.

The Busyness Trap

Today's fast-paced lifestyle can also be a distraction. Our schedules are packed between school, sports, hobbies, and social events. It's easy to think we're too busy for prayer, Bible reading, or just being still and knowing He is God. This busyness can make us feel like we're wearing our helmets backward, unable to see or remember the direction we should be going—toward God.

Keeping Our Helmets On

Remembering to keep our "helmets" on means making a conscious effort to focus on what truly matters. It means setting aside time each day to talk to God, read His Word, and reflect on His love and the salvation He's given us. It's about choosing activities and entertainment that uplift and strengthen our faith rather than pull us away from it.

We can also use the tools of our modern world for good, like listening to worship music, watching uplifting content, or using apps designed to help us learn more about the Bible and stay connected to our faith community. It's about finding balance and making sure our hearts and minds are centered on Jesus.

Staying Focused in a World of Distractions

Staying focused on our salvation in a world full of distractions isn't always easy, but it's possible with God's help. Just like a ship uses an anchor to stay in place amidst the waves, our faith in Jesus is the anchor for our souls, keeping us steady and secure. When we feel ourselves getting pulled away by the distractions of the world, we can pray, asking God to help us refocus and remember the incredible love and salvation He offers.

By wearing our spiritual armor daily, especially the Helmet of Salvation, we can navigate the distractions of modern life with wisdom and discernment, keeping our eyes fixed on Jesus, the author, and perfecter of our faith.

Young Testimonies: Coming to Christ

There are many stories of kids, just like you, who have found hope and joy in Jesus. These young testimonies remind us that no one is too young to experience God's love and start a new life with Him. Hearing how others came to Christ can encourage us to share our stories and help our friends understand God's amazing salvation.

Activities and Reflections

Quiz: Test Your Knowledge of Salvation

Take a fun quiz with your friends or family to see what you know about salvation. Questions could include stories from the Bible, verses that discuss God's love and, Jesus' sacrifice, and what it means to be saved.

Crafting: Designing a Symbolic Helmet

Using paper, cardboard, or any other materials you like, craft a helmet that represents the salvation we have in Jesus. You can decorate it with symbols like crosses, hearts, or anything that reminds you of Jesus' love and the new life He gives us.

Family Discussion: Personal Salvation Stories

Gather with your family and share your own stories of how you came to understand what Jesus did for you. If some family members aren't sure yet, this can be a beautiful time to talk about any questions or thoughts they have about God and salvation. Sharing your personal journeys can help everyone see how real and life-changing God's love is.

The Helmet of Salvation is more than just a piece of armor; it's a constant reminder of our new life and our hope in Jesus. Keeping our minds focused on God's love helps us live out our salvation daily, showing the world the difference Jesus makes. So, let's put on our helmets, hold onto the truth of salvation, and step forward in faith, ready for whatever adventures God has in store for us!

The Sword of the Spirit

For the word of God is living and powerful, and sharper than any two-edged sword, piercing even to the division of soul and spirit, and of joints and marrow, and is a discerner of the thoughts and intents of the heart. Hebrews 4:12

Next, we will explore a super cool piece of the Armor of God: The Sword of the Spirit. Imagine a sword that's not too heavy, not too light, and shines brighter than the sun. This isn't just any sword; it's special because it represents God's Word, the Bible!

Understanding the Bible's Power – Wielding God's Word

The Bible is like a treasure chest filled with amazing stories, powerful lessons, and God's promises to us. But it's not just a book to read at bedtime; it's like a sword that helps us in life.

When we learn what the Bible says, we're like warriors learning how to use their swords. It helps us know right from wrong and teaches us about God's incredible love.

The Dual Nature of the Sword: Defense and Offense

Our Sword of the Spirit has two super important jobs. First, it's a weapon that protects us. When we remember Bible verses, we can use them to take captive bad thoughts or help us avoid wrong choices. Second, our sword can also be used like a scalpel, separating anything that is not of God from our lives. This would be like removing wrong thinking about different things. Things like selfishness, envy, unforgiveness, and so much more.

When you begin to know and walk in the word of God, you will feel a heaviness if you are carrying unforgiveness in your heart. In the Word, Jesus tells us to "forgive, and you will be forgiven" (Luke 6:37). You decide to forgive the person you held unforgiveness over, and suddenly, you feel free from that burden because you also know that God has forgiven you.

Bible Stories of the Word in Action

There are many wonderful Bible stories where God's Word is like a superhero's sword. Remember when Jesus was in the desert, and the sneaky devil tried to trick Him? Jesus used God's Word to stop the devil's tricks, saying, "It is written..." (Matthew

4:1-11). And then there's David, a young shepherd boy who defeated the giant Goliath not with a big sword but with his faith in God and a little sling (1 Samuel 17). These stories show us that knowing and believing God's Word gives us strength, just like a mighty sword. Besides Jesus in the desert and David facing Goliath, there are numerous other instances that highlight the Word in action.

Joshua and the Walls of Jericho

In the book of Joshua, we find the remarkable story of the walls of Jericho falling down. Joshua and the Israelites were facing a formidable obstacle: the massive walls of Jericho stood between them and the land God promised them. But God gave Joshua specific instructions, which might have seemed unusual at first. For six days, they were to march around the city once each day, and on the seventh day, they were to march around seven times; then, the priests would blow their trumpets, and everyone would shout. Joshua followed God's commands precisely, and on that seventh day, the walls of Jericho collapsed (Joshua 6). This story illustrates the power of obedience to God's Word and how faith in His instructions, no matter how unconventional they may seem, can lead to miraculous outcomes.

Elijah and the Prophets of Baal

The confrontation between Elijah and the prophets of Baal on Mount Carmel is another vivid example of God's Word in action. At a time when the Israelites were wavering between worshipping God and Baal, Elijah proposed a test to prove who the true God was. Each would prepare a bull as a sacrifice but not set fire to it; the god who answered by fire would be deemed the true God. Despite the prophets of Baal's loud cries and rituals, their god did not answer. But when Elijah prayed, God sent fire from heaven that consumed not only the sacrifice but even the stones and soil around it, and all the water in the trench Elijah had made. This powerful demonstration led the people to proclaim, "The Lord, He is God!" (1 Kings 18). Elijah's unwavering faith in God's promise and courage to stand alone against 450 prophets showcase the strength of adhering to God's Word.

Shadrach, Meshach, and Abednego

The story of Shadrach, Meshach, and Abednego in the fiery furnace is a stirring testament to the power of faith and God's Word. When King Nebuchadnezzar ordered everyone to worship a golden statue, these three young men refused, staying true to God's commandments. As a result, they were thrown into a blazing furnace, but their faith in God's protection was so strong that they were not harmed by the fire. In fact, a fourth figure, resembling a son of the gods, was seen walking with them in the furnace. Astonished, Nebuchadnezzar called them out, unharmed by the flames, and acknowledged the power of their

God (Daniel 3). This story highlights how faith in God's Word can protect us in the face of life's fiercest trials.

The Centurion's Faith

In the New Testament, the story of the Roman centurion's faith in Jesus' authoritative word is a compelling example of belief in action. The centurion approached Jesus, asking Him to heal his servant. When Jesus offered to come to his house, the centurion expressed his unwavering faith in Jesus' spoken word alone, believing that if Jesus merely said the word, his servant would be healed. Marveling at such faith, Jesus declared it done, and the servant was healed at that very hour (Matthew 8:5-13). This account underscores the power inherent in Jesus' words and the miracles that faith in His word can bring about.

The Story of Nehemiah

In the bustling city of Jerusalem, a man named Nehemiah took on a great challenge. Jerusalem's walls were in ruins, leaving the city vulnerable. Nehemiah, guided by his faith and God's words, decided to rebuild these walls to protect his people. Despite facing many who wanted to stop him, Nehemiah used wisdom from God's word to stay strong and encourage his people. He prayed and kept God's promises close to his heart, which helped him complete the seemingly impossible task of rebuilding the walls of Jerusalem (Nehemiah 2-6). Nehemiah's story teaches us that we can face big challenges and make a difference with God's word in our hearts.

Each of these stories, from the fall of Jericho's walls to the unwavering faith of a Roman officer, teaches us about the extraordinary power of God's Word. Like a mighty sword, it has the power to break down barriers, protect us from harm, and heal the broken. As we learn and live by these words, we embark on a grand adventure, wielding the Sword of the Spirit to face challenges with courage, uphold truth, and spread God's love, just like the heroes of the Bible.

So, let's pick up our Sword of the Spirit and prepare for adventure! By learning and living by God's Word, we're not just reading stories; we're becoming part of the greatest adventure of all.

Challenges of Maintaining Spiritual Discipline

Staying disciplined in reading the Bible and praying every day can sometimes feel like a big task, especially when we'd rather play video games or watch TV. But just like a warrior practices with their sword every day to stay sharp, we need to keep our Sword of the Spirit sharp by reading God's Word and talking to Him in prayer. It might seem tough at first, but the more we do it, the stronger and wiser we'll become.

Kids Who Memorized and Used the Scripture

There are many stories of kids, just like you, who have memorized parts of the Bible and used them in amazing ways. Some kids have shared verses with friends who were sad or scared, and those words helped bring comfort and hope. Others have remembered verses when they felt afraid about courage, like "This is my command- Be strong and courageous! Do not be afraid or discouraged. For the Lord your God is with you wherever you go." (Joshua 1:9). By keeping God's Word in their hearts, these kids were able to spread light and love to those around them, showing the true power of the Sword of the Spirit.

Activities and Reflections

Memorize & Recite: A Verse a Day

Challenge yourself to learn a new Bible verse every day. You can write them on cards, draw pictures about them, or even make up a song. Start with verses about Courage, Love, Patience, Faith, and Hope. Share these verses with your family and friends, and encourage them to learn with you. By the end of the week, you'll have a collection of verses you know by heart, ready to use whenever you need them.

Family Discussion: The Bible's Role in Our Home

Gather your family and talk about how the Bible is like a treasure map for life. Discuss how everyone can help make sure that reading the Bible and praying together becomes a special part of your daily routine. Share your favorite Bible stories or verses and talk about how they have helped you or can help you in the future. This conversation will help make the Bible an important part of your family's adventure together.

We have learned that wielding the Sword of the Spirit is not just about knowing God's Word but living it out in our daily actions. By diving into stories of the past, practicing discipline, and sharing what we learn, we become true warriors of faith, ready to face the world with God's wisdom as our guide. So let's embark on this adventure with excitement, knowing that with our Sword of the Spirit in hand, we're never alone and always prepared.

The Shield of Faith

"You are my refuge and my shield; your word is my source of hope."
Psalm 119:114

As we continue learning about the Armor of God, we come to the final piece: The Shield of Faith. Imagine carrying a shield so strong that no matter what comes flying your way, you can stand safe and secure. This shield isn't made of wood or metal but of faith—your trust and belief in God's power and love.

Understanding Faith's Protective Role – Guarding Against Attacks

Faith is like an invisible shield that protects us. It's like holding up a shield in a battle when we believe in God and trust Him. This shield can stop all kinds of things that might try to hurt us, like fear, doubt, or feeling alone. It's not always easy to hold up our shield, especially when things get tough, but remembering God's promises helps keep our shield strong and in front of us. The more we carry our shield, the stronger we get. The stronger we get carrying our shield, the bigger our shield becomes as our faith continues to grow.

Biblical Battles and the Power of Faith

The Bible is full of stories where faith acts as a powerful shield. Think about David, a young shepherd boy who faced a giant warrior named Goliath. David didn't wear heavy armor or carry a big sword as King Saul tried to have him do. No, he had faith in God and a simple slingshot. His trust and faith in God was his shield, and it was strong enough to defeat Goliath (1 Samuel 17). David's story teaches us that no matter how big our problems seem, our faith in God can help us overcome them.

Sometimes, we might feel doubt creeping into our thoughts, trying to make our shield of faith feel smaller and weaker. Maybe it's a scary situation or a time when a prayer feels unanswered. But remember Peter, who walked on water towards Jesus? When he kept his eyes on Jesus, he was walking just fine. But the moment he looked at the stormy waves and doubted, he began to sink (Matthew 14:29-31). Jesus helped him up, reminding him to keep his faith strong, no matter the storm.

Noah builds an Ark

Imagine being one of only a few people who believed it was important to follow God. And because you were the only one whom God found to be righteous in His sight, you were the one

He chose to give a plan that would save your family and animals to one day replenish the earth. God chose Noah to offer the plans to build the ark. In obedience to God, he and his family would work building the ark for the next 100 years and making it ready. Now, you should know that before this time, they had not seen the rain; water came up from the ground to water the plants and provide water for the people.

Do you think people were making fun of Noah for building the ark in obedience to God? Because Noah was faithful to do all God instructed, when the great flood came, his family and all of the animals went into the ark, and the Lord closed the door. The storms and rains came, and all life was lost except Noah, his family, and the animals in the ark. This story shows us that our faith can do amazing things when we follow God's guidance, even when it's hard to understand.

Modern Challenges to Faith and Overcoming Them

Today, we might not face city walls like Jericho, but we will still face challenges. Maybe it's feeling left out at school, worrying about a test, or seeing bad things happen in the world. These situations can test our faith, but just like Joshua, we can remember God's promises and keep our Shield of Faith up. Talking to God, reading the Bible, and sharing our feelings with family or friends can help make our shield even stronger.

Real-life Testimonies of Unyielding Faith

Many people, even kids, have amazing stories of how their faith helped them through tough times. These real-life testimonies inspire us and show that God is always with us, helping us hold our Shield of Faith high. Can you remember a time when you made a decision to do the right thing even when your friends were encouraging you to do something you might get in trouble for? Your faith shield got a little bigger when you chose to do the right thing. Remembering to do what is right in the eyes of the Lord, even when it is hard, shows your trust in the Lord to protect you and keep you safe.

Activities and Reflections

DIY: Crafting a Personal Shield

Let's get creative and make our own Shield of Faith! Use cardboard, paint, markers or crayons, and decorations to create a shield that represents your faith. You can draw symbols that remind you of God's love, strength, and promises. Whenever you see your shield, let it remind you of your faith in God.

Memory Verse Challenge: Strengthening Faith

Choose a Bible verse about faith that you love, and try to memorize it. You can write it down, make a drawing about it, or even set it to a tune to help you remember. This verse will be like a mini-shield you can carry in your heart, ready to use whenever you need a boost of faith.

Family Discussion: Remembering Moments of Faith

Gather with your family and share stories of times when your faith was like a shield for you. It could be a moment when you were scared but prayed and felt peace or when you trusted God with a big problem and saw Him help you through it. Sharing these moments can help everyone remember how powerful and important our faith is.

Holding up the Shield of Faith might take effort, especially when challenges come our way, but remember, with faith in God, we're never fighting alone. So, let's march forward with our shields held high, ready for whatever comes our way.

Understanding the Real Battle

We have reviewed all of the different pieces of the Armor of God. Now, we will uncover the mysteries of the real battle we face every day. It's not like the battles you see in cartoons or video games; it's a special kind of fight that needs a special type of armor—the Armor of God!

Ephesians 6:12 Explained – Beyond Flesh and Blood

Ephesians 6:12 tells us that our real battle isn't against people we can see but against powerful forces in the spiritual world that we can't see with our eyes. These forces try to make us do wrong things or feel scared and alone, but God gives us special protection to stand strong against them.

The Spiritual Realm and Its Reality

Just like there's a world around us with trees, mountains, and oceans, there's also a spiritual world that we can't see. This world is filled with God's love and His angels, but also with principalities of spiritual darkness that bring challenges that we face in our hearts and minds. That's why we must put on the Armor of God to keep our hearts, minds, and spirits safe. In 2 Corinthians 10:4-5, Paul is telling the people, "We use God's mighty weapons, not worldly weapons, to knock down the strongholds of human reasoning and to destroy false arguments. We destroy every proud obstacle that keeps people from knowing God. We capture their rebellious thoughts and teach them to obey Christ."

The only way that Paul can do this is to know the word of God, to answer and proclaim the truth in the word, so that these people would be set free from their wrong thinking. Through prayer and taking authority over the lies of the enemy, they are able to reach the people with the word of God, setting them free from the spiritual enemy.

Bible Stories of Spiritual Warfare

There are many stories in the Bible where God's people faced big challenges with the help of God's strength. Remember David and Goliath? David didn't win because he was the biggest or the strongest; he won because he had faith in God's power to protect and help him (1 Samuel 17).

One of the Bible's foundational stories of spiritual warfare is the Exodus, where Moses leads the Israelites out of Egypt, away from Pharaoh's tyranny. The plagues that God sent upon Egypt, culminating in the Passover and the parting of the Red Sea, were not just physical manifestations of God's power but also acts of spiritual warfare against the gods of Egypt and the oppressive spirit of slavery. Moses' confrontations with Pharaoh and his reliance on God's instructions demonstrate a profound trust in God's sovereignty and power, highlighting the spiritual battle behind the physical liberation of the Israelites (Exodus 7-14).

The Apostle Paul's missionary journeys were fraught with both physical and spiritual opposition. In Ephesus, for example, Paul's preaching led to a significant decrease in the business of local silversmiths who made idols, causing a riot. This wasn't just a socio-economic conflict but a spiritual battle against the stronghold of idolatry in the city. Despite imprisonment, beatings, and shipwrecks, Paul's persistent ministry is a testimony of the ongoing spiritual warfare faced by those spreading the Gospel, emphasizing the victory that comes through perseverance and faith (Acts 19, 2 Corinthians 11:23-27).

Adventures Beyond Sight

The Armor of God in Action

The story of David and Goliath from 1 Samuel 17 is a compelling reflection of being ready for battle by embodying the principles of the whole armor of God. Although the story in the Bible doesn't directly mention the Armor of God as described in Ephesians 6, David's faith, actions, and words demonstrate what it means to be spiritually equipped for battle.

In this story, David, a young shepherd boy, faces Goliath, a giant warrior intimidating the armies of Israel. David's readiness for battle doesn't come from physical armor; in fact, he rejects King Saul's offer of traditional armor because it's cumbersome and unfamiliar to him. Instead, David goes into battle with a sling, five smooth stones, and, most importantly, an absolute faith in God.

David's trust in God as his protector and deliverer reflects the Shield of Faith, deflecting the figurative "fiery darts" of fear and doubt cast by Goliath's threats. His choice to face Goliath with just a sling and stones, relying on God's strength, mirrors the Sword of the Spirit, using God's word and promises as his offensive weapon. David declares to Goliath, "You come against me with sword and spear and javelin, but I come against you in the name of the Lord Almighty, the God of the armies of Israel, whom you have defied" (1 Samuel 17:45, NIV), showcasing his spiritual armor in action.

David's story vividly illustrates how faith, reliance on God's word, and righteousness (right standing with God) equip us for life's battles, aligning with the metaphorical Armor of God that Paul describes in Ephesians 6. This narrative teaches that true strength and victory come not from physical armor or weapons but from being spiritually prepared and grounded in faith.

Recognizing the Signs of Spiritual Battles

Sometimes, we might feel worried, scared, or tempted to do things we know are wrong. These feelings can be signs of the spiritual battles we face. Just like David, we can remember to put on our Armor of God to help us stand strong and overcome these challenges with God's help.

Overcoming through the Armor of God

No matter what we face, the Armor of God is always there to protect us and give us strength. Whether we're dealing with a tough day at school, a fight with a friend, or feeling worried about how something will turn out, we can pray and remember each piece of God's Armor to help us through.

Activities and Reflections

Pictionary: Spiritual vs. Physical Battles

Play a game of Pictionary with your friends or family. In this game, you draw things related to physical battles (like knights and castles) and spiritual battles (like prayer, love, and kindness).

This will help you see the difference and remember how to fight the real battle with God's help.

Spiritual Warrior Badge of Honor

Create a special badge that represents each piece of the Armor of God. You can draw, color, and decorate your badges and wear them as a reminder that you're a strong warrior for God, ready for any battle that comes your way.

Family Discussion: Supporting Each Other in Battles

Sit down with your family and talk about times when you've faced tough challenges and how you've helped each other through them. Share how putting on the Armor of God (like being truthful, choosing what's right, and remembering God's love) helped you overcome these challenges together.

Understanding the real battle and learning how to wear the Armor of God makes you a warrior in God's kingdom! Remember, no matter what battles we face, with God's Armor, we're never fighting alone. So, let's stand strong, support each other, and face every challenge with courage and love!

Embracing the Full Armor

"Therefore take up the whole armor of God, that you may be able to withstand in the evil day, and having done all, to stand." Ephesians 6:13

Dear young warriors, we've journeyed together through the incredible Armor of God, discovering each piece and its unique power. Now, as we reach the end of this adventure, let's understand how all these pieces work together to protect and empower us every single day.

The Interconnectedness of the Armor

Imagine each piece of the Armor of God like parts of a noble knight's armor. Just like a knight needs every part of their suit to be fully protected and strong, we need every piece of God's armor. The Belt of Truth keeps us rooted in honesty, the Breastplate of Righteousness protects our hearts, the Shoes of Peace guide our steps, the Shield of Faith defends against doubts, the

Helmet of Salvation keeps our minds safe, and the Sword of the Spirit, which is God's Word, gives us wisdom and strength. When we wear all these pieces together, we're fully equipped to face anything that comes our way.

Kids Being Prepared for Their Daily Spiritual Journey

Every day is an adventure filled with new challenges and opportunities. Just like getting ready for school in the morning, putting on the Armor of God prepares you for the day ahead. It's not about wearing physical armor but about remembering God's truths, choosing what's right, finding peace in His promises, trusting in His protection, knowing His love saves us, and using His word to guide us. This way, no matter what you face—whether it's a tough test, a disagreement with a friend, or feeling scared or alone—you're ready and strong because you're wearing God's special armor.

Stand Firm in Faith

Now, brave adventurers, it's your turn to stand tall and confident in your faith. Remember, you are never alone on this journey. God is always with you, offering His Armor to protect and strengthen you. When you wake up each day, think about putting on each piece of the Armor of God. You can even say a little prayer as you imagine putting on each piece, asking God to help you live out His truths, make choices that please Him, and spread kindness and peace wherever you go.

You are God's mighty warrior, equipped with an incredible Armor that makes you ready for anything. With the Armor of God, you can be a shining light of faith, hope, and love to everyone around you. So, stand firm, keep the faith, and take on each new day with courage and joy, knowing you're wearing the most powerful armor there is—the Armor of God.

Thank you for joining this adventure through the Armor of God. You're now fully equipped to face your daily challenges with strength, courage, and wisdom. Wear your armor proudly, young warriors, and go forth in the strength of God's mighty power!

Adventures in Scriptures for Kids: The Parable Teachings of Jesus

Lorie Eubank

The Power of Stories

Why Parables?

Imagine sitting around a campfire, listening to someone tell an exciting story that keeps you on the edge of your seat. That's the power of a good story - it can transport you to different places, introduce you to unique characters, and teach you important lessons without you even realizing it! Parables are special stories that Jesus told to help people understand big ideas in a simple way. Just like how we use pictures and examples to explain things, Jesus used parables to make his teachings clear and memorable. They're like puzzles; as you piece them together, you discover truths that can help you in your everyday life. The use of parables illuminates the unique and powerful method Jesus employed to impart wisdom and moral teachings.

Parables serve as bridges between the known and the unknown, transforming abstract concepts into tangible realities. Through the simplicity of everyday scenarios, such as a farmer sowing seeds or a woman searching for a lost coin, Jesus connected with people from all walks of life. These stories were not just for entertainment; they were shared to provoke thought, inspire introspection, and invite listeners into a deeper understanding of spiritual truths. The beauty of a parable lies in its ability to encapsulate complex ideas in relatable narratives, making profound truths accessible to everyone, regardless of their background or level of education.

Jesus: The Master Storyteller

Over 2,000 years ago, in the lands of deserts and seas, hills and valleys, Jesus shared his teachings with everyone who would listen - from fishermen and farmers to merchants and mothers. He chose to tell stories, or parables, because he knew that was the best way to reach the hearts of all these different people. These parables were about everyday things like seeds, lamps, and lost coins, but they had deeper meanings about love, kindness, and forgiveness. Jesus was a master at using the world around him to explain life's greatest lessons in a way that everyone, young and old, could understand and remember if they were listening.

His choice of parables as a teaching method was strategic and intentional. In a time and place where oral teaching was the standard, stories were not just remembered; they were felt and lived. By embedding his teachings in parables, Jesus ensured that his messages were not only heard but also experienced emotionally and spiritually by his listeners.

The foundational explanation for Jesus' use of parables is found in Matthew 13:10-17. Here, Jesus explains to his disciples that parables are a means to reveal the mysteries of the kingdom of heaven to those who are open to understanding while also concealing these truths from those who are not receptive. This passage underscores the dual function of parables: to enlighten those who are seeking truth and to obscure it from those who are indifferent or hostile. The use of parables is thus a form of divine teaching tailored to the spiritual openness of the listener.

Adventure Awaits!

Are you ready for an adventure like no other? In this book, we'll journey through the parables of Jesus, discovering the treasures hidden within each story. Each chapter will be like opening a new door to a world filled with valuable lessons, exciting discoveries, and fun activities that will help you see the world in a whole new way. We'll explore the lessons behind the stories and think about how they apply to things like making friends, solving problems, and doing the right thing. So, grab your explorer's hat and get ready to set out on aa adventure through the parables of Jesus!

The Parable of the Sower (Matthew 13:1-23)

"For God is the one who provides seed for the farmer and then bread to eat. In the same way, he will provide and increase your resources and then produce a great harvest of generosity in you." 2 Corinthians 9:10 NLT

Setting the Scene

On a sunny day, beside a sparkling lake, a crowd gathered around a man known for his wisdom and kindness. This man was Jesus, and people from all over had come to hear him speak. The gentle lapping of the water and the distant calls of fishermen casting their nets set a peaceful backdrop for what was about to be a powerful lesson. Jesus chose this moment, with nature all around and a diverse crowd in front of him, to share a story that would unfold the mysteries of life and growth through the simplicity of a sower and his seeds.

Purpose of Parables: Jesus used parables, stories that used everyday experiences to explain deeper truths and to reach the hearts of everyone, no matter their age or background. He knew that a story about a farmer scattering seeds would be something everyone could picture, making the spiritual lessons more relatable and easier to understand.

Breaking Down the Parable

In the parable, a sower goes out to sow seeds, which fall onto four different types of soil:

The Path: Some seeds fall on a walking path, like a sidewalk, where they can't take root and are quickly eaten up by birds.

Rocky Ground: Other seeds land on rocky soil, where they sprout quickly but soon wither away because they don't have deep roots.

Among Thorns: Some seeds fall among thorns, which grow up and choke the tender plants, preventing them from ever bearing fruit..

Good Soil: Finally, some seeds fall on fertile soil, where they grow strong and produce a bountiful harvest.

The Meaning of the Seeds: The seeds represent the teachings and wisdom that Jesus shares. Just like seeds need the right conditions to grow, these teachings need an open and ready heart to truly take root and flourish.

Challenges of Growth and Nurturing: The parable highlights the different challenges we face in life that can prevent us from growing and reaching our full potential, like distractions, difficulties, and competing priorities, symbolized by the birds, rocks, and thorns.

Jesus Explains to His Disciples

After sharing the parable with the crowd, Jesus takes a moment to explain its deeper meaning to his closest followers, his disciples.

The Mystery of Parables: Jesus tells his disciples that parables are a way to reveal the secrets of the kingdom to those who are ready to hear and understand them, while also concealing the truth from those who are not open to it.

Interpretation of the Soils: Each type of soil represents a different response to Jesus' teachings:

The path symbolizes those who hear the message but don't understand it, allowing it to be taken away easily.

The rocky ground represents those who receive the message with joy but give up when faced with challenges because they lack a strong foundation.

The thorns are like the worries of life and the lure of wealth that suffocate spiritual growth.

The good soil stands for those with an open and receptive heart who listen, understand, and produce a rich harvest of good deeds and character.

Emphasis on Understanding and Fruitfulness: Jesus emphasizes the importance of truly understanding his teachings and allowing them to transform our lives. Just like the good soil produces a plentiful harvest, a heart that truly embraces Jesus' words will lead to a life full of positive actions and deep, lasting joy.

Making it Personal

Imagine you have a handful of seeds you want to plant in your garden to grow beautiful flowers or yummy vegetables. But what if you tossed those seeds on the sidewalk, among rocks, or into a thorny bush? They wouldn't grow very well, would they? That's because seeds need good soil to grow strong and healthy.

Jesus told a story about seeds to help us understand something important about our hearts and minds. Think of the seeds as lessons about love, kindness, and sharing. Our hearts are like the soil where we plant these lessons. If our heart is like the sidewalk (hard and closed), we won't understand or remember these important lessons. If it's like rocky or thorny ground (filled with too many distractions or not caring enough), the lessons might start to grow but then get lost or forgotten. But if our heart is like good soil (open and ready to learn), these lessons will grow big and strong, just like the best plants in the garden.

So, Jesus' story teaches us to be like good soil—always ready and eager to learn, listen, and grow from the good things we hear, without letting distractions or stubbornness stop us. This way, we can grow into the best versions of ourselves, full of kindness and love, just like a beautiful, thriving garden.

The Parable of the Prodigal Son (Luke 15:11-32)

"A single day in your courts is better than a thousand anywhere else! I would rather be a gatekeeper in the house of my God than live the good life in the homes of the wicked." Psalm 84:10 NLT

Setting the Scene

In a time and place where family and tradition held the fabric of society together, Jesus tells a story that would challenge the very core of these values, yet in a way that brings a deeper understanding of forgiveness and love. This parable, set in a rural household, revolves around a father and his two sons. Each character in this parable provides an example of profound life lessons.

The Context of the Parable: Jesus shares this parable at a time when he is being criticized for associating with sinners and outcasts. He uses this story to illustrate God's boundless mercy and to challenge societal norms about worthiness and redemption.

Introducing the Main Characters:

The Father, who represents God's unconditional love and forgiveness.

The Younger Son, who seeks independence and adventure but finds himself in dire straits due to his reckless choices.

The Older Son, who stays home, dutifully working on his father's land, embodying obedience and responsibility.

Breaking Down the Parable

The Departure and Rebellion: The younger son, restless and eager for independence, asks for his inheritance early and leaves home. He travels far and squanders his fortune on a reckless lifestyle, only to find himself destitute and alone. This situation forces him to reflect on his actions and helps him realize the blessings of the life he left behind.

The Return and Redemption: Swallowing his pride, the younger son returns home, prepared to beg for forgiveness and work as a servant. To his surprise, his father welcomes him with open arms, celebrating his return as if he were welcoming back someone from the dead, symbolizing the joy of reconciliation and the possibility of a fresh start.

The Older Brother's Response: The older son's reaction introduces a contrast to the father's joy. He feels angry and betrayed, questioning the fairness of the celebration for his wayward brother when he himself has never disobeyed. This high-lights the challenge of unconditional love and forgiveness, even for those who feel they've earned their righteousness.

Jesus Explains to His Disciples

God's Unconditional Love: Through the character of the father, Jesus illustrates God's boundless and unconditional love, which welcomes back the lost and the repentant without hesitation or reservation, celebrating their return to the right path.

The Joy of Repentance: The story emphasizes the beauty of repentance, not just as an act of saying sorry, but as a transformative process that brings one back into harmony with oneself, with others, and with God. The celebration for the younger son symbolizes the joy in heaven over one sinner who repents.

Challenge of Unconditional Forgiveness: The older son's struggle reflects the human challenge of accepting God's grace towards others, especially when we feel they don't deserve it. It calls into question our understanding of justice and fairness and invites us to embrace a higher standard of love and forgiveness, just as the father in the parable does.

This parable, rich in imagery and emotion, not only reveals the depths of God's love and the joy of forgiveness but also challenges us to reflect on our own capacity for compassion, understanding, and unconditional love toward others.

Making it Personal

Imagine you have two siblings: one decides to go on a big adventure with their savings and ends up spending it all, while the other stays home, helping out and doing what's expected. The sibling who left eventually runs out of money, and things get really tough. They remember how good they had it at home and decide to come back, hoping maybe, just maybe, they can be forgiven and work as a helper in their own home.

When they return, expecting to be in big trouble, they're surprised to find open arms and a big welcome back party just for them! This is like the dad in the story, who is so happy to have his child back that he doesn't care about the mistakes; he's just glad they're safe and sound. But the sibling who stayed home feels a bit upset. They think, "I've been here all along, doing everything right. Where's my party?"

This story shows us how everyone makes mistakes, but it's never too late to come back and apologize. It's also about how important it is to forgive, just like the dad in the story, who represents how loving and forgiving God is. It teaches us that even when we feel overlooked or undervalued, like the sibling who stayed home, everyone is loved and important, and everyone deserves a second chance.

The Parable of the Good Samaritan (Luke 10:25-37)

"The Lord will not reject his people; he will not abandon his special possession." Psalm 94:14 NLT

Setting the Scene

In a moment filled with tension and curiosity, an expert in religious law stands up to test Jesus with a question that has puzzled hearts and minds for ages: "Who is my neighbor?" This question is not just about geography or family ties; it's about the essence of human connection and compassion. Jesus chooses to answer this profound question with a story that would redefine the concept of 'neighbor' for generations to come.

The Expert's Question: The question posed by the expert isn't just a matter of curiosity but a test aiming to challenge Jesus and possibly justify his own views on whom to consider worthy of love and whom to overlook.

Defining a Neighbor: Rather than giving a direct answer, Jesus describes a situation that illustrates the true meaning of 'neighbor,' transcending social boundaries, ethnic lines, and religious divisions and placing love and compassion at the heart of the relationship.

Breaking Down the Parable

The Injured Man and the Bypassers: The story begins with a man traveling from Jerusalem to Jericho, who is robbed and beaten and is left half-dead by the roadside. A priest and then a Levite, both respected figures in society, pass by the injured man, choosing to keep their distance. Their actions, or rather their inaction, highlight the ease with which people can ignore suffering when it inconveniences them or challenges their norms.

The Unexpected Helper: Enter the Samaritan, a figure least expected to show compassion, given the deep-seated prejudices between Jews and Samaritans at the time. Yet, it is he who stops, moved with pity, to tend to the man's wounds and ensure his recovery, even at personal cost. This act of kindness from an unexpected source challenges stereotypes and invites a broader understanding of community and care.

The Challenge to Act: The Samaritan's actions serve not only as a demonstration of compassion but also as a call to action. He goes beyond basic aid, ensuring the man's continued care and promising to return, embodying the essence of commitment to the well-being of another.

Jesus' Direct Message

True Neighborly Love: Through this parable, Jesus illustrates that neighborly love knows no boundaries and is not confined to those we know or are comfortable with. It's about recognizing the inherent dignity and worth of every individual and responding to their needs with compassion and kindness.

Overcoming Biases and Prejudices: The choice of a Samaritan as the hero of the story is deliberate, confronting the audience's prejudices head-on and challenging them to see beyond societal divisions. This parable calls for a radical reevaluation of who merits our love and care, urging us to extend our compassion to all, regardless of background, belief, or status.

Taking Action on Compassion: The Good Samaritan parable powerfully reminds us that compassion is not a passive emotion but a call to action. It's about seeing the needs around us, feeling moved by them, and doing something to help. Jesus ends the parable by instructing, "Go and do likewise," making it clear that the essence of the story is not just to feel but to act, not just to empathize but to engage in tangible acts of love and kindness.

In this simple yet profound parable, Jesus redefines what it means to be a neighbor, setting a standard of love and compassion that transcends all human-made barriers, calling us to a higher purpose of unity and mutual care.

Making it Personal

Let's imagine you're walking through your school hallway, and you see someone who tripped and dropped all their books. Some people might walk right past, maybe because they're late or they don't want to get involved. But then, someone unexpected, maybe someone from a different grade or someone you wouldn't think would help, stops to help pick up the books and makes sure the other person is okay. This story is a bit like the one Jesus told about the Good Samaritan.

In Jesus' story, a man is hurt by the side of the road, and people you'd expect to help, like a priest and a Levite (who were kind of like community leaders), just walk on by. Then, someone from a group that wasn't liked very much by others, a Samaritan, stops to help the hurt man. He even takes him to a place to rest and pays for his care. Jesus told this story to show that being a good neighbor or a good friend isn't about who lives next to you or who's just like you. It's about helping and caring for others, no matter who they are or where they come from.

So, the story teaches us that anyone can be a neighbor, and being a good one means helping others when they need it, not just when it's easy or when they're just like us. It's about being kind and caring, just like the Samaritan in the story, and doing the right thing, even when it's hard or when no one else is.

The Parable of the Mustard Seed (Matthew 13:31-32)

"Do not despise these small beginnings, for the Lord rejoices to see the work begin..." Zechariah 4:10 NLT

Setting the Scene

In a moment of teaching, surrounded by those eager to hear his wisdom, Jesus shares a parable that highlights the beauty and mystery of growth from the smallest of beginnings. This story, simple yet profound, draws from the natural world to reveal spiritual truths.

The Wonder of Growth: Jesus begins by drawing attention to the natural process of growth, which is both gradual and transformative. It's a process that's often overlooked in its early stages but leads to outcomes that far exceed the initial expectations.

The Power of Small Beginnings: The focus on a mustard seed, one of the tiniest seeds known to his audience, serves to illustrate that the size of a beginning does not determine its potential. This message encourages listeners not to underestimate the significance of small starts, emphasizing that great things often have humble beginnings.

Breaking Down the Parable

The Tiny Seed's Potential: The mustard seed, despite its minuscule size, has the potential to grow into a tree. This inherent potential is a metaphor for the latent possibilities within small acts of faith, kindness, and the smallest beginnings of a spiritual journey.

The Expansive Growth: The growth of the mustard seed into a tree is symbolic of an expansion that exceeds natural expectations. It represents how the kingdom of Heaven, or the influence of spiritual truths, grows in ways that can't be contained or predicted by its humble beginning.

Shelter and Refuge for Many: The image of the fully grown mustard tree providing shelter for birds speaks to the inclusive and nurturing nature of the kingdom of Heaven. It suggests that spiritual growth not only benefits the individual but provides a haven for others, offering support, comfort, and refuge.

Jesus Explains to His Disciples

The Kingdom of Heaven's Nature: Through this parable, Jesus conveys to his disciples that the kingdom of Heaven is not about grandiose beginnings or visible strength; it's about the incredible potential of even the smallest seed of faith to grow into something that offers shelter and refuge to many.

Growth Through Faith: The mustard seed's journey from a tiny seed to a large tree mirrors the journey of faith. It starts small, with the initial acceptance of spiritual truths, and grows in depth and width through experiences, challenges, and the nurturing of one's relationship with God.

Nurturing Our Spiritual Journey: Just as the mustard seed requires the right conditions to grow, Jesus highlights the importance of nurturing one's spiritual journey. This nurturing involves embracing faith, engaging in practices that deepen understanding and connection, and being open to the transformative growth that follows.

In this parable, Jesus uses the simple example of a mustard seed to illustrate profound spiritual truths about the kingdom of Heaven, growth, and potential. It reminds us that greatness often begins in small and seemingly insignificant forms, inviting listeners to reflect on the expansive potential within their own small starts and acts of faith.

Making it Personal

Think about the tiniest seed you've ever seen, like the one you might find in a fruit or vegetable. It's so small you might almost lose it if you're not careful. Now, imagine that tiny seed growing into a huge tree, so big that birds can build nests in its branches.

This is the picture Jesus painted with the Parable of the Mustard Seed.

In this story, Jesus tells us that something as small as a mustard seed can grow into a big, strong tree. He wants us to understand that even the smallest things, like a kind word, a small act of helping someone, or even a little bit of faith in something good, can grow into something much bigger and more wonderful than we could imagine. It's like when you learn something new, and it seems small at first, but then it helps you in many ways as you grow up.

This parable teaches us not to overlook the small things or think they're unimportant. Just like the mustard seed, these small beginnings can grow into something big and beautiful that can help and shelter others, just like the tree that gives birds a place to rest. So, every kind act or good thought, no matter how small, is important and can make a big difference in the world.

The Parable of the Unforgiving Servant (Matthew 18:21-35)

"When you forgive this man, I forgive him too. And when I forgive whatever needs to be forgiven, I do so with Christ's authority for your benefit." 2 Corinthians 2:10 NLT

Setting the Scene

In a moment ripe for teaching, Peter approaches Jesus with a question that challenges the limits of forgiveness: "How often should I forgive someone who sins against me? Seven times?" Jesus responds not with a simple number but with a parable that would encapsulate the boundless nature of forgiveness and the expectations placed upon those who have been forgiven.

Peter's Question on Forgiveness: Peter's question reflects a common human desire to quantify forgiveness, to put a limit on how much one should forgive before it's considered enough. Jesus uses this opportunity to teach about the inexhaustible nature of forgiveness in the kingdom of Heaven.

The King's Mercy: The story begins with a king settling accounts with his servants. When one servant is unable to pay an enormous debt, the king initially orders that the man and his family be sold to repay the debt. The servant's plea for mercy touches the king's heart, leading him to cancel the debt entirely—a gesture of profound compassion and forgiveness.

Breaking Down the Parable

The Forgiven Servant's Heart: The servant, after just being forgiven a debt he could never repay, sees a fellow servant who owes him a much smaller amount. Instead of extending the mercy he received, he demands repayment and has the man thrown into prison. This stark contrast highlights the servant's failure to internalize the grace he was shown, revealing a heart untouched by the profound forgiveness he experienced.

The Consequence of Unforgiveness: When the king learns that the servant he forgave has refused to show the same mercy to another, he is enraged. The forgiven servant is then handed over to be tortured until he can repay his debt—an impossible task. This severe turn of events underscores the grave consequences of harboring an unforgiving spirit, particularly after receiving forgiveness oneself.

The Heart of Mercy: The king's initial act of canceling the debt exemplifies a heart of mercy, one that is willing to absorb the cost of forgiveness. This element of the parable serves as a model for the kind of forgiveness and compassion expected from those who have been forgiven.

Jesus' Direct Message

God's Boundless Forgiveness: Through this parable, Jesus communicates the nature of God's forgiveness—vast, unmerited, and freely given. It's a divine forgiveness that releases us from debts we could never repay on our own, inviting us into a life of freedom and grace.

The Call to Forgive Others: Jesus makes it clear that receiving forgiveness comes with the responsibility to extend it to others. The parable serves as an important reminder that to embrace the forgiveness offered by God, one must also be willing to forgive, reflecting God's mercy in our relationships with others.

The Dangers of a Hardened Heart: The unforgiving servant's fate illustrates the dangers of allowing one's heart to become hardened by resentment and an unforgiving spirit. Such a state not only harms relationships and communities but also alienates the individual from the very essence of God's kingdom, which is grounded in forgiveness and reconciliation.

In this parable, Jesus delivers a powerful message about the nature of forgiveness, the expectation for those who have been forgiven, and the perilous path of an unforgiving heart. It's a call to reflect God's boundless mercy in our lives, recognizing that forgiveness is not just an act but a state of being that transforms hearts and relationships.

Making it Personal

Imagine you borrowed a really cool toy from a friend, one that's super rare and maybe even your favorite. But, oh no! It accidentally breaks while you're playing with it. You feel terrible and scared about what your friend might say. When you tell them what happened, expecting them to be really upset, they surprise you by saying, "It's okay, I forgive you. Let's just play with something else." You feel a huge relief and are super thankful for their kindness.

But then, later on, your brother borrows a small toy from you, and they lose it. It's not as big of a deal as the rare toy you broke, but you get really upset and don't want to forgive them, even though your friend forgave you for something much bigger. This is what Jesus was talking about in the Parable of the Unforgiving Servant.

Jesus wants us to understand that just like we make mistakes and need forgiveness, we should also be ready to forgive others, especially since we've been forgiven for so much already. It's like passing on a kindness. If someone shows you a big kindness, like your friend did when they forgave you for breaking their toy, you should remember that feeling and be kind to others too, even if they make mistakes with your things. It's about sharing kindness and forgiveness with each other, just like it was shared with you. In doing so, you show the love of God through your act of forgiveness.

The Parable of the Lost Sheep (Luke 15:1-7)

"Some wandered in the wilderness, lost and homeless. Hungry and thirsty, they nearly died. "Lord, Help!" they cried in their trouble, and he rescued them from their distress. He led them straight to safety, to a city where they could live." Psalm 107:4-7 NLT

Setting the Scene

As murmurs of discontent rise among the Pharisees and scribes, critical of Jesus' open-hearted association with sinners and outcasts, Jesus chooses this moment to share a parable that would vividly illustrate the heart of divine compassion and the value placed on every individual, no matter their status or past.

Addressing the Grumblings: The discontent stems from a viewpoint that sees association with sinners as defilement, a challenge to religious purity. Jesus, aware of their judgments, responds not with rebuke but with a story that offers a profound perspective on God's priorities and love.

The Shepherd's Heart: The parable centers on a shepherd, a familiar figure in Jesus' time, known for their dedication and the lengths they would go to care for their flock. This shepherd's willingness to leave behind the many to seek out the one lost sheep showcases a level of care and commitment that transcends mere duty, embodying a deep, personal love for each individual under his watch.

Breaking Down the Parable

The Lost One Versus the Ninety-Nine: The decision of the shepherd to leave the ninety-nine in the open country to search for the one lost sheep might seem illogical from a purely numerical standpoint. However, it underscores the genuine value of each individual, illustrating that each person's worth is not diminished by their wandering or lostness.

The Joy of Finding the Lost: The shepherd's joy upon finding the lost sheep is profound, highlighting the emotional investment in the well-being of each member of the flock. This joy is not kept private but is shared with friends and neighbors, emphasizing the communal nature of redemption and the shared happiness in recovering the lost.

Celebrating Redemption: The celebration that follows the sheep's return is symbolic of the broader celestial jubilation over any sinner's repentance. It's a festivity that transcends earthly rejoicing, tapping into the very heart of heaven's joy over restored relationships and reclaimed lives.

Jesus' Direct Message

God's Relentless Love: Through this parable, Jesus conveys the message of God's relentless pursuit and unconditional love for every individual, especially those who have strayed or feel lost. It's a love that goes beyond the boundaries, seeking out each one until they are brought back into the fold.

Value of Each Soul: Jesus highlights the immense value placed on every soul, teaching that in the eyes of God, each person holds irreplaceable worth. This message serves as a direct counter to any societal norms that might deem certain individuals as less worthy of attention, care, or redemption.

Rejoicing in Salvation: The parable centers on the rejoicing in heaven over one sinner who repents, underscoring the joyous nature of salvation. This rejoicing is not just a heavenly affair but invites all who understand and embrace this heavenly perspective to celebrate the transformative power of repentance and the restoration of every lost soul to their rightful place in God's heart.

In this parable, Jesus masterfully uses the imagery of a shepherd and a lost sheep to communicate profound truths about God's love, the intrinsic value of every individual, and the heavenly celebration that accompanies the return of one who was lost. It's a vivid illustration that invites reflection on personal worth, God's priorities, and the joyous nature of spiritual recovery and redemption.

Making it Personal

Imagine you have a box full of your favorite toys, and one day, you notice that one of them, a small but special toy, is missing. Even though you have so many other toys, you start searching everywhere for that one missing toy because it means a lot to you. You look under the bed, behind the couch, and even in the garden until, finally, you find it hidden in a corner. You're so happy to have it back that you might even do a little dance or shout, "I found it!"

This is similar to the story Jesus told about the Lost Sheep. In the story, a shepherd has 100 sheep, but one wanders away and gets lost. Even though he still has 99 sheep left, the shepherd goes out to find the one lost sheep because every single sheep is important to him. When he finds it, he's so happy that he carries it back on his shoulders and even throws a party with his friends to celebrate.

Jesus told this story to show that just like the shepherd didn't forget about his one lost sheep, God doesn't forget about anyone, no matter how unimportant they might seem to others. Everyone is special to God, just like your one toy was special to you, and there's a big celebration for every person who finds their way back to Him, just like you celebrated when you found your toy.

The Parable of the Ten Virgins (Matthew 25:1-13)

"So you, too, must keep watch! For you do not know the day or hour of my return." Matthew 25:13 NLT

Setting the Scene

In a story set against the backdrop of a wedding, a time of great celebration and joy in ancient communities, Jesus speaks of ten virgins awaiting the arrival of the bridegroom. This setting is charged with anticipation and excitement, as weddings were significant social and religious events, symbolizing union and new beginnings.

The Awaiting Bridegroom: The bridegroom's arrival is eagerly anticipated, but the exact time of his coming is unknown. This uncertainty adds a layer of tension to the anticipation, highlighting the importance of being prepared for his arrival at any moment.

Preparedness and Anticipation: The virgins represent those awaiting the coming Kingdom, each tasked with keeping their lamps lit as a sign of readiness and anticipation. This readiness is not just about waiting but being actively prepared for the moment the bridegroom arrives, symbolizing the active state of preparedness expected of believers.

Breaking Down the Parable

Wise and Foolish Virgins: The ten virgins are split into two groups: five wise, who bring extra oil for their lamps, and five foolish, who do not. The wise virgins' foresight contrasts sharply with the foolish virgins' lack of preparation, illustrating the difference between mere outward readiness and true, thoughtful preparedness.

The Value of Readiness: The point of the parable lies in the moment the bridegroom arrives; the wise virgins are ready to join the procession, while the foolish find themselves scrambling for oil. This moment underscores the value of being prepared, not just in the moment but in all the moments leading up to the crucial one.

The Closed Door: When the foolish virgins return, ready at last, they find the door to the wedding banquet closed to them. This stark image of the closed door serves as a powerful metaphor for the finality of some opportunities and the importance of being prepared before it's too late.

Jesus' Direct Message

Being Spiritually Prepared: Jesus uses this parable to drive home the message of spiritual vigilance and preparedness. Just as the wise virgins were ready for the bridegroom's arrival, so too must individuals be ready for the coming of the Kingdom of God, living in a state of constant readiness through faith, obedience, and spiritual vigilance.

Eternal Consequences of Choices: The fate of the foolish virgins highlights the eternal consequences of one's spiritual state and choices. The closed door is a sobering reminder that there comes a point when it is too late to prepare, underscoring the gravity of spiritual readiness.

The Uncertainty of Time: The unknown hour of the bridegroom's arrival speaks to the uncertainty of time in relation to the Kingdom of God. It emphasizes the need for constant readiness, as the timing of critical spiritual moments cannot be predicted and may come when least expected.

Through the Parable of the Ten Virgins, Jesus communicates the critical importance of spiritual vigilance, the irrevocable nature of some spiritual outcomes, and the need to live in a state of continual readiness for the Kingdom's coming. It's a call to prioritize spiritual preparedness, recognizing that the time to prepare is always now, and the consequences of readiness—or the lack thereof—are eternal.

Making it Personal

Imagine you're invited to a super cool surprise party for your best friend. You're told it's going to be a big celebration, but the exact time it starts is a secret; you just need to be ready to go when it's time. You and your friends are told to bring flashlights because the party might start when it's dark. Some of your friends think ahead and bring extra batteries for their flashlights, just in case, but others don't.

Suddenly, you get the call that the party is starting, but it's already dark outside. The friends with extra batteries quickly put them in their flashlights and are ready to go, lighting up their path to the party. The others, whose flashlights have gone out, have to rush to find batteries, but by the time they're ready, everyone is gone, and the party has already started, and the door is closed. They missed out on all the fun because they weren't prepared.

This story is a lot like the one Jesus told about the Ten Virgins. The wise ones are like the friends who brought extra batteries, always ready for the party to start. The foolish ones are like the friends who didn't bring extra batteries and weren't ready when the call came. Jesus told this story to teach us the importance of always being ready for important things, like being kind, helping others, and living in a way that shows we're ready for God's promises because we don't know when the time will come for his return.

The Parable of the Talents (Matthew 25:14-30)

"The integrity of the upright will guide them, but the perversity of the unfaithful will destroy them." Proverbs 11:3 NKJV

Setting the Scene

In this parable, Jesus speaks of a man going on a trip who gives some of his property to his servants to look after, each according to their ability. This scenario is rich with expectations and trust, highlighting the relationship between a master and his servants, based not only on duty but also on the belief in each servant's potential and capabilities.

Entrusting Responsibilities: The master's act of entrusting his servants with substantial amounts of money (talents) signifies a profound level of trust and expectation. It reflects a test of stewardship and faithfulness, with each servant given responsibility according to their perceived capacity.

Different Abilities and Gifts: The distribution of talents according to each servant's ability underlines the recognition of individual differences and strengths. It emphasizes that responsibilities and expectations are tailored to each person's unique capabilities, setting the stage for a test of personal initiative and resourcefulness.

Breaking Down the Parable

Varied Returns on Investment: The servants who receive five and two talents each put their money to work, doubling their initial amount. Their actions demonstrate initiative, focus, determination to succeed, courage, and diligence, leading to substantial growth. In contrast, the servant given one talent allows fear to paralyze him, resulting in no growth.

The Reward of Diligence: Upon his return, the master praises and rewards the first two servants for their diligence and faithful stewardship. Their success is met not just with material reward but also with an invitation to share in their master's happiness, symbolizing a deeper relational and spiritual reward.

The Consequence of Fear and Laziness: The third servant, who hid his talent, faces the master's disappointment and condemnation. His actions—or lack thereof—stem from fear and a fundamental misunderstanding of his master's character, leading to the loss of his talent and being removed from the master's service.

Jesus' Direct Message

Utilizing God-given Gifts: Through this parable, Jesus emphasizes the importance of utilizing the gifts and abilities God has given to each individual. It's a call to action, urging believers not to waste their God-given potential but to invest it wisely in the service of God and others.

Faithfulness in Small and Large: The parable highlights that faithfulness in small responsibilities leads to trust in larger ones. It suggests that how one manages current duties, no matter how insignificant they may seem, reflects their readiness for greater tasks and responsibilities.

Accountability and Reward: Jesus teaches that there will be a time of accounting for how one has used their talents and gifts. Faithful stewardship is rewarded, not just with material gain but with deeper spiritual fulfillment and increased responsibilities. Conversely, neglect and fear lead to loss and separation from the joy of serving.

In the Parable of the Talents, Jesus shares profound truths about stewardship, responsibility, and the use of gifts and abilities. It's a reminder that each person is entrusted with unique talents by God, with the expectation not of equal results but of maximum effort and faithfulness, leading to personal growth and the expansion of God's kingdom.

Making it Personal

Think about when you and your friends get together to build a big brick castle. Imagine if one of your friends has to leave, but they have a big box of bricks they've been saving for just this castle. They decide to leave it with you and your friends, trusting you'll use them well to make the castle even cooler.

Your friend who left is like the man going on a journey in Jesus' story. The box of bricks is like the money (talents) he leaves with his servants. Some of your friends might get more bricks because they're really good at building, and some might get fewer, but what matters is what each of you decides to do with what you've got.

In the story, two servants use the talents to create more, just like if you and some friends used the bricks to add awesome towers and walls to the castle, making it the best it could be. But one servant hides his talent away, like if someone took their bricks and just hid them under a chair, not using them at all. When the friend comes back, they're super happy with the amazing castle but really sad about the unused bricks under the chair. Jesus tells this story to teach us that it's important to use what we're given, whether it's bricks, talents, or kindness, to make something good and share it with others, instead of hiding it away.

The Parable of the Rich Fool (Luke 12:13-21)

"Don't store up treasures here on earth, where moths eat them and rust destroys them, and where theives break in and steal. Store your treasures in heaven, where moths and rust cannot destroy, and thieves do not break in and steal. Wherever your treasure is, there the desires of your heart will also be." Matthew 6:19-21 NLT

Setting the Scene

The parable unfolds against the backdrop of a man's plea to Jesus to settle a family inheritance dispute with his brother, highlighting the common human preoccupation with material wealth and possessions. Jesus seizes this moment to teach a profound lesson on the futility of earthly accumulation through the story of a wealthy man whose life becomes consumed by his riches.

The Desire for Wealth: The request made to Jesus underscores a deep-seated human desire for wealth and the common disputes that arise over material possessions, reflecting the broader societal tendency to equate success and security with the abundance of possessions.

Earthly Accumulation: The stage is set for a narrative that critically examines the pursuit of material wealth, questioning the value and purpose of accumulating goods beyond one's needs and the implications of such pursuits on one's spiritual well-being.

Breaking Down the Parable

The Rich Man's Prosperity: The parable introduces a rich man whose land yields a bountiful harvest, presenting him with an opportunity to reflect on the blessings he has received. Instead of gratitude or generosity, his focus turns to how he might store this surplus, leading him to plan the construction of larger storage facilities.

The Folly of Hoarding: In his decision to hoard his wealth, the rich man reveals a misplaced trust in material possessions as a source of security and happiness. His plans are centered on self-satisfaction and the belief that ample goods can secure a life of ease and pleasure, devoid of any consideration for others or for God.

The Unpredictability of Life: The parable reaches its climax when God addresses the rich man, calling him a fool for not considering the fragility and unpredictability of life. The man's sudden death renders his earthly plans meaningless, highlighting the folly of placing one's ultimate trust in temporary possessions.

Jesus' Direct Message

True Riches in God: Jesus uses the parable to redirect the listener's understanding of true riches, emphasizing that wealth in the eyes of God is not measured by earthly possessions but by one's relationship with God and the richness of one's spiritual life.

The Danger of Greed: The parable serves as a stark warning against the dangers of greed and the constant desire for more. Jesus challenges the prevailing cultural norms that equate wealth with success, urging his followers to guard against the tendency to find security in material wealth.

The Value of Eternity Over Temporal: The ultimate message of the parable lies in the contrast between the temporary nature of earthly wealth and the eternal value of spiritual riches. Jesus invites his listeners to invest in their relationship with God and in the well-being of others, suggesting that such investments yield eternal dividends, far outweighing the fleeting satisfaction of material accumulation.

Through the Parable of the Rich Fool, Jesus offers a profound critique of the human preoccupation with wealth and possessions, urging a reevaluation of priorities in light of the brief nature of life and the enduring value of spiritual riches. It's a call to live with an awareness of life's uncertainties and to seek treasures that transcend the material, aligning one's life with the values of God's kingdom.

Making it Personal

Imagine you've just won the biggest, coolest toy store shopping spree, where you can grab as many toys as you can in ten minutes. You fill up cart after cart, and soon your room is overflowing with toys, more than you could ever play with. You start thinking about where you're going to store all these toys. Maybe you think about getting bigger toy boxes, or even turning another room into your toy room. But in all this planning, you forget to play with the toys or share them with friends. You're just worried about keeping them all to yourself.

This is kind of like the story Jesus told about the Rich Fool. This man had a farm that did really well, so well that he didn't have enough room to store all his crops. Instead of sharing or being thankful, he decided to knock down his barns and build even bigger ones just for himself. He thought that with all these crops stored up, he could take it easy for the rest of his life. But God told him that he was being foolish because that very night his life would end, and then who would get all the stuff he stored up?

Jesus told this story to teach us that it's not smart to keep piling up things for ourselves without thinking about what really matters, like being kind, our relationship with Jesus, helping others, and being thankful for what we have. It's like having all those toys and not playing with them or sharing them—it doesn't make us happy in the end. It's better to share and care for others, which makes us truly rich in what matters most.

The Parable of the Sheep and the Goats (Matthew 25:31-46)

"He is ready to separate the chaff from the wheat with his winnowing fork. Then he will clean up the threshing area, gathering the wheat into his barn but burning up the chaff with never-ending fire." Luke 3:17 NLT

Setting the Scene

In a vivid depiction of the final judgment, Jesus portrays a scene where the Son of Man, referred to as the King, separates people into two groups as a shepherd separates sheep from goats. This imagery sets a solemn tone, emphasizing the coming day of judgment and the clear distinction that will be made between the righteous and the wicked based on their actions.

The Coming Judgment: The scene is set with all the grandeur and seriousness of an ultimate judgment, where all nations are gathered before the throne of God for judgment. This moment points to the critical and final judgment that all mankind will face regardless of their status or background, their race or religion.

Distinguishing the Righteous from the Wicked: The separation of the sheep from the goats serves as a powerful metaphor for the divine discernment between those who have lived according to God's will and those who have not. The criteria for this separation are based not on religious observance or public fulfillment of religious obligations but on acts of compassion and kindness as well as a devotion to following God's will.

Breaking Down the Parable

The King's Commendation and Condemnation: The King commends the righteous, the 'sheep,' for their acts of kindness, listing specific examples such as feeding the hungry, giving drink to the thirsty, welcoming a stranger, and visiting the sick or imprisoned. Conversely, the 'goats' are condemned for their failure to perform such acts, highlighting the intrinsic value placed on compassionate action.

Acts of Kindness as Service to the King: The commendation of the righteous is rooted in the principle that acts of kindness to the least privileged are considered as direct service to the King Himself. This reveals a profound biblical principle that service to others, particularly the needy, is equated with service to God.

Eternal Consequences: The parable concludes with the declaration of eternal destinies based on the actions of the individuals.

The righteous are invited into eternal life, while the wicked are consigned to eternal punishment, underscoring the lasting implications of one's choices and actions.

Jesus' Direct Message

Recognizing Christ in the Needy: Through this parable, Jesus teaches that He is to be recognized in the faces of the needy, the poor, and the suffering. The call to see Christ in others challenges superficial religious practices, urging a deeper, more compassionate engagement with the world.

Serving Others as Serving God: The parable elevates acts of kindness and service to a divine mandate, making clear that true discipleship involves practical, tangible expressions of love and compassion. Serving others, especially the most vulnerable, is not just a moral duty but a form of worship and devotion to God.

The Weight of Choices on Eternal Destiny: The final judgment scene emphasizes the profound impact of one's choices and actions on their eternal destiny. It serves as a strong reminder that faith must be lived out in acts of love and kindness, with eternal implications for both the giver and the receiver of such acts.

In the Parable of the Sheep and the Goats, Jesus presents a compelling vision of the final judgment, where the true measure of one's life is revealed through their response to the needs of others. It's a call to authentic discipleship, marked by compassion, service, and a recognition of the inherent dignity and worth of every individual, reflecting the very heart of God's kingdom.

Making it Personal

Imagine you're in a big classroom and the teacher announces a surprise "kindness test" based on all the good things you've done when no one was watching. On one side, there are kids who shared their lunches, helped others with homework, and were kind to new students. On the other side, there are kids who didn't share, didn't help, and ignored those who needed a friend. The teacher explains that the kind acts were like secret assignments, and those who did them passed the test because they showed they cared about others just like they would care for their own family or friends. Those who passed the test were able to go outside and play on the playground, the others would have to stay inside and study.

This is similar to the story Jesus told about the Sheep and the Goats. In the story, the 'King' separates people like a teacher separates kids into two groups based on the kind things they've done, like helping others when they're hungry, sick, or need a friend. Jesus explains that whenever we help someone in need, it's like we're helping Him, and that's what passes the "kindness test." He wants us to understand that being kind and caring for others is really important and shows that we're following God's way of love. It's like being on the team that chooses to make the classroom (and the world) a better place with each kind act.

The Parable of the Persistent Widow (Luke 18:1-8)

"My eyes will be open and my ears attentive to every prayer made in this place." 2 Chronicles 7:15 NLT

Setting the Scene

The Context of Jesus' Teaching About Prayer and Persistence: Imagine a warm afternoon with people sitting around eager to learn from Jesus. He wanted to teach them something very important about never giving up when they need help, especially from God. So, He decided to tell them a story that would help them understand why they should always keep trying and never lose hope, especially when talking to God through prayer.

Introduction of the Characters: In Jesus' story, there are two main characters. First, we meet a judge in a town. This judge was known for not being very nice or fair to people. He didn't really care about what was right or wrong. Then, we have a widow. In those times, widows often had no one to protect or stand up for them. This widow had been treated unfairly and wanted help to make things right.

The Widow's Quest for Justice in an Unjust World: The widow in the story faces a big problem. Someone has treated her wrongly, and she wants to make things right. But to do that, she needs the help of the judge, who isn't known for being kind or fair. Despite this, the widow is determined to get the justice she deserves.

Breaking Down the Parable

The Widow's Repeated Pleas for Justice: Every day, the widow goes to see the judge, asking him to help her. "Please make things right for me!" she says. But every day, the judge ignores her. He doesn't want to be bothered. But the widow doesn't give up; she keeps going back, again and again.

The Judge's Initial Reluctance and Eventual Capitulation: The judge, tired of seeing the widow come back every day and not wanting to hear her pleas anymore, thinks to himself, "Even though I don't care about what's right, this widow is not giving up. To stop her from bothering me, I will finally help her." So, after many days of the widow asking, the judge finally decides to help her get the justice she's been seeking.

The Power of Persistence Demonstrated by the Widow's Actions: The widow's never-give-up attitude in the story teaches us something amazing about persistence. Even when it seemed like the judge would never listen, her continual effort and determination to seek justice paid off in the end. She showed that not giving up can lead to the help and answers we need.

Jesus Explains to His Disciples

The Contrast Between the Unjust Judge and God: Jesus then explains to His friends, listening to the story, that God is nothing like the unjust judge. Unlike the judge, God cares deeply about each of us and what's fair and right. Jesus wants us to understand that if even an unfair judge can eventually give in to someone's repeated requests, imagine how much more willing God is to listen to and help us when we need Him.

The Encouragement to Pray Persistently Without Losing Heart: Jesus uses this story to encourage everyone to keep talking to God, especially when things are tough. He says, "Don't lose hope or give up, even if you don't get an answer immediately. Keep praying and telling God what you need."

The Assurance of God's Justice for His Chosen Ones Who Cry out to Him: Jesus ends the story by reassuring everyone that God hears their prayers and sees their struggles. He promises that God will make sure justice is served for those who don't give up asking for His help. It's like Jesus is saying, "Trust that God is listening and will make things right at just the right time."

Through the Parable of the Persistent Widow, Jesus teaches us the incredible value of not giving up, especially when seeking help or justice. It reminds us that even when things seem unfair and tough, we should keep talking to God about our problems, trusting He cares for us and will always do what's right for us.

Making it Personal

Imagine you're playing a video game where you need to ask a character for help to move to the next level, but this character is grumpy and doesn't want to be bothered. You ask once, and the character says, "No." But you really want to get to the next level, so you keep asking again and again. Finally, the character says, "Okay, okay, I'll help you!" so you'll stop asking and leave them alone. You're super happy because now you can move forward in the game.

This is similar to Jesus's story about a widow who needed help. She went to a judge who wasn't very nice and didn't care about people. The widow wanted the judge to help her because someone was being unfair to her, but the judge kept ignoring her. However, she didn't give up; she kept going back, asking for help over and over. Eventually, the judge got so tired of her asking that he decided to help, not because he wanted to do the right thing but because he wanted her to stop bothering him.

Jesus told this story to teach us about never giving up when we ask God for help. He wanted us to know that if even a grumpy judge can give in to someone's requests after they keep asking, God—who loves and cares about us so much more—will definitely listen to us when we talk to Him. It's like Jesus is saying, "Keep asking God for help, don't lose hope, and trust that He's always listening and ready to give you what you need at the right time."

The Parable of the Lost Coin (Luke 15:8-10)

"In the same way, there is joy in the presence of God's angels when even one sinner repents." Luke 15:10 NLT

Setting the Scene

The Woman's Home: Imagine a small, cozy house filled with the signs of daily life—a place where every item has its place and value. In this home lives a woman, perhaps a lot like people we know, who takes care of her house with diligence and care.

The Daily Life and Tasks: Each day, the woman goes about her chores—sweeping the floors, preparing meals, and taking care of her family. Her days are filled with the simple, yet important tasks that keep her home running smoothly.

The Introduction to the Concept of Something Valuable Being Lost: Amidst her daily routine, the woman realizes that one of her ten silver coins is missing. This isn't just any coin; it's valuable, not only in money but perhaps as a keepsake or a reminder of something dear. The loss of this coin disrupts her day and fills her with concern—it's something valuable that needs to be found.

Breaking Down the Parable

The Loss of One Coin: The missing coin turns the woman's day upside down. She counts her coins again and again, hoping she might have miscounted, but the truth remains—one precious coin is gone. It's a small thing, but its absence is deeply felt.

The Exhaustive Search: Determined to find the lost coin, the woman lights a lamp, providing light to every corner of her home, and begins an exhaustive search. She sweeps every inch of her house, moving furniture and looking in places she rarely needs to check. Her determination shows us the effort she's willing to put in to recover what's lost.

The Moment of Finding and the Ensuing Joy: Finally, her efforts pay off—the glint of the coin catches her eye from a dark corner of the room. Relief and joy wash over her as she picks up the lost coin. It's a moment of pure happiness in recovering something she thought might be gone forever.

Jesus Explains to His Audience

The Value of Each Individual to God: Jesus uses this moment to teach a profound truth: just like the woman searched for her lost coin, God searches for His lost children. Each person is incredibly valuable to God, much like the coin was to the woman. No one is too small or insignificant in God's eyes.

The Joy in Heaven Over One Sinner Who Repents: The woman's joy in finding her coin is a reflection of the joy in heaven when one person decides to turn back to God. Jesus explains that whenever someone chooses to return to God, there's a celebration in heaven, much like the woman's relief and happiness when she found her coin.

The Call to Share in the Joy of Recovery and Redemption: Jesus invites us to share in this joy, to recognize the beauty in recovery and redemption. Just as the woman might have shared her joy with her neighbors, we're encouraged to rejoice when someone finds their way back to God, celebrating each return as a precious victory.

Through the Parable of the Lost Coin, Jesus teaches us about God's relentless search for each of us, the immeasurable value He places on every individual, and the joyous celebration that occurs with every heart that returns to Him. It's a reminder that, in God's eyes, everyone is worth searching for, and every return is a cause for heavenly joy.

Making it Personal

Imagine you have a special collection of stickers, and you know exactly how many you have because they're your favorites. One day, you realize one of your best stickers is missing. It's not just any sticker; it's one you got from a friend and means a lot to you. So, what do you do? You start looking everywhere for it. You clean your room, look under your bed and behind your desk, and you don't stop searching until you find it. When you finally find that sticker stuck to the back of a book, you're super happy and relieved. You might even tell your family, "I found it!"

This is similar to the story Jesus told about a woman who lost one of her ten silver coins. The coin was very important to her, not just because it was worth money, but maybe it was special for another reason too. She turned her house upside down, looking for it, sweeping and searching until she finally found it. And when she did, she was so happy that she wanted to share the good news with her friends and neighbors.

Jesus told this story to show us how much God cares about each and every one of us. Just like the woman looking for her coin, God looks for us, especially when we're lost or feeling alone. And when someone decides to be friends with God again, it's like a big celebration, not just at home, but all over heaven! It's a way of showing that everyone is important, no matter how small or lost they might feel.

The Parable of Wedding Banquet (Matthew 22:1-14)

"For Many are called, but few are chosen." Matthew 22:14 NLT

Setting the Scene

The Kingdom of Heaven Likened to a King Preparing a Wedding Banquet for His Son: Picture a grand palace bustling with preparations for an event of a lifetime—the wedding of the King's son. The air is filled with anticipation and excitement, as such a banquet symbolizes joy, unity, and celebration.

The Initial Invitation to the Invited Guests: Invitations, written on fine parchment, are sent out to esteemed guests. These guests are honored to be called to such a significant occasion, reflecting their standing in the King's regard.

The Rejection of the Invitation by the Guests: Surprisingly, when the messengers deliver the invitations, the invited guests find reasons to decline. Some are too caught up in their daily affairs, while others are indifferent, disrespecting the invitation and the King and his son.

Breaking Down the Parable

The King's Response to the Initial Rejection and the Sending Out of More Servants: The King, undeterred by the initial rejection, sends out more servants. He insists on sharing the joy of his son's wedding, showing persistence in the face of disappointment.

The Mistreatment of the Servants and the King's Subsequent Judgment on the Murderers and Their City: In a shocking turn, some of the invited guests mistreat and even kill the servants. The King's response is swift and severe, dealing justice to those who harmed his messengers and showed contempt for his generous invitation.

The Extension of the Invitation to Everyone, Filling the Wedding Hall with Guests: In a generous move, the King extends the invitation to everyone, not just the elite. The banquet hall fills with a diverse crowd, symbolizing an inclusive community where all are welcome.

The Twist in the Parable

The King's Interaction with a Guest Not Wearing Wedding Clothes: Amidst the celebration, the King notices a guest not wearing wedding clothes, a sign of disrespect and disregard for the significance of the event.

The Guest's Removal from the Banquet: The guest, unable to explain his inappropriate attire, is removed from the banquet. This act underscores the importance of being prepared and respectful of the King's generosity.

The Statement, "Many are Called, but Few are Chosen": This profound statement concludes the parable, highlighting the distinction between being invited and being fit to participate in the Kingdom's joys.

Jesus Explains the Parable

The Representation of God's Invitation to the Kingdom Through Jesus: The parable mirrors God's invitation to humanity to partake in the Kingdom through Jesus. Just as the wedding banquet was open to all, so is the Kingdom of God accessible to everyone through faith in Christ.

The Rejection of Jesus by Many, Leading to the Opening of the Kingdom to All, Not Just the Initially Chosen: The rejection faced by the servants reflects the resistance and indifference Jesus met from many. This rejection, however, opened the way for all people, not just a select few, to enter the Kingdom.

The Emphasis on the Appropriateness of Response to the Invitation (Represented by Wearing Wedding Clothes): The parable stresses the need for an appropriate response to God's invitation. Accepting the invitation to the Kingdom involves a transformation—a readiness to be clothed in righteousness and live in a manner worthy of the King's call. To be clothed in righteousness is to put on the righteousness of Christ. We must repent our sins and accept Jesus as our Lord and Savior.

Through the Parable of the Wedding Banquet, Jesus teaches about the generous invitation of God to join in the Kingdom's celebration, the tragic rejection by those who are indifferent to His call, and the joyful inclusion of all who respond with a heart ready to embrace the Kingdom's values. It's a call to recognize the honor of being invited by God and to respond with readiness and respect.

Making it Personal

Imagine you're invited to the most amazing party ever by the coolest, kindest person in town—let's say they're the mayor. This isn't just any party; it's a huge celebration with all the best games, treats, and fun you can imagine. The mayor sends out fancy invitations, and everyone's excited. But then, something strange happens. Some of your friends start saying they're too busy to go. They have homework and chores or just want to play video games at home. They ignore this awesome invitation because they're caught up in everyday stuff or don't care about how special the invitation is.

This story is like the one Jesus told about a king who threw a big wedding party for his son. He sent out invitations, but the people who were invited made excuses and didn't come. Some were too busy with their work, and others didn't treat the invitation with respect. So, the King decided to invite everyone else instead—people from all over, not just the important ones, to fill the party with guests.

Jesus told this story to show that God invites everyone to be part of His special celebration, like being part of God's family and sharing in His happiness. However, not everyone pays attention to the invitation. Some people ignore it or don't think it's important. The story tells us we should be excited and ready for God's invitation and not miss out on the amazing things He has for us because we're too busy or don't care. It's about saying "yes" to God and joining in the joy He offers us.

The Parable of the Net (Matthew 13:47-50)

"For Everyone who calls on the name of the Lord will be saved."

Romans 10:13 NLT

Setting the Scene

Introduction to the Kingdom of Heaven Being Like a Net Thrown into the Sea: Picture a vast, sparkling sea under the bright sky. Fishermen cast a large net into these waters, symbolizing the kingdom of heaven reaching out into the world, drawing people in with its wide embrace.

The Gathering of All Kinds of Fish Within the Net: As the net settles into the depths, it captures many fish, each different from the next. This mix of fish represents the diverse people who come into the kingdom, each with their own stories and backgrounds.

The Eventual Pulling of the Net Ashore, Signifying the End of an Age: With a great heave, the fishermen pull the net ashore, full of the day's catch. This moment of bringing the net to land symbolizes the end of time when all people will be brought before God for the final judgment.

Breaking Down the Parable

The Sorting of the Good Fish from the Bad by the Fishermen: The fishermen begin sorting through their catch on the shore. They carefully select the good fish suitable for keeping and separate them from those that are not. This careful selection process mirrors the discernment of righteousness in people.

The Good Fish Being Kept, While the Bad Are Thrown Away: The good fish are placed into baskets, destined for the market or the fishermen's homes, symbolizing the reward of the righteous. The bad fish, however, are discarded, representing the rejection of those who turn away from God's ways.

The Imagery of the Net Capturing a Variety of Fish, Representing the Inclusivity of the Kingdom's Message: The net, indiscriminate in its catch, illustrates the kingdom's open invitation to all. It shows that the message of God's love and salvation is for everyone, regardless of who they are or where they come from.

The Conclusion of the Parable

The Likeness of the Sorting of Fish to the End Times When Angels Will Separate the Wicked from the Righteous: Just as the fishermen sorted the fish, angels will one day separate the righteous from the wicked. This separation will mark the fulfillment of God's promise of justice and redemption.

The Fate of the Wicked, Being Thrown into a Fiery Furnace Where There is Weeping and Gnashing of Teeth: The parable concludes with a stark warning: those who choose a path away from God will face a dire fate, symbolized by the fiery furnace, a place of regret and sorrow.

Jesus' Explanation

The Parable as an Illustration of the Final Judgment: Jesus uses this story to illustrate the final judgment, a time when God will look into all hearts and discern the true nature of their faith and deeds.

The Emphasis on the Coexistence of Good and Evil Until the End of the Age: The parable acknowledges the reality of good and evil coexisting in the world. It reassures us that a time will come when righteousness will be honored and wrongdoing will be addressed.

The Role of the Angels in the Final Sorting, Ensuring Justice and Fulfillment of God's Will: In the conclusion of the parable, angels play a crucial role in executing God's justice, ensuring that each person's choices and actions are fairly assessed in the light of God's eternal truth.

Through the Parable of the Net, Jesus teaches us about the inclusive call of the kingdom of heaven, the certainty of judgment, and the ultimate separation of good from evil. It's a reminder of the vastness of God's love, the reality of final judgment, and the importance of living a life aligned with the values of the kingdom of God.

Making it Personal

Imagine you and your friends decide to have a big toy cleanup day where you sort all your toys into two piles: the ones you love and want to keep and the ones you're ready to give away because they're broken or you don't play with them anymore. You spread out a huge blanket and dump all your toys on it, just like casting a net full of toys instead of fish.

In this big mix, there are all sorts of toys—some are awesome action figures, cool cars, and cuddly stuffed animals you want to keep. But there are also broken toys, puzzles with missing pieces, and games you never play. So, you start sorting through them, deciding which ones are keepers and which ones you'll let go.

This is similar to a story Jesus told about fishermen who throw a big net into the sea. When they pull it in, they find all kinds of fish in the net. They sit down and sort the fish, keeping the good ones and throwing the bad ones back. Jesus said this is like what will happen at the end of the world. God will look at all the people, like the fishermen looked at their fish, and see who has chosen to be kind, to follow Him, and to treat others well—these are the "good fish." And just like you did with your toys, God will know which ones are keepers based on the love of Christ in their hearts and a life that was lived to honor God.

Embarking on Our Own Adventure

"The Lord is compassionate and merciful, slow to get angry and filled with unfailing love." Psalm 103:8

Lessons Learned

As we reflect on the journey through these parables, we are reminded of the timeless wisdom they contain and the transformative power they hold for our lives today. Each story, while simple in nature, reveals profound truths about the kingdom of God, the nature of true righteousness, and the path to spiritual fulfillment.

The parables we've explored encompass a wide range of teachings, from the importance of preparedness and stewardship in the Parables of the Ten Virgins and the Talents, to the boundless mercy and forgiveness of God illustrated in the Parable of the Prodigal Son. We've seen the value of humility and service in the Parable of the Good Samaritan and the folly of placing one's ultimate trust in worldly possessions through the Parable of the Rich Fool. Each parable, with its unique characters and scenarios, conveys aspects of Jesus' message, emphasizing the universal nature of His teachings, applicable across time and cultures.

Applying the Parables Today

In modern life, these parables serve as more than just old stories; they act as mirrors reflecting our own lives and hearts, inviting us to look deep within ourselves. They challenge us to examine our priorities, our relationships, and our daily choices, urging us to align more closely with the values of the kingdom of God. These stories encourage us to look inward and assess our own actions and attitudes in light of the teachings of Jesus. They prompt questions about how we use our resources, how we treat others, and how prepared we are for the unexpected moments of life, both big and small.

The Role of Parables: Parables remain relevant as they address fundamental human experiences and moral dilemmas, offering wisdom and guidance that transcend historical and cultural boundaries. They invite us to see beyond the surface of our lives and to consider deeper spiritual truths.

A Call to Action

As we close this lesson on the Parable Teachings of Jesus and look ahead, the parables beckon us to live out the lessons they teach. This is not a passive journey but an active walk with God, marked by deliberate choices and actions that reflect the heart of Jesus' teachings.

Spreading Love, Understanding, and Forgiveness: We are called to be agents of love in a world that often seems dominated by indifference and division. By practicing understanding and extending forgiveness, we can break down barriers and build bridges, embodying the reconciliatory spirit of the gospel.

Embracing Spiritual Growth: The journey doesn't end with understanding; it's about transformation. Embracing spiritual growth means continually seeking to let our lives and our actions look more like the principles illustrated in these parables, cherishing a heart that mirrors the compassion, generosity, and humility of Jesus.

Continuing the Journey with Jesus: The adventure doesn't stop with the last parable. We are invited to continue walking with Jesus, exploring deeper truths, facing new challenges, and growing in our faith. This journey is one of constant learning, serving, and becoming, as we seek to live out the kingdom values in our everyday lives.

In embracing the lessons of these parables, we embark on our own adventure, one marked by growth, challenge, and the ever-present guidance of Jesus' teachings. It's a journey of becoming, as we strive to live out the profound truths captured in these timeless stories, making them a living reality in our lives.

Adventures in Scripture for Kids: Exploring The Great Men of the Bible

Lorie Eubank

Setting the Stage for Adventure

Welcome, young adventurers! Are you ready to set off on an epic journey through time and faith? The Bible is not just any book; it's an adventure book filled with stories of courage, battles, miracles, and, most importantly, ordinary people like you and me, called by God to do extraordinary things.

Why the Bible is Like an Adventure Book

Imagine opening a treasure chest filled with stories of great heroes, epic quests, and incredible miracles. That's what the Bible is like! Each story is a piece of a grand adventure, showing us how God works in amazing ways. From the bravery of David facing Goliath with just a sling to Moses parting the Red Sea, these adventures teach us about courage, faith, and the power of God.

Understanding the Purpose of Reading About These Great Men

You might wonder, "Why should we read about these great men?" Well, these stories are not just for entertainment; they're lessons from the past that teach us how to live today. Through the lives of these great men, we learn about faith, perseverance, forgiveness, and trust in God. They teach us that no matter how big our challenges may seem, with God's help, we can overcome them.

The Journey of Faith and What It Holds for Young Readers

As you dive into these stories, think of yourself as a character in the adventure. The journey of faith is like being on a path filled with challenges, surprises, and treasures. Along the way, you'll learn to trust in God's plan, find courage in difficult times, and discover the amazing plan God has for your life.

Always remember, the heroes in the Bible were not born extraordinary; they were just like you and me. They placed their trust in God and heeded His call on their lives. They stumbled, they faced their fears, and at times, they even questioned. But through their stories, we discover that God can work wonders through anyone, including you. You have the potential to achieve great things.

So, don your explorer's hat and let's embark on this thrilling expedition together! Are you prepared to witness the marvels of God's power and love as they unfold through the lives of the great men in the Bible? Let the adventure commence!

Adam - The First Man and His Choices

"Those who listen to instruction will prosper; those who trust in the Lord will be joyful." Proverbs 16:20

The Garden of Eden

In the beginning, God created a beautiful place called the Garden of Eden. It was a place of perfect harmony, where the first man, Adam, lived in close relationship with God.

Adam walked and talked with God, and all animals were brought before Adam to give a name. Imagine a world without pain, fear, or sadness—a place filled with stunning landscapes, delicious fruits, and crystal-clear waters. This was Adam's home, a gift of love from God.

In this paradise, God gave Adam a special gift: free will. This meant Adam could make his own choices, he could go where he wanted and do what he wanted. God made every tree grow that was good for food. There was only one rule God gave Adam: do not eat from the tree in the center of the garden, the tree of knowledge of good and evil. God warned Adam that if he ate from that tree, he would surely die.

The Consequences of Choices

Despite the beauty and perfection of Eden, Adam faced a pivotal choice when Eve was tempted by the serpent. Choosing to eat the forbidden fruit, Adam and Eve made a decision that would change everything. This act of disobedience had severe consequences. Adam and Eve, his wife, were no longer able to stay in the Garden of Eden. They faced a new reality filled with hardship, pain, and separation from God's direct presence.

Losing paradise was a terrible consequence, but within this story, there's a glimmer of hope. God promised redemption, a plan to restore the broken relationship between humanity and Himself. This promise hinted at a future where the consequences of Adam's choice could be overcome.

Lessons from Adam

Adam's story is a powerful lesson for us, especially as young adventurers on our own journeys of faith. First, we learn about the importance of obedience. Like Adam, we face choices every day. Choosing to follow God's way shows our trust and love for Him.

Despite Adam's mistake, his story also teaches us about God's incredible love for us. Even when we make mistakes, God continues to love us and offers forgiveness. He doesn't give up on us, no matter what.

Lastly, Adam's story points to the eternal hope of salvation. Just as God promised a way to mend the brokenness caused by Adam's choice, He offers us salvation through Jesus Christ. This is the ultimate adventure—a journey from loss to hope, from separation to reconciliation with God.

Making it Personal: The Choice in the Park

Imagine you're at the park with your friends, playing your favorite game. Everyone's having a great time until you notice a new kid sitting alone, looking like they wish they could join in but are too shy to ask. You think about inviting them to play, but you also worry—what if your friends don't want the new kid to join? What if it makes the game less fun? It's a moment where you have to choose: Do you keep playing as if you didn't notice, or do you go over and invite the new kid, making them feel welcome?

This situation is a bit like Adam's choice in the Garden of Eden. You're not choosing between eating fruit or not, but you are deciding between the easy route of doing nothing or the potentially harder choice of including someone new. Think about it: What feels right to you? What would make the park a happier place for everyone?

Choosing to invite the new kid to play might feel a bit scary at first, but it's a choice that can change everything—for the better. Just like Adam faced consequences for his choice, your choices have outcomes too. In this case, making the inclusive choice not only makes the new kid's day but also sets an example for your friends about kindness and inclusion. It shows them (and reminds you) that being welcoming and friendly is way cooler than just sticking to what's familiar. This kind of choice strengthens your character and builds a community where everyone feels like they belong. And just like the hope and redemption that followed Adam's story, your choice brings a little more joy and friendship into the world, which is pretty awesome.

So, as we reflect on Adam's life and choices, let's remember the lessons of obedience, God's unfailing love, and the hopeful promise of salvation that shines through even our mistakes. These lessons guide us as we navigate our own adventures in faith.

Noah - The Righteous Man in a Wicked World

"Just as the body is dead without breath, so also faith is dead without good works." James 2:26 NLT

Building the Ark

Noah's story is a powerful testament to the strength of faith and the importance of obedience, even in the most challenging circumstances. During a time when the earth was filled with wickedness and every thought or imagination of man was consistently evil. As this saddened the Lord, he decided to destroy everything he created on the face of the earth. Only Noah found favor with God, so he and his family would be saved if he followed the Lord's instructions.

In a world overwhelmed by wickedness, Noah stood out because of his righteousness and unwavering faith in God. His life took a dramatic turn when God, disappointed by the corruption and wickedness of mankind, gave Noah an extraordinary mission: to build an ark, a massive boat that would save Noah, his family, and pairs of every animal species from a flood meant to cleanse the world.

Imagine Noah's astonishment as he received these instructions from God. The ark was to be a colossal structure made of gopher wood and waterproofed with pitch. This wasn't just a boat; it was a symbol of God's salvation plan, and it took a lot of faith to do such an important job. Can you imagine how many trees would need to be cut down to build this ark? What about all the food they would have to gather to feed the animals and their family while in the ark?

The Significance of Faith in Action

Noah's immediate response was to put his faith into action. Building the ark was a monumental task, requiring physical labor and immense spiritual resilience. His faith was active, demonstrated through his diligent work with his family to build the ark. If you read Genesis 5:32, Noah was 500 years old when his sons were born. Later, after the ark was completed, Genesis 7:11 says he was 600 years old when God closed him and his family, along with all of the animals, up in the ark, and the flood covered the earth. Can you imagine how sad God must have been, considering that no one changed their ways in the 100 years it took for the ark to be built?

The Challenge of Obedience in a Scoffing World

Although the bible doesn't detail it, I can only imagine how he was mocked for what he was doing to build the ark. During that time, they had not seen the rain. Water came up from the ground in the form of a mist (Gen. 2:5-6) to water the plants. Considering the massive size of the ark, many people possibly thought he was crazy and that a boat of that size would never be able to move. Despite the ridicule, his commitment to God's command shows the courage it takes to stand firm in one's faith, especially when it goes against popular opinion.

The Flood and God's Promise

The arrival of the flood was a pivotal moment, not just for Noah but for all creation. As the rains began and the waters rose, the ark became a refuge in the midst of a great storm that brought immense destruction.

The flood was both a tragic end and a necessary cleansing, washing away the corruption that had marred creation. It was a sobering reminder of the consequences of widespread disobedience and moral decay.

The Salvation of Noah's Family

Amidst this destruction, the ark stood as a beacon of hope. Noah, his family, and the animals aboard were saved from the waters and the corruption outside. Their survival was a testament to God's mercy and the protection afforded to those who remained righteous.

The Promise of a Rainbow

After the flood, God made a covenant with Noah, symbolized by a rainbow, promising never to destroy the earth with a flood again. This rainbow was more than just a beautiful natural phenomenon; it was a sign of God's enduring promise and grace, a reminder of His covenant with humanity and all living creatures.

Lessons from Noah

Noah's story teaches us invaluable lessons about faith, obedience, and God's justice and mercy.

Standing Strong in Faith – Noah's unwavering faith in the face of adversity is a model for us all. It shows the strength that comes from trusting God, even when His plans seem incomprehensible or impossible.

The Cost of Disobedience – The reminder of the great flood illustrates the consequences of collective disobedience and moral failure. It serves as a warning of what can happen when societies turn away from God's divine guidance found in his word, the Bible.

God's Commitment to Those Who Trust Him

Above all, Noah's life story highlights God's profound commitment to those who remain faithful. Despite the corruption of the world, God provided a means of salvation for Noah and his family, reaffirming His love and mercy towards those who trust and obey Him.

Making it Personal: Standing Out in the Crowd

Imagine you're at school, and there's a big project coming up. The popular opinion is to take the easy route, maybe even cut some corners to finish it quickly. Everyone seems to be on board with this idea, laughing off the rules and joking about how they can outsmart the system. You know deep down that this isn't right, that the project is meant to be done with effort and honesty. This is your "ark-building" moment, much like Noah's. Do you go with the flow to fit in, or do you stand up for what you believe is right, even if it means doing it alone?

This scenario is about more than just a school project; it's about making choices that reflect your values, even when it's not the popular thing to do. Noah faced something similar, choosing to follow God's instructions in a world that had lost its way. He stood out, not just for building an ark, but for his unwavering faith and obedience.

When you decide to take the high road and do the project the right way, it might feel like you're building your own "ark" — a big, challenging task that sets you apart. But just like Noah, making the right choice can have a profound impact. It shows your teachers and classmates that integrity matters to you and might even inspire others to think twice about their choices. In the end, standing firm in your beliefs not only builds your character but can also encourage a wave of change around you, proving that one person's decision to do right can be a beacon of hope and inspiration for many.

As we reflect on Noah's life, let's remember the importance of standing firm in our faith, the serious consequences of turning away from God, and the profound promise of His protection and blessing for those who remain faithful.

Abraham - The Father of Nations

"He was fully convinced that God is able to do whatever he promises. And because of Abraham's faith, God counted him as righteous." Romans 4:21-22 NLT

The Call to a New Land

Abraham's journey from Ur to becoming the patriarch of a great nation is a story of remarkable faith and obedience to God's call.

Abraham's story begins with a summons from God that would set him on a path to becoming the father of nations. This call was not just about a physical journey but a walk of faith with God. Imagine Abram, his name before God made a covenant with him and changed his name to Abraham (See Genesis 17:5), had just settled with his father and family in Haran after leaving Ur. He is out watching over all his possessions, and he hears the voice of God telling him he should leave his family and this land and travel to a new land he had never seen.

Abram was 75 years old when he left his father and other family and began his journey. He only took his wife and nephew Lot and the rest of the people he brought into his household at Haran.

The Promise of Descendants

Since they were much older and had no children to pass on their great wealth, Abraham thought he would give his inheritance to one of his trusted servants, Eliezer of Damascus. However, in Genesis 15:4-6, God told Abraham that he would have more descendants than the stars in the sky. God's promise to Abraham was staggering: despite his and his wife Sarah's old age, they would have descendants as numerous as the stars! How could this be? This promise wasn't just about biological offspring but the birth of a multitude of nations and kings, including spiritual descendants through faith.

The Test of Faith: Famine and Journey to Egypt

One of the early tests of Abraham's faith came when a severe famine struck the land God had led him to inhabit. This famine was not just a physical challenge but a spiritual one, testing Abraham's reliance on God's promises. Despite God's assurance that he would inherit this land and become a great nation, the immediate reality of starvation and scarcity conflicted with the promise of abundance and prosperity.

Faced with this dire situation, Abraham decided to go down to Egypt to find sustenance. This decision, while practical, led to a series of moral and ethical challenges. Fearful for his own safety due to his wife Sarah's beauty, Abraham asked her to say she was his sister, hoping to protect himself from potential harm from the Egyptians. This act of deception showed a lapse in Abraham's faith, as he relied on his own ideas rather than trusting in God's protection.

The Pharaoh of Egypt, believing Sarah was unmarried, took her into his palace, which could have jeopardized the divine promise of a lineage through Sarah. However, God intervened by afflicting severe plagues on Pharaoh and his household, revealing the truth about Sarah's relationship with Abraham. Realizing the truth, Pharaoh reproached Abraham for his deceit but also spared his life and allowed him to leave Egypt with his wife and considerable wealth.

The Birth of Ishmael: Struggling with God's Timing

Another significant test of Abraham's faith occurred with the birth of Ishmael. As years passed without the fulfillment of God's promise of an heir, Sarah and Abraham grew impatient. Sarah suggested that Abraham have a child with her Egyptian servant, Hagar, a common practice at the time for childless couples. Abraham consented, and Ishmael was born to Hagar.

This action represented another moment of Abraham's reliance on human solutions rather than divine provision. The birth of Ishmael led to further complications: tension arose between Sarah and Hagar, affecting the entire household and creating a rift that would have lasting implications for generations.

Despite these actions, God's plan remained unaltered. He reaffirmed His original promise to Abraham, explicitly stating that the covenant would be established through a son born to Sarah, who would be named Isaac. This reiterated God's commitment to His word and His timing, emphasizing that human actions cannot thwart divine purposes.

Lessons from Abraham's Tests of Faith

- **Trust in God's Provision:** The famine and subsequent journey to Egypt highlight the importance of trusting in God's provision even when circumstances seem dire. Abraham's decision to go to Egypt reflects a natural human impulse to seek immediate solutions, yet it also shows the importance of relying on divine guidance in all decisions.

- **Patience with God's Timing:** The birth of Ishmael teaches the value of patience in waiting for God's promises to unfold. Abraham's attempt to fulfill God's promise through his own methods instead of waiting for God's timing led to strife and division. This underscores the lesson that God's timing is perfect, even when it differs from human expectations.

- **Learning from Mistakes:** Abraham's story is also a testament to God's grace and mercy. Despite Abraham's failures and moments of doubt, God remained faithful, correcting and guiding Abraham back to the right path.

This shows that God's promises and plans for us are not nullified by our mistakes; rather, they are opportunities for growth and deeper reliance on Him.

Abraham's life, filled with various tests of faith, invites believers to trust in God's provision, await His timing, and learn from their missteps, assured that God remains faithful to His promises.

Demonstrating Unparalleled Faith – Sacrificing Isaac

One of the most profound tests of Abraham's faith came when God asked him to sacrifice his son Isaac, the very child through whom God's promises were to be fulfilled.

Abraham's willingness to sacrifice Isaac is a powerful testament to his faith. He didn't understand why God asked this of him but was willing to obey, trusting that God had a plan and could even raise the dead if necessary.

At the moment of the ultimate test, God provided a ram as a substitute sacrifice, sparing Isaac. This act underscored a critical lesson: God will provide in our moments of greatest need, often in ways we cannot predict or understand.

After the test, God reaffirmed His covenant with Abraham, promising that his descendants would be as numerous as the stars and that all nations of the earth would be blessed through them. This incident not only highlighted Abraham's faith but also foreshadowed God's ultimate provision of a sacrificial lamb in Jesus Christ, who would take away the sins of the world.

Making it Personal: Trusting God in New Beginnings

Imagine you're about to start something completely new and a bit scary—maybe it's moving to a new city, starting a new school, or even joining a new sports team. This is much like what Abraham faced when God told him to leave everything familiar behind and move to a place he'd never seen before. You might feel nervous or uncertain about what's ahead, wondering if you'll make friends or if you'll fit in.

In this new chapter of your life, you have a choice to make: do you let fear hold you back, or do you trust that God has a good plan for you in this new place? Think about it: How can trusting in God's faithfulness help you take the first steps with confidence?

Choosing to trust God and stepping out in faith, you decide to embrace the new opportunities with a hopeful heart. By joining clubs, talking to new classmates, or trying out for the team, you start to see that God is guiding you through each new challenge. Just as Abraham discovered the promises of God unfolding with each step of obedience, your trust in God's plan reveals new friendships and exciting opportunities. This act of faith not only enriches your experience but also strengthens your trust in God's goodness and care for you. It shows how faith can transform uncertainty into a journey of growth and blessing, reinforcing that God is always faithful to His promises.

Moses - The Deliverer

"The Lord is my rock, my fortress, and my savior; my God is my rock, in whom I find protection. He is my shield, the power that saves me, and my place of safety." Psalms 18:2 NLT

From Palace to Desert

Moses' life is a profound story of transformation and deliverance, showcasing God's power to use unlikely heroes for His grand purposes. Moses' journey from a basket in the Nile to leading Israel out of Egypt is marked by God's intervention and Moses' personal growth.

Moses was born into a world where his very existence was threatened by Pharaoh's decree to kill all of the Hebrew baby boys. His mother's desperate act of placing him in a basket on the Nile River led to his rescue by Pharaoh's daughter. His sister was watching over him in the river and told the Pharaoh's daughter she could get a nursemaid who could help nurse him, and she did. Moses was a little older; he was taken back to the Pharaoh's daughter, who adopted him as her own. This illustrates how God can turn difficult situations into remarkable stories of salvation.

Growing up in Pharaoh's Household

Raised in the luxury of Pharaoh's palace, Moses received the best education and upbringing, preparing him in ways he couldn't have imagined for his future role. This part of his life highlights the unexpected ways God equips His chosen for their appointed missions.

The Burning Bush Encounter

Moses' encounter with God at the burning bush was a pivotal moment. It was here, while tending his father-in-law Jethro's flock in the solitude of the desert that Moses heard God's call to deliver the Israelites from Egypt. This encounter not only signified Moses' calling but also showed the personal relationship God seeks with those He calls to serve.

Confronting Pharaoh

Moses' return to Egypt to demand the Israelites' release was a bold move met with resistance from Pharaoh. Moses, once a member of Pharaoh's household, now stood before him as God's representative, showing the transformative power of God's call. Moses' leadership was characterized by monumental challenges and miraculous victories, demonstrating God's power and guidance.

The Ten Plagues

The ten plagues were both a judgment against Egypt for the bondage of the people of Israel and a powerful demonstration of God's sovereignty. Through each plague, from turning the Nile to blood to the death of the firstborns, God systematically dismantled Pharaoh's resistance while showcasing His protective care over the Israelites. Do you know what the 10 plagues were? Here is the list of those plagues:

1. **Water Turned to Blood** (Exodus 7:14-24): The waters of the Nile turned to blood, killing all fish and making the water undrinkable.

2. **Frogs** (Exodus 8:1-15): Frogs swarmed the land, invading houses and covering the Egyptian territory.

3. **Lice** (Exodus 8:16-19): Dust turned into lice or gnats that attacked people and animals alike.

4. **Flies** (Exodus 8:20-32): Swarms of flies plagued Egypt, corrupting the land and entering the houses of Egyptians.

5. **Livestock Pestilence** (Exodus 9:1-7): A severe pestilence killed the Egyptian livestock, including horses, donkeys, camels, cattle, sheep, and goats.

6. **Boils** (Exodus 9:8-12): Painful boils broke out on Egyptians and animals.

7. **Hail** (Exodus 9:13-35): Fiery hail rained down, devastating the land and killing both people and animals caught outside.

8. **Locusts** (Exodus 10:1-20): Locusts came and con-

sumed all the crops and every tree growing in the fields, causing severe famine.

9. **Darkness** (Exodus 10:21-29): A darkness that could be felt covered Egypt for three days, but the Israelites had light where they lived.

10. **Death of the Firstborn** (Exodus 11:1-10, 12:29-30): The firstborn of every Egyptian family died, including the firstborn of livestock. This final plague culminated in the Exodus of the Israelites out of slavery.

Each plague was a manifestation of God's power and was intended to challenge the gods of Egypt, demonstrating to the Egyptians and the Israelites that the God of Israel was the one true God.

Crossing the Red Sea

When the Pharaoh finally released the people of Israel, there were over 600,000 men, women, children, and flocks and herds. When Pharaoh was told the people had fled, his heart was hardened against them, and he gathered an army to pursue them. The crossing of the Red Sea was the definitive sign of God's deliverance. As Moses stretched out his staff, the waters parted, allowing the Israelites to escape Pharaoh's pursuing army. God was with them, and He helped them cross the Red Sea on dry ground. This miraculous event not only secured Israel's freedom but also demonstrated God's unmatched power and faithfulness.

Lessons from Moses

Moses' life offers invaluable lessons on leadership, faith, and obedience to God.

Humility in Leadership

Despite his initial reluctance and self-doubt, Moses grew into a leader who led not by personal strength but by reliance on God. His humility allowed him to be an effective leader, mediator, and prophet, setting an example for all who are called to lead.

Perseverance during Challenges

Moses faced numerous challenges, from Pharaoh's hardened heart to the Israelites' frequent complaints and rebellions. Yet, he persevered, trusting in God's promises and leading with patience and resilience.

Being a Vessel for God's Will

Moses' life underscores the theme that God uses imperfect individuals to fulfill His will. Despite his flaws and mistakes, Moses was a vessel for God's purposes, playing a crucial role in the salvation history of God's people. As we reflect on Moses' story, let us be inspired to embrace humility, persevere through trials, and be open to being used by God to accomplish great things, no matter how insurmountable the challenges may seem.

Making it Personal: The Test of Integrity

Picture yourself in a challenging situation at school, where you're given a group project to work on. Your group decides to take the easy way out by copying someone else's work, reasoning that it's the quickest path to a good grade. You're faced with a dilemma: go along with the group and compromise your values, or stand up for what you know is right, even if it means potentially facing conflict or making the project harder for yourself.

This scenario mirrors Moses' journey in many ways. Just as Moses faced immense challenges and had to make tough decisions while leading the Israelites, you too are faced with a choice that tests your integrity and faith. Think about it: How will your actions now affect your character and future? What does it mean to trust that following God's way, even when it's difficult, is the right choice?

Choosing to advocate for honesty and hard work, you convince your group to take the right path, emphasizing the importance of integrity. This decision may not be the easiest, but it builds trust and respect among your peers and teachers. Just as Moses remained faithful to God's commands amidst adversity, your choice to stick to your principles not only sets a positive example for others but also reinforces your own character development. In the long run, maintaining your integrity shapes you into a leader like Moses, someone who is trusted and looked up to, demonstrating that God blesses and upholds those who act justly and walk faithfully with Him.

David - The Shepherd King

"Create in me a clean heart, O God, and renew a steadfast spirit from within me. Do not cast me away from your presence, and do not take your Holy Spirit from me. Restore to me the joy of Your salvation, and uphold me by Your generous Spirit." Psalms 51:10-12 NKJV

The Anointing of a Future King

David's life story is a compelling narrative of faith, fall, and forgiveness, from his humble beginnings as a shepherd boy to his reign as one of Israel's greatest kings. Humble beginnings marked David's early years as a shepherd caring for his father's sheep. One visit from the Prophet Samuel, and he was chosen by God to become the second king of Israel. Although most saw David as insignificant, considering his youth and small size compared to his brothers, God saw his heart.

David, spending most of his time alone in the fields, knew he was not alone and was known as a man after the heart of God. David's anointing by Samuel as the future king of Israel, while still a young shepherd, marked him as God's chosen, setting the foundation for his future. This event highlighted the theme throughout the Bible that God looks at the heart, not outward appearances.

Facing Goliath

David's encounter with Goliath is not just a story of faith and courage, but a testament to his unwavering resilience and trust in God's protection and power. As a young shepherd, David faced the giant Goliath with nothing but a sling and a few stones, relying solely on his faith. This victory was a powerful demonstration of God's ability to use the least likely individuals to achieve His purposes, inspiring us to trust in His strength even in the face of our own 'Goliaths'.

Friendship with Jonathan

David's friendship with Jonathan, King Saul's son, is a beautiful example of loyalty, love, and mutual respect. Despite the potential rivalry, Jonathan recognized David's future kingship and formed a covenant with him, demonstrating a selfless love that sought the best for his friend above personal ambition.

Reign and Challenges

David's reign was a time of great achievements and profound challenges, reflecting the complexities of leadership and the human condition.

Ascending the Throne

David's ascent to the throne was a fulfillment of God's promise, yet it came with its own set of challenges. His leadership was marked by military victories, expansion of the kingdom, and the establishment of Jerusalem as the political and spiritual center of Israel, showcasing his strategic and spiritual leadership.

The Temptation with Bathsheba

David's affair with Bathsheba and the subsequent cover-up, including the orchestration of Uriah's death, marked a significant moral failure in David's life. This event illustrates the dangers of temptation and the far-reaching consequences of sin, even in the lives of those after God's own heart.

Facing Betrayal from Within

David faced betrayal from those closest to him, including his son Absalom, who sought to take over the throne. These internal conflicts revealed the complexities of David's personal and political life, testing his faith, patience, and forgiveness.

Lessons from David

David's life offers profound lessons on the nature of true worship, the importance of a repentant heart, and the complexities of human nature. You can be a great person and still make mistakes. It is how we handle those mistakes through repentance that sets a path for forgiveness and true diligence in our walk with God.

The Heart That Seeks God

Despite his flaws, David is remembered as 'a man after God's own heart' because of his deep faith and desire to follow and please God in all that he did. His life serves as a comforting reminder that God's mercy and grace are not withheld from us when we repent of our sins. It reassures us that there is nothing we can do in our life that would remove God's love from us, offering a sense of comfort and security in His unfailing love.

Repentance and Restoration

David's sincere repentance after his sin with Bathsheba, as expressed in Psalm 51, is a powerful reminder of the importance of acknowledging our mistakes and seeking God's forgiveness. It shows us that no failure is final when we turn back to God with a genuine heart, inviting us to reflect on our own lives and consider areas where we may need to seek forgiveness and restoration.

The Power of Worship

David's role as a psalmist highlights the power of worship in drawing near to God and finding strength in Him. His psalms express a wide range of human emotions, from despair to exuberant joy, teaching us that worship is a powerful way for us to connect with God in every circumstance of life. As we reflect on David's life, let's draw inspiration from his faith, learn from his failures, and embrace the healing and restoration that come through sincere repentance and worship.

Making it Personal: The Underestimated Player on the Field

Imagine you're part of a sports team, maybe it's soccer or basketball, and it's time to pick teams for an important inter-school tournament. As everyone lines up, the usual picks are the taller, stronger players—the ones who have always shone in practice games and matches. But this time, the coach decides to give a chance to someone who's always been overlooked, someone smaller than the rest. This time that someone is you. How would you feel stepping into this new role? What would you do with this unexpected opportunity?

This situation is much like the story of David, who, despite his small stature and youthful appearance, was chosen by God for a great purpose. Like David facing Goliath, you face your own giants on the field—not with physical strength but with your agility, determination, and heart. Your teammates and opponents might initially doubt your abilities, wondering why the coach would pick someone like you for such a critical role.

As the tournament progresses, you prove your worth not through brute strength but through strategic thinking, quick reflexes, and a cooperative spirit that uplifts your entire team. Each game is a chance to show that true athletic prowess isn't just about physical size but about heart, perseverance, and the courage to face challenges head-on. Your success helps shift the team's perspective on what makes a player valuable, demonstrating that often, the most unlikely candidates can make the greatest impact when given a chance. This teaches you and your teammates an important lesson: that God often uses the least likely among us for greatness, and by prioritizing faith and courage, even the smallest player can lead a team to victory.

Solomon - The Wise King

"If any of you lacks wisdom, let him ask of God, who gives it to all liberally and without reproach, and it will be given to him." James 1:5NKJV

Praying for Wisdom – The Dream at Gibeon

Solomon's reign is a tale of unparalleled wisdom, grand achievements, and powerful lessons on the pitfalls of compromise and the quest for true fulfillment. Solomon's story begins with a heartrending plea for wisdom, setting the tone for his rule as a king known for his discernment and understanding. In a dream at Gibeon, the Lord appeared to Solomon and asked him, "What shall I give you?" Solomon made a request that would define his legacy.

Instead of asking for long life, riches, or the defeat of his enemies, he asked for wisdom to lead God's people. God's response to Solomon's humble request was to grant him unmatched wisdom, riches, and honor beyond any king before or after him.

Discernment in Judgment

Solomon's wisdom was first showcased in his famous judgment between two women claiming to be the mother of a child. By divine inspiration, he proposed to divide the child in half. This revealed the true mother's love, earning him widespread acclaim for his discernment. This incident exemplifies how divine wisdom can illuminate truth and bring justice in complex situations.

Building the Temple

One of Solomon's crowning achievements was building the Temple in Jerusalem, a dwelling place for God's presence among His people. This monumental task, completed with grandeur and precision, symbolized Israel's central place in worshiping the one true God and underscored Solomon's devotion to God.

Achievements and Downfall

Despite his wisdom and accomplishments, Solomon's reign also illustrates the dangers of compromise and turning away from God.

Solomon's contributions to the Bible, including Proverbs and Ecclesiastes, offer great insights into human nature, the fear of God, and the pursuit of wisdom. These writings reflect Solomon's deep understanding of life's complexities and the ultimate source of true wisdom.

Marrying Foreign Wives

Solomon's political alliances solidified through marriages to foreign princesses, which led to his greatest downfall. His wives turned his heart to other gods, leading him into idolatry. This breach of faith marked a stark contrast to his earlier devotion and wisdom, serving as a cautionary tale about the dangers of compromise and disobedience. Even with the greatest wisdom known to man, he still made wrong choices that significantly impacted his life.

Turning from God

Solomon's turn from God had significant repercussions, not only for his own life but for the entire kingdom. His idolatry and abandonment of the ways of God led to divine judgment, resulting in the kingdom's eventual division. This tragic end to Solomon's reign is a powerful reminder of the consequences of turning away from God.

Lessons from Solomon

Solomon's life offers invaluable lessons on wisdom, the perils of compromise, and the human heart's quest for meaning.

The Significance of Wisdom

Solomon's story underscores the immeasurable value of wisdom—rooted in the fear of God and the pursuit of His will. It reminds us that true wisdom is a gift from God, meant to guide us in living lives that honor Him and serve others.

The Dangers of Compromise

Solomon's downfall illustrates how even the wisest can fall through compromise and disobedience. His life warns us to guard our hearts and remain faithful to God's commands, resisting the allure of worldly temptations that can lead us astray.

Vanity and the Search for Meaning

Ecclesiastes, attributed to Solomon, effectively addresses the vanity of worldly pursuits and the elusive nature of true fulfillment. Solomon's reflections teach us that meaning and purpose are found not in earthly achievements or pleasures but in fearing God and keeping His commandments.

As we reflect on Solomon's life, let us seek divine wisdom to guide our choices, be vigilant against compromise, and anchor our lives in the eternal purpose and meaning found only in God.

Making it Personal: Choices in the Digital Age

Imagine you're navigating the complex world of social media, where every day, you're bombarded with choices about what to post, whom to follow, and how to react to various opinions and trends. These choices might seem trivial, but like Solomon's decisions, they can significantly impact your life and how you are perceived by others.

Now, think about the wisdom required to make these choices. Are you seeking to build up and encourage others, or are you drawn into conflicts and controversies that stir up negativity? Solomon asked for wisdom to lead his people rightly, and similarly, you need wisdom to navigate the digital landscape in a way that reflects your values and integrity.

When you choose to post something encouraging, truthful, and kind, you are using wisdom to positively impact your community. Conversely, when you decide to engage in harmful or divisive behavior online, it can lead to consequences that echo Solomon's downfall—relationships can be strained, and your reputation can suffer. Solomon's story teaches us that wisdom is not just about knowing a lot or being clever; it's about making decisions that align with God's will and lead to health and life. Each time you log in, think about how the content you choose to engage with and share can either build up or tear down. Choosing wisely can help you maintain a positive and influential presence that honors God and embodies the wisdom He values.

Daniel - Integrity in Exile

"Have I not commanded you? Be strong and of good courage; do not be afraid, nor be dismayed, for the Lord Your God is with you wherever you go." Joshua 1:9 NKJV

Life in Babylon

Daniel's life is a compelling testament to living a life of unwavering faith and integrity amidst the challenges of exile and the pressures of a foreign empire. Daniel's journey in Babylon begins with his and his friends' captivity. Yet, it's marked by divine favor and wisdom, enabling them to navigate the difficult life in an empire that often opposed their faith.

The King's Food Dilemma

Upon their arrival in Babylon, Daniel and his friends faced a test of their commitment to God's laws when they were ordered to eat the king's food, which was against their dietary restrictions. Daniel's request for a diet of vegetables and water—and the subsequent improved health and appearance that followed—demonstrated God's faithfulness in honoring those who honor Him.

Interpretation of Nebuchadnezzar's Dream

Daniel's God-given ability to interpret King Nebuchadnezzar's troubling dream set him apart in a land of magicians and astrologers. His interpretation revealed the dream's meaning and affirmed God's sovereignty over all kingdoms and empires, establishing Daniel's reputation as a man of exceptional wisdom and insight.

Promotion in a Foreign Land

Daniel's integrity and God-given wisdom led to his promotion within the Babylonian empire. Despite his foreign status and the jealousy it provoked among other officials, Daniel's abilities and faithfulness positioned him as a trusted advisor to the king, showcasing the potential for God's people to thrive and witness in non-Christian environments.

Faith Under Pressure

Daniel's and his friends' faith was tested repeatedly, yet each trial highlighted their steadfastness and God's miraculous deliverance.

In the Lions' Den

Daniel's unwavering practice of praying to God, despite King Darius's decree that made such prayer a capital offense, resulted in his being thrown into a den of lions. God's intervention to shut the lions' mouths and preserve Daniel's life demonstrated

His power and faithfulness, leading even Darius to proclaim the greatness of the God of Daniel.

Lessons from Daniel

Daniel's life in Babylon offers timeless lessons on faithfulness, the sovereignty of God, and the impact of living with integrity.

Steadfastness in Faith

Daniel's consistent devotion to God, regardless of the circumstances or consequences, exemplifies the steadfastness of faith that can withstand the trials and temptations of life, encouraging us to remain faithful in all situations.

God's Sovereignty Over Kingdoms

The stories of Nebuchadnezzar's dream and the subsequent rulers who acknowledged God's power through Daniel's life affirm God's ultimate sovereignty over all earthly kingdoms and rulers, reminding us that human empires cannot thwart God's plans and purposes.

The Reward of Integrity

Daniel's integrity, characterized by his unwavering commitment to God's laws and courage in the face of opposition, was rewarded with divine protection, favor, and influence. His life teaches us that while integrity may not always prevent trials, it will bring God's presence, deliverance, and eventual vindication.

As we reflect on Daniel's life, let us be inspired to live with uncompromising integrity, steadfast in our faith, and confident in the sovereignty of God over all aspects of our lives.

Making it Personal: Standing Firm in Your Beliefs

Imagine you're on a sports team, and there's pressure from teammates to skip practice for a not-so-important reason, maybe to hang out or attend a party instead. Everyone is going along with the plan because it seems like harmless fun and no one wants to be the odd one out. However, you know that commitment and discipline are what the coach expects and are crucial for the team's success.

This scenario echoes Daniel's experience in Babylon, where he faced the king's food dilemma. Like Daniel, you are faced with a choice: go along with what everyone else is doing, which is easier and more fun, or stand firm in your commitments, honoring the principles of dedication and responsibility you value. What does it mean to be faithful to your commitments, and how might this integrity shape your character and influence on the team?

Choosing to attend practice instead of joining your teammates in skipping not only sets a positive example but also strengthens your character. Just as Daniel's choice to stick to his dietary convictions led to divine favor and health and promotion, your choice to prioritize team commitments can lead to personal and collective benefits. Your coaches and teammates will likely notice and respect your dedication, which could even inspire others to reconsider their priorities. Like Daniel, standing firm in your beliefs, especially when faced with peer pressure, prepares you for greater responsibilities and opportunities. It's a testament that obedience to what you know is right, despite hardship, leads to victories not just on the field but in life's broader scope.

Shadrach, Meshach, and Abednego - Unyielding Faith in the Fiery Furnace

"As for me, I will call upon God, and the Lord shall save me."
Psalm 55:16 NKJV

Standing Up Against the King's Decree

The story of Shadrach, Meshach, and Abednego is a powerful testament to the strength of faith and the courage to stand firm in the face of overwhelming adversity. In the heart of Babylon, these three young men faced a monumental challenge to their faith and lives.

King Nebuchadnezzar erected a massive golden statue and decreed that at the sound of music, everyone in the kingdom was required to bow down and worship this image. This edict put Shadrach, Meshach, and Abednego in direct conflict with the king's command, as bowing to the statue would violate their unwavering commitment to worship only the God of Israel.

The Command to Bow and the Trio's Refusal

When the music sounded, the vast majority complied with the king's decree, yet Shadrach, Meshach, and Abednego stood firm, refusing to bow. Their refusal was not an act of defiance against the king but a steadfast commitment to their faith, even in the face of severe consequences.

The Threat of the Fiery Furnace

Infuriated by their defiance, Nebuchadnezzar threatened them with death in a fiery furnace, giving them one last chance to renounce their faith and do as they were commanded. Their response was unwavering—they would not serve the king's gods or worship the golden statue, even if it meant facing the flames.

Miraculous Deliverance

The faith of these three men was about to be tested in the most extreme manner, leading to a miraculous demonstration of God's power and presence.

Bound and cast into the furnace, heated seven times its usual temperature, the situation seemed dire. Yet, what happened next would astonish the entire kingdom and change the course of their faith journey.

The Fourth Figure in the Flames

Nebuchadnezzar and his officials witnessed an astounding sight—the three men walking unbound in the flames, accompanied by a fourth figure, whom the king described as looking like "a son of the gods." This fourth person protected them, ensuring not even a hair on their heads was singed, nor did their clothing smell of smoke from the fire.

Emerging Unharmed and Unchanged

Shadrach, Meshach, and Abednego emerged from the furnace completely unharmed, a miraculous testament to God's power to save. This event led Nebuchadnezzar to praise their God and issue a decree that no one should speak against the God of Shadrach, Meshach, and Abednego, acknowledging His ability to rescue in ways no other god could.

Lessons from Shadrach, Meshach, and Abednego

Their story is not just a historical account but a source of timeless lessons on faith, courage, and the nature of God's deliverance.

The Courage to Stand Up for One's Beliefs

The unyielding faith of Shadrach, Meshach, and Abednego inspires us to have the courage to stand firm in our beliefs, even when faced with life-threatening challenges. Their story teaches us that true faith often requires standing alone, against the crowd, and sometimes against the most powerful forces in our lives.

God's Presence in Our Most Challenging Moments

Their experience in the furnace is a profound reminder that God is with us in our most challenging moments, providing protection and companionship even when we feel most alone. It reassures us that in times of trial, we may find ourselves not only surviving but also accompanied by a divine presence that brings peace amid the flames.

The Impact of Unwavering Faith on Even the Most Powerful Rulers

These three men's faith saved their lives and influenced one of the most powerful rulers of their time. Their unwavering faith led to a royal decree that acknowledged the supremacy of their God, showing that true faith can have far-reaching effects, often beyond what we can imagine.

By exploring the unwavering faith of Shadrach, Meshach, and Abednego, young readers can find inspiration to stand firm in their own beliefs, understanding that God's presence is a constant source of strength and protection in every circumstance.

Making it Personal: Standing Up for Others

Imagine you're at school and you notice a group of students teasing someone just because they're different—maybe they dress uniquely, are from another country, or simply don't fit in with the usual crowd. Everyone else seems to be laughing or ignoring the situation because it's easier to go along with the majority or stay out of trouble.

This scenario echoes the courage shown by Shadrach, Meshach, and Abednego, who stood firm in their beliefs despite the immense pressure to conform. Like them, you face a decision: do you ignore the bullying and blend in with the crowd, or do you stand up for the person being teased, showing kindness and support?

Choosing to be kind and defending the person being bullied can feel as daunting as facing a fiery furnace, especially when no one else is standing up. However, your actions can have a profound impact, not just on the person being bullied but also on those around you. It sends a message that kindness and bravery are more important than fitting in. By standing up, you also set a moral example that encourages others to rethink their actions and inspire them to act with compassion in the future.

Taking such a stand can be a powerful testament to your faith and character, reflecting a commitment to doing what's right in the eyes of God. It can also shift the culture in your school, showing that it's not only possible but commendable to support and respect each other's differences. Your choice to stand up and be kind can resonate far beyond that moment, helping to create an environment where everyone feels safe and valued.

Elijah - Prophetic Power and Humanity

"Be still, and know that I am God; I will be exalted among the nations, I will be exalted in the earth!" Psalms 46:10

Confronting the Prophets of Baal — Fire from Heaven

Elijah's story intertwines moments of divine power and human vulnerability, illustrating the profound impact of faith and the reality of God's presence in both triumph and despair. Elijah's ministry was marked by bold actions that demonstrated God's power and sovereignty in the face of idolatry and unbelief.

The Challenge on Mount Carmel

In one of the most dramatic confrontations in the Bible, Elijah challenged the prophets of Baal on Mount Carmel to a test that would prove whose god was real. Each side would prepare a bull for sacrifice and call on their god to send fire from heaven. This event was not just a contest between Elijah and the prophets but a pivotal moment for Israel to return to God.

While the prophets of Baal called on their god from morning till noon without any response, Elijah rebuilt the altar of the Lord, used twelve stones representing the tribes of Israel, and drenched the altar in water to demonstrate the undeniable power of God. When Elijah prayed, God answered with fire from heaven that consumed the sacrifice, the wood, the stones, the soil, and even the water in the trench around the altar, leaving no doubt about His supremacy.

Victory against False Gods

The miraculous display on Mount Carmel led to the decisive defeat of the prophets of Baal and a turning point for the people of Israel. This victory was a powerful demonstration of God's might and His demand for exclusive worship, reaffirming His status as the one true God.

Personal Struggles

Despite Elijah's bold faith and prophetic victories, he also faced moments of fear, exhaustion, and despair, revealing his humanity.

After the triumph on Mount Carmel, Elijah fled for his life from Jezebel, who vowed to kill him. His flight into the wilderness, driven by fear and a sense of isolation, underscores the personal costs of prophetic ministry and the reality of spiritual warfare.

Encountering God on Mount Horeb -God's Gentle Whisper

In a moment of deep despair, Elijah encountered God on Mount Horeb. God instructed him to stand on the mountain as He passed by. There were powerful displays of wind, earthquake, and fire, but God was not in them; instead, He revealed Himself in a gentle whisper.

This encounter with the gentle whisper, or "still small voice," highlights that God's presence is not always in the dramatic or spectacular but often in the quiet and simple moments, requiring us to listen closely and attentively.

Lessons from Elijah

Elijah's life offers valuable lessons on faith, the nature of God, and how we encounter Him.

The Supremacy of God

Elijah's confrontations with the prophets of Baal and his other prophetic acts underscore the central biblical theme of the supremacy of God over all other powers and deities, calling us to acknowledge and worship Him alone.

Finding Strength in Vulnerability

Elijah's moments of vulnerability remind us that strength is not always in power or certainty but often in acknowledging our weaknesses and fears. In these moments, we can experience God's comfort, guidance, and provision in deeper ways.

Listening for God's Voice in the Quiet

The encounter on Mount Horeb teaches us the importance of quietness and stillness in experiencing God's presence. In a world filled with noise and distractions, Elijah's story invites us to find time for silence to listen for God's gentle whisper to guide and comfort us.

Elijah's life, woven with themes of divine power and human frailty, encourages us to live boldly for God while also seeking Him in the quiet places of our hearts, where His gentle whisper can guide and sustain us.

Making it Personal: Navigating the Noise of Everyday Life

Imagine you're in the middle of a hectic week; school projects are due; if you have a phone, your social media notifications are blowing up, and your schedule is packed with activities. In this whirlwind of activity, you feel overwhelmed and stressed, barely finding a moment to pause or breathe. In times like these, your faith feels most distant, and you wonder how you can reconnect with God amid such chaos.

Elijah's encounter on Mount Horeb teaches a valuable lesson about finding God not in the thunderous and the grandiose but in the quiet and subtle moments. Reflect on how you can create moments of stillness in your busy day. What steps can you take to reduce the noise that distracts you from God's presence?

Choosing to set aside specific times for prayer and reflection can be a start. Perhaps it means turning off your phone or the TV for a few minutes each day, finding a quiet spot during breaks, or starting your mornings a little earlier to meditate on a Bible passage. As you make these small adjustments, notice how they affect your ability to hear God's "gentle whisper." Just as Elijah found renewal and direction in the quietness, you, too, can discover that these moments of stillness strengthen your faith and provide clarity amidst life's chaos. By actively seeking these quiet times, you remind yourself of God's nearness and His desire to lead you through each day, showing that even in a busy world, there is power and peace in stillness and seeking God.

John - The Beloved Disciple

"And so it happened just as the Scriptures say: "Abraham believed God, and God counted him as righteous because of his faith." He was even called a friend of God. James 2:23 NLT

Who is John?

John, known as the "Beloved Disciple," was one of Jesus Christ's closest followers. A fisherman by trade, John left his nets along with his brother James when Jesus called them. This chapter explores John's unique relationship with Jesus, his key contributions to the early Christian church, and his profound writings that continue to inspire millions around the world.

Following Jesus

John's journey with Jesus began on the shores of Galilee, where he and his brother James were called to be disciples. From the moment John left his nets to follow Jesus, he became part of an inner circle that experienced moments with Christ that the other disciples did not witness. At key events such as the Transfiguration, John saw Jesus in divine form, talking with Moses and Elijah, which not only underscored the messianic identity of Jesus but also deepened John's understanding of Jesus' divine mission.

During the Last Supper, John was positioned close enough to lean against Jesus, a gesture indicating not just physical proximity but immense trust and brotherly love. This placement at the table during such a critical moment in Jesus' ministry highlights John's role as a confidant and beloved friend. John's insights into Jesus' teachings during these intimate moments are reflected in the unique depth of understanding expressed in the Gospel of John, which emphasizes the divinity of Christ and the meaning of His love.

At the Cross

John's steadfastness and loyalty are nowhere more evident than at the foot of the Cross, where he stood by Jesus in His most agonizing hours—a time when most of the other disciples had fled in fear. This act of loyalty and courage illustrates the depth of John's love for Jesus. Here, amid despair and suffering, Jesus entrusted the care of His mother, Mary, to John, symbolizing a significant transfer of responsibility and trust. Jesus' words, "Woman, here is your son," and to John, "Here is your mother," (John 19:26-27) further signify the personal relationship they shared, binding John and Mary in a familial relationship that would have required great emotional and spiritual strength from John.

This moment is pivotal, as it shows John's dual role as both disciple and family, tasked with a mission of care that would extend beyond Jesus' earthly life. It underscores John's understanding of the community and love central to Jesus' teachings, tasks he carried forward in his care for Mary and in his later writings.

John's Ministry and Writings

After Jesus' resurrection and ascension, John took a leading role in the early Christian church. His ministry, particularly in Ephesus, nurtured and strengthened early believers amidst growing persecution. John's pastoral role is evident in the way he addressed the churches in his epistles, offering both correction and comfort, underscoring themes of love, truth, and eternal life. His letters to various congregations, as found in the New Testament, reflect a deep understanding of Jesus' teachings and a passionate commitment to spreading the Gospel.

John's Gospel differs from the other gospels (Matthew, Mark, and Luke) in that it focuses on the spiritual rather than the chronological order of events in Jesus' life. It begins with the profound proclamation: "In the beginning was the Word, and the Word was with God, and the Word was God." (John 1:1). This declaration showcases John's intent to convey not just the events of Jesus' life but also their eternal significance. Furthermore, the Book of Revelation, a prophetic work received by John on the Isle of Patmos, reveals visions of the ultimate triumph of

God over evil, providing hope and instruction for the church enduring persecution.

John's writings collectively serve as a biblical foundation for understanding the identity and mission of Jesus Christ, the importance of love in the believer's life, and the ultimate hope of every Christian. Through his gospel, letters, and prophetic writings, John continues to guide and influence Christian thought and devotion, emphasizing his profound relationship with Jesus, both as a disciple and as a friend.

Lessons from the Isle of Patmos

During a time of persecution, John was exiled to the Isle of Patmos, where he received the visions recorded in Revelation. These writings reflect not only a future hope but also the immediate presence of God during times of suffering. John's resilience and unwavering faith during his exile encourage believers to persevere in faith, even when faced with great trials.

John's Legacy and Lessons for Today

John's legacy is one of profound love and faithful witness. His life teaches us the importance of a deep, personal relationship with Jesus, characterized by love that acts and faith that endures. For young readers today, John's story is a call to love Jesus and others fully, to remain faithful through trials, and to bear witness to the truth of God's grace in their own lives.

The Timeless Message of John

John's life and writings serve as a powerful reminder of God's love and the transformative power of faith. As we close this chapter, let us reflect on how we, like John, can draw closer to Jesus daily, loving Him and those around us with the heart of the Beloved Disciple. Let us pray for the courage to stand firm in our faith and the wisdom to see God's hand in every part of our lives.

Making it Personal: Living as a Beloved Disciple Today

Imagine you're at school and notice a classmate sitting alone during lunch, looking a bit sad and isolated. Everyone else is busy with their groups, and it would be easy for you to join your friends and ignore the situation. However, John, the Beloved Disciple, showed us through his actions and writings that true discipleship involves showing love and kindness, especially to those who might be overlooked or in need.

John's deep commitment to caring and compassion, as exemplified when Jesus entrusted him with the care of His mother, Mary, challenges us to look for ways to demonstrate this "beloved disciple" kind of love in our own lives. How can you, in a similar spirit, extend friendship and kindness to someone who might feel left out or alone? It could be as simple as inviting them to join your table, offering a listening ear, or sharing a kind word that brightens their day.

Reflect on the impact these actions might have on your classmate and your understanding of what it means to live out your faith. By choosing to act with love and compassion, you're not only following in the footsteps of John but also actively participating in transforming your school into a more inclusive and caring environment. This kind of love—a love that seeks out the lonely and uplifts the downtrodden—echoes the teachings of Jesus and carries powerful potential to change lives, including your own.

Peter - The Rock on Which the Church is Built

"For it is by believing in your heart that you are made right with God, and it is by openly declaring your faith that you are saved."
Romans 10:10 NLT

Who is Peter?

Simon Peter, originally a simple fisherman from the shores of Galilee, emerged as one of the most prominent figures in Christian history. Called by Jesus to abandon his nets and follow Him, Peter's life was transformed from the pursuit of fish to the pursuit of souls. Known for his fiery spirit and impulsive nature, Peter's journey with Jesus shaped him into a pivotal leader whose strengths and flaws illuminate his profound humanity.

The Calling of Peter

Jesus' invitation to Peter, "Come, follow me, and I will make you fishers of men," marked the beginning of Peter's transforma-tion. As one of Jesus' closest companions, Peter witnessed miracles, heard parables firsthand, and often acted as the spokesperson for the group of disciples. His journey was punctuated by profound moments, such as when he walked on water towards Jesus, showcasing his fleeting bravery and human doubts. His declaration that Jesus was the Messiah revealed his deep insight and connection with Jesus, who, in turn, recognized Peter's foundational role in the early church.

Peter's Denial and Redemption

Peter's journey through denial to redemption is one of the most moving narratives of human fallibility and divine grace. On the eve of Jesus' crucifixion, Peter vehemently promised loyalty but ended up denying Jesus three times, just as Jesus had predicted. This betrayal occurred during Jesus' most vulnerable moment, intensifying the sting of Peter's actions. However, his story did not end there. After the resurrection, Jesus appeared to Peter, offering him a chance for redemption through a profound and tender exchange where Jesus asked Peter three times if he loved Him, mirroring Peter's three denials. Each affirmation from Peter was met with Jesus' command to "Feed my sheep," signifying not only forgiveness but also reestablishing Peter's role as a leader in nurturing the Christian community.

Peter's Ministry and Leadership

Following his reinstatement, Peter embraced his role with newfound vigor and divine guidance. His ministry was marked by powerful miracles and preaching, beginning with his bold proclamation at Pentecost, which led to the conversion of about

3,000 people. Peter's faith allowed him to perform miraculous acts through the power of the Holy Spirit, including healing a lame man at the temple gate, which not only demonstrated his divine authority but also affirmed his leadership in the early Church. Another notable miracle was the raising of Tabitha (Dorcas) from the dead, which mirrored the compassionate miracles of Jesus and underscored the continuation of Jesus' work through His apostles.

Peter also experienced remarkable spiritual milestones that deepened his understanding of Jesus' mission. He was one of the few disciples who witnessed the Transfiguration of Jesus on the mountain, an event that revealed the divine nature of Christ and significantly bolstered Peter's faith and understanding of the Messianic prophecies. This event was pivotal, confirming Jesus as the Son of God and deeply impacting Peter's perception of his Master's true identity and mission.

Lessons from Peter's Life

Peter's life offers profound lessons in faith, leadership, and the dynamics of grace. His initial impulsive nature was gradually transformed into a hallmark of bold, faith-driven leadership. Peter's personal failures, particularly his denial of Christ, coupled with his later redemptive acts, illustrate the transformative power of repentance and forgiveness. These experiences convey that no failure is too great to overcome with faith and that restoration is always possible with God.

Moreover, Peter's experiences with miracles—from walking on water to significant healings—highlight the theme that with faith, believers can act as conduits for God's power, impacting lives and advancing God's kingdom on Earth. These miracles not only served to affirm the early Church but also to reinforce Peter's faith and leadership.

Peter's close relationship with Jesus, marked by moments of both profound revelation and deep personal failure, illustrates a critical message: leadership in the Christian context is not about perfection but about perseverance, humility, and an unyielding commitment to follow Christ. Peter's life encourages all believers to seek a deeper, more personal relationship with Jesus, promising that such a connection can lead to remarkable spiritual growth and impact.

The Enduring Legacy of Peter

Peter's life, intertwined with moments of great faith and profound failure, teaches us about the beauty of redemption and the strength that comes from true conviction. As we reflect on his story, let each of us strive to be as bold and steadfast in our faith as Peter was, guided by the enduring love of Jesus Christ.

Making it Personal: Standing Strong in Your Faith

Imagine you're in the school cafeteria, and the conversation turns to a topic involving faith, perhaps a recent news event related to religion or a moral issue. Some of your peers start making jokes about religious beliefs or perhaps challenge the idea of faith as outdated or irrelevant. You feel that stirring inside you, a call to respond, but you're also aware of the eyes that might turn your way, the snickers, or even outright disagreement that could follow. This is your Mount Carmel moment, much like Peter's challenges, where you're faced with the decision to either blend in silently or stand firm in your faith.

Think about this: How can you, like Peter, find the courage to speak up for what you believe in? Peter, once fearful and denying Jesus to save himself, found his strength in the Holy Spirit and became a bold preacher, unafraid of persecution. His transformation and eventual bravery offer a blueprint for facing opposition. Reflect on the times Peter spoke with conviction before authorities, not with aggression, but with firmness and a clear articulation of his faith.

You could start by expressing your views calmly and respectfully, using this as an opportunity to share why your faith is important to you. It isn't about winning an argument but about being true to your convictions. You might say, "I understand how you feel, but for me, faith provides a strength and perspective that are very important." It's also alright to ask for respect, as mutual respect is the foundation of meaningful dialogue. Standing firm doesn't always mean standing alone; often, displaying your commitment can inspire others to reflect on their views and even garner support from those who might have remained silent. Each time you choose to stand firm, you strengthen not only your own faith but also encourage others to consider their stances, building an environment where diverse perspectives can be shared respectfully.

Paul – From Persecutor to Preacher

"And do not be conformed to this world, but be transformed by the renewing of your mind, that you may prove what is that good and acceptable and perfect will of God." Romans 12:2

The Damascus Road Experience

Paul's transformation from a fierce persecutor of Christians to one of the most influential apostles of Christ is a testament to the transformative power of God's grace. Paul's faith journey began with a dramatic encounter that forever changed the course of his life and the history of Christianity.

Before his conversion, Paul, then known as Saul, was a zealous Pharisee who vehemently persecuted the early Christian church. His dedication to Judaism led him to believe that he was serving God by arresting Christians and disrupting the spread of the new faith.

The Blinding Light, a Voice, and a Transformation in Christ

On his way to Damascus to persecute more Christians, Paul was struck by a blinding light from heaven, and he heard the voice of Jesus asking, "Saul, Saul, why do you persecute me?" This supernatural encounter not only halted Paul's mission of persecution but also opened his eyes to the truth of Jesus Christ.

Paul's conversion was marked by three days of blindness, during which he neither ate nor drank. His sight was restored by Ananias, a disciple in Damascus, who baptized him. From that moment, Paul became a fervent preacher of the faith he once tried to destroy, demonstrating the radical nature of God's grace and the potential for transformation in Christ.

Apostle to the Gentiles – Missionary Journeys

Paul's ministry expanded the reach of the Gospel beyond Judaism, making a lasting impact on the early Christian church and beyond.

Paul embarked on several missionary journeys across the Roman Empire, from Asia Minor to Europe, facing both receptiveness and resistance. His travels were fueled by a mandate from Jesus to spread the Gospel, and his efforts led to the establishment of numerous Christian communities.

Beyond his missionary travels, Paul's legacy includes the planting of churches in key cities and the writing of letters to these communities. These epistles, many of which are included in the New Testament, addressed theological issues, practical problems, and ethical conduct, guiding believers in their faith and practice.

Perseverance Amidst Persecutions

Paul's ministry was marked by constant challenges, including imprisonment, beatings, and shipwrecks. Despite these hardships, he remained steadfast, driven by his commitment to Christ and the Gospel. His perseverance serves as a powerful example of faith in action.

Lessons from Paul

Paul's life and ministry offer invaluable lessons on faith, suffering, and the Christian perspective on life and eternity.

The Power of God's Transformative Love

Paul's dramatic conversion highlights the power of God's love to transform the most unlikely individuals. His life is a testimony to the fact that no one is beyond the reach of God's grace and redemption.

The Joy in Suffering for Christ

Paul's writings often reflect on the paradox of finding joy in suffering for the sake of Christ. He viewed his trials as a way to share in Christ's sufferings and as an opportunity to demonstrate the power of the Gospel in the midst of adversity.

The Eternal Perspective

Paul's teachings consistently point believers to an eternal perspective, emphasizing that the trials of this life are temporary compared to the glory that awaits in Christ. His focus on the eternal kingdom of God encourages believers to live lives of hope, purpose, and anticipation of Christ's return.

Paul's journey from persecutor to preacher underscores the transformative impact of encountering Christ, inspiring believers to embrace God's grace, endure trials with joy, and keep their eyes on the eternal promises of God.

Making it Personal: Staying Anchored in a Digital World

Consider your daily routine, which likely includes scrolling through social media, watching TV and streaming videos, and consuming a wide array of digital content. Each day, you're bombarded with messages, trends, and lifestyles that often reflect worldly values and priorities. Amid this constant stream of information, how do you maintain your Christian values and not be swayed by the world?

Paul's transformative encounter on the road to Damascus highlights the profound impact of God's Word in renewing our minds. Just as God's grace radically changed Paul's life, you, too, can experience transformation through daily engagement with the Scriptures. Reflect on how often you read the Bible compared to how much time you spend on social media or other activities. Are your daily habits helping you grow in faith, or are they pulling you into the world's mold?

By choosing to dedicate time each day to reading the Bible and prayer, you set a foundation that helps guard against the temptations and distractions of this world. This practice of renewing your mind isn't just about resisting negative influences; it's about embracing God's truth in a way that transforms how you think, act, and interact with others. As you make this a priority, you'll find that you can discern God's will more clearly, but you're also equipped to live it out, demonstrating what is good, acceptable, and perfect before God. This ongoing renewal is essential for staying true to your faith and influencing those around you positively, proving that a life rooted in Christ can thrive even in a world that often goes in the opposite direction.

Embracing the Legacy of Wisdom

As we close this book, filled with stories of courage, faith, and transformation from the lives of great men in the Bible, let us reflect on what it means to truly live a life that is pleasing to God. From Adam's garden to Paul's journeys, each story offers us a glimpse into the challenges and triumphs of walking with God. These men were not perfect; they faced doubts, made mistakes, and sometimes fell short. But their stories share a common thread—a relentless pursuit of a relationship with God, no matter the circumstances.

Adam, Noah, Abraham, Moses, David, Elijah, and Paul—these men teach us that following God's will is not always about doing grand, heroic acts. It is about making daily choices that reflect our faith and commitment to God. Whether it's choosing honesty over deceit, courage over fear, or forgiveness over bitterness, these choices shape who we are and influence those around us. Like a small stone creating ripples in a vast lake, our choices send waves into the world that can spread far beyond what we might initially see.

To live a life that reflects God's good, acceptable, and perfect will, it's essential to cultivate a daily relationship with Him. This doesn't mean just praying before meals or attending church on Sundays. It means making God a part of your everyday experiences—talking to Him about your fears, asking for His guidance in your decisions, and thanking Him for the little joys that come your way. Just as Daniel remained faithful amid Babylon's pressures, or as young David trusted God against Goliath, your faith can stand strong against the challenges of modern life.

Let these stories be more than just ancient tales; let them be a guide for your journey. Seek God daily as your constant companion and greatest ally, not just in times of trouble. When you make your relationship with Him your highest priority, you open your life to the endless possibilities of His grace and power. You become a light in your community, a beacon of hope, and a living testament to God's love.

So, as you move forward, remember that you are part of a grand story that continues with each choice you make. Stand firm in your faith, seek wisdom, show kindness, and above all, cherish your walk with God. Through your actions, thoughts, and words, strive to live a life that honors Him, and you will surely find the path that leads to true fulfillment and joy. Let your life be an example of God's love as you grow each day in His grace and walk in His perfect will.

Adventures in Scripture for Kids: Exploring The Great Women of the Bible

Lorie Eubank

A Brand New Adventure

Hey there, young adventurer! Are you ready to dive into an incredible journey through time? "Adventures in Scriptures for Kids: Exploring the Great Women of the Bible" is your personal invitation to explore the stories of some truly remarkable women whose lives helped shape the course of biblical history. This book isn't just about reading; it's about discovering, learning, and growing. The examples we are given in these great women of the Bible help us to see that God doesn't expect perfection, just a submitted heart and a desire to please Him.

Embark on a Journey of Faith and Courage

Each page of this book is packed with engaging stories and thought-provoking discussions about women who demonstrated faith, perseverance, courage, and love. These great women—from queens and prophetesses to ordinary everyday heroes—played important roles in God's divine plan. Their stories are here to inspire and guide you, showing that no matter who you are, you have a purpose.

Why Women of the Bible?

Our adventure starts by revealing why these women are so important. Though often overlooked, their contributions were important to the unfolding of biblical events and God's overall plans. As we explore their lives, you'll gain a new appreciation for how central women were in these stories and how their influence is still felt today.

With each chapter, you'll meet different women of the Bible—like Eve, starting humanity in the Garden of Eden, or Queen Esther, making brave choices to save her people. These stories cover a wide range of emotions and lessons, highlighting God's grace and the power of faith even in tough times.

Be Inspired to Make a Difference

We invite you to see yourself in these stories. Find inspiration in the resilience and faith of these women, and understand how these ancient tales reflect in your own life. The book includes fun activities, reflective questions, and practical applications to help engage your mind and heart, encouraging you to think deeply and live out the virtues you admire.

A Journey of Faith and Purpose

"Adventures in Scriptures for Kids: Exploring the Great Women of the Bible" merges historical insights with spiritual lessons, creating a unique and enriching experience that goes beyond just learning history—it's about discovering how to live a life filled with faith and purpose.

Join us on this adventure to learn from the great women of the Bible and see how their lives can inspire you to be courageous, faithful, and loving in your own unique way. Let's start this exciting journey together!

Eve - The First Mother (Genesis Ch 2:18 - 3:24)

"And the Lord God said, "It is not good that man should be alone; I will make him a helper comparable to him." Genesis 2:18 NKJV

Creation and Paradise

In the serene beauty of the Garden of Eden, where all creation was in harmony, lived Eve, the first woman, alongside Adam, the first man. As significant as her role as the mother of all living, Eve's story is foundational to understanding humanity's origin and the complexities of human choice and divine intention.

The Creation of Eve

God saw that it was not good for Adam to be alone, so He created a companion for him. Eve was formed from one of Adam's ribs, symbolizing her integral role as a partner in life's journey. This act of creation illustrates that companionship and equality are inherent to human relationships as designed by God. Eve's introduction into Eden marked the beginning of human partnership, highlighting themes of unity and mutual support.

Life in the Garden of Eden

Eden was a place of perfect peace and abundance, where Adam and Eve lived in close communion with God and nature. They were stewards of a perfect world, tending to the garden and enjoying the fruits of their paradise. This period of time reflects an ideal state of human existence, free from pain and suffering, where their every need was met.

Relationship with Adam

Adam and Eve's relationship was founded on equality and mutual respect. They shared responsibilities and the joys of Eden, representing the ideal partnership. This union was a model partnership that set the foundation for all human relationships to follow.

The Temptation and the Fall

The tranquility of Eden was disrupted when Eve encountered the serpent, who tempted her with the fruit from the Tree of Knowledge of Good and Evil, which God had forbidden them to eat. The serpent's persuasive words sparked curiosity and desire in Eve, leading to her decision to eat the fruit and share it with Adam. This act of disobedience, often called the Fall, introduced sin and its consequences into the world.

Consequences of Their Actions

The immediate effect of their actions was the loss of innocence; Adam and Eve became aware of their nakedness and felt shame for the first time. They were expelled from Eden to prevent them from eating from the Tree of Life and becoming immortal sinners. This expulsion marked the beginning of the human struggle with sin, labor, and pain—an enduring consequence that altered the course of human history.

God's Promise for Mankind

Despite the severity of the Fall, God did not abandon Adam and Eve. The curses laid upon them, and the serpent also contained the seeds of future redemption. God made garments of skin for Adam and Eve, showing His continuing care. More importantly, He promised that Eve's offspring would eventually crush the serpent's head, hinting at the eventual victory over sin and death, a prophecy to foreshadow the coming of Christ.

Understanding Consequences

Eve's story is a profound lesson in the ramifications of our choices. The decision to eat the forbidden fruit had far-reaching effects, impacting not just their immediate circumstances but the spiritual state of all their descendants. It teaches the importance of obedience and the high costs of transgression.

The Importance of Wisdom and Discernment

Eve's interaction with the serpent underscores the necessity for wisdom and discernment in decision-making. It illustrates the vulnerability of innocence and the need for vigilance against deceit. This part of her story encourages us to seek God's wisdom and be cautious of the influences that can lead us astray.

Redemption and New Beginnings

Despite the tragedy of the Fall, Eve's story is also about hope and redemption. The promise of a savior provided a glimpse of restoration and a new beginning. It reflects the overall biblical theme of God's plan for salvation—a plan that redeems the falls of humanity and restores them to a right relationship with Him.

Fun Family Activity

Fruit Tasting Activity: Get a plate and various types of fruit, including an apple, and have a fruit-tasting session. Discuss how something as simple as fruit led to such significant consequences for Eve and all of humanity. And though it was not just about a specific type of fruit, it helps us to understand the importance of obedience and the repercussions or consequences of our actions.

Making it Personal

Reflective Questions

1. **What about you?**: Consider a time when you faced a difficult choice, knowing your decision could have significant consequences. Perhaps it was a moment when you were tempted against your better judgment due to peer pressure or strong desire. How did you respond? Did you consider the long-term effects of your decision, or did you focus only on immediate gratification?

2. **Understanding Consequences**: Eve made a choice that had big consequences for herself and others. Can you think of a time when you made a choice that affected not just you but others around you? What did you

learn from that experience?

3. **Wisdom and Discernment**: Why do you think Eve was tempted to eat the fruit, even though she knew it was against God's command? What does this tell us about the importance of being careful in our decisions?

4. **The Role of Temptation**: What are some temptations that kids face today? How can you apply the lesson of Eve's experience to resist temptations in your own life?

5. **Redemption and New Beginnings**: Despite the mistakes Eve made, God still cared for her and made garments of skins to clothe her and Adam. What does this tell us about forgiveness and new beginnings? How can we seek forgiveness when we make mistakes?

Reflecting on Eve's experience, think about the importance of seeking wisdom and making choices that align with your values that would be pleasing to God. Every decision has the potential to shape not only your own life but also impact those around you. By applying the lessons from Eve's story, you can approach life's choices with greater thoughtfulness and a deeper understanding of their potential consequences, always striving for decisions that bring about growth, unity, and alignment with God's principles.

Sarah - Mother of Nations (Genesis Ch. 12:1 - 23:2)

"For I know the thoughts that I think towards you, says the Lord, thoughts of peace and not of evil, to give you a future and a hope. Then you will call upon Me and go and pray to Me, and I will listen to you. And you will seek me and find Me, when you search for Me with all your heart." Jerimiah 29:11-13

Early Life and Promises

In the records of biblical history, few figures are as central and revered as Sarah, the wife of Abraham. Her story unfolds across several chapters of Genesis, portraying her as a figure of immense faith and complexity. Known initially as Sarai, which means "my princess," she was later renamed Sarah, meaning "princess to all," by God to signify her role in the divine covenant He had with Abraham.

Introduction to Sarah and Abram

Sarah and Abram, later Abraham, begin their journey in Ur

of the Chaldees. The narrative swiftly moves to God's call to Abram, urging him to leave his homeland for a place He would show him, promising that He would make of him a great nation. Sarah, as Abram's wife, was an important part of this promise, although personal trials and deep-seated desires marked her own journey.

God's Promise to Abram and Sarai

The promise of descendants as numerous as the stars was extraordinary, considering both Abraham and Sarah were well beyond the age of childbearing. This pledge frames much of Sarah's story, highlighting her struggles with faith, patience, and the fulfillment of God's promises.

Challenges Faced Due to Barrenness

Sarah's barrenness is a continuous source of pain and societal stigma. During that time in history, a woman's value was often measured by her ability to bear children, and Sarah's inability to do so tested both her faith and her identity. This challenge led to significant decisions, including her arrangement for Abram to have a child with Hagar, her Egyptian maid, a common practice at the time but one that would lead to further familial strife.

The Birth of Ishmael

Hagar's subsequent pregnancy with Ishmael brought additional tension and strife within the family. Sarah's relationship with Hagar soured, leading to conflict and the eventual mistreatment of Hagar. This part of the story reveals the complexities of Sarah's character and underscores the human flaws and emotions accompanying her faith journey.

God Reaffirms His Promise

Despite these challenges, God reaffirms His covenant with Abraham, explicitly including Sarah in the promise this time, indicating that she would bear a son named Isaac. This reaffirmation is a life-changing moment for Sarah, directly addressing her role in the covenant and her doubts about the promise.

Birth of Isaac in Sarah's Old Age

Upon hearing she would have a child, Sarah's laughter reflects both amazement and joy. Her reaction is a human response showing the struggle of faith against doubt. The eventual birth of Isaac is a triumph, fulfilling God's promise and affirming Sarah's role as a mother of nations.

The Virtue of Patience

Sarah learned to wait patiently for God's promises to unfold throughout her life. Her story teaches that patience is not passive waiting but faithful endurance based on God's assurances, even when circumstances seem impossible.

Trusting in God's Timing

Sarah's journey emphasizes the importance of trusting in God's perfect timing. Despite her efforts to hasten God's promise through the birth of Ishmael, it was only through Isaac that the covenant was fulfilled. This shows us that God's timing often does not align with human expectations but always fulfills a greater purpose.

The Value of Perseverance

Sarah's life was marked by perseverance through doubt, societal pressures, and personal disappointments. Her enduring faith under these pressures highlights her strength and resilience, providing a powerful example for those facing their own trials.

Fun Family Activities

1. **Create a Starry Night Sky**: Using black construction paper and stickers or white paint for stars, create your own representation of a starry night sky, similar to what Abraham might have seen when God promised him countless descendants. This activity can help visualize the magnitude of God's promise to Sarah and Abraham.

2. **Tent Craft**: Since Sarah and Abraham lived in tents, traveling as they needed to, try building a model tent using sticks and fabric. This can help you understand their lifestyle. Discuss the challenges and adventures of frequently living in tents and moving as part of God's plan. If you have been tent camping, you may have been in the tent for a few days or even a week. Imagine living in a tent your whole life.

Making it Personal

Reflective Questions

1. **What about you?**: Consider a long-held dream or goal you have struggled to achieve, facing setbacks that

sometimes make the dream seem unreachable. Perhaps it's getting on a sports team, an academic goal, or a personal project. How do you respond to these challenges? Do you feel tempted to give up or find ways to renew your commitment and continue standing in faith?

2. **Understanding Patience**: Sarah waited a very long time for God's promise of a child to be fulfilled. Can you think of something you had to wait a long time for? How did you feel during the wait, and what was the outcome?

3. **Trusting in God's Timing**: Why do you think it was important for Sarah to have a child at such an old age? What does this tell us about how God's plans might be different from our expectations?

4. **The Impact of Decisions**: Sarah decided to take matters into her own hands by giving Hagar to Abraham. What were the consequences of this decision for everyone involved? How does this story help us understand the importance of waiting for God's timing?

5. **The Joy of Fulfillment**: How do you think Sarah felt when she finally held Isaac in her arms? Have you ever experienced joy or relief when something you hoped for finally happened? How did you react?

Reflecting on Sarah's story, consider the importance of perseverance, patience, and trust in something greater than immediate circumstances. Like Sarah, you may find that the greatest achievements require time and faith, often coming to fruition in ways you might not expect but that ultimately fulfill a greater plan. By adopting Sarah's virtues, you can approach your goals with renewed focus and a deeper understanding of the value of waiting and working in faith toward a promised future.

Ruth - The Loyal Daughter-in-law (Ruth Ch. 1-4)

"Let all that I am praise the Lord; may I never forget the good things He does for me." Psalms 103:2 NLT

Tragedy and Hope

Ruth's story, beautifully shared in the Book of Ruth, is a tender picture of loyalty, love, and redemption. Set during the time of the Judges—a period marked by social and moral chaos—Ruth's story shines with hope and faithfulness. As a Moabite woman who leaves her homeland for Bethlehem, her journey from widowhood to an esteemed position in the lineage of David, and ultimately in the genealogy of Jesus Christ, is a profound testament to the power of devotion and divine providence.

Ruth's Marriage and Early Tragedies

Ruth's life in Moab began with her marriage to Mahlon, son of Elimelech and Naomi, an Israelite family that had migrated due to famine. However, her new beginning was soon marred by the death of her husband, followed by the deaths of her brother-in-law and father-in-law. These successive tragedies left Ruth and her mother-in-law, Naomi, without any immediate male relatives, thrusting them into a difficult social and economic position.

The Decision to Stay with Naomi

When Naomi decided to return to Bethlehem after hearing that the famine had ended, she urged her daughters-in-law to remain in Moab and remarry. Orpah, Ruth's sister-in-law, tearfully departed; however, Ruth clung to Naomi, uttering the iconic words, "Where you go, I will go, and where you stay, I will stay. Your people will be my people and your God my God" (Ruth 1:16). This heartfelt declaration not only shows Ruth's unwavering loyalty but also her adoption of Naomi's faith and people as her own.

Arrival in Bethlehem

Upon arriving in Bethlehem, Ruth, the Moabite, found herself in a foreign land, grappling with the challenges of her widowhood and outsider status. Yet, her story of resilience and loyalty was only beginning to unfold.

Ruth Meets Boaz

To support herself and Naomi, Ruth went to glean in the fields during the barley harvest, adhering to the Levitical law that allowed the poor and foreigners to pick up leftover grains. There, she met Boaz, a wealthy and kind relative of Naomi's late husband. Impressed by her devotion to Naomi and by her faithfulness, Boaz offered Ruth protection and allowed her to gather grain more freely, ensuring she had enough to eat.

Boaz's Kindness and Protection

Boaz's actions towards Ruth were not merely acts of charity; the Jewish laws of kindness and redemption governed them. His respect for Ruth grew as he learned more about her sacrifices for Naomi. He provided her safety among his workers, extra food, and a sense of belonging, breaking social norms that often isolated foreigners.

Their Eventual Marriage

The relationship between Ruth and Boaz developed through a beautiful blend of respect and admiration. Naomi, recognizing Boaz's role as a kinsman-redeemer, guides Ruth in matters of tradition and law, which leads to Ruth approaching Boaz to take up his role as redeemer. This resulted in their marriage, restoring Ruth's and Naomi's inheritance and securing their positions within the community of Bethlehem.

What is a Kinsmen-Redeemer? A kinsman-redeemer is like a special family hero who helps when someone in the family is in trouble or needs support. Imagine having a cousin or big brother who promised to always help you if you ever lost something important or needed help with a big problem. This family hero could protect you, help you get back something important like your home if you lost it, or even make sure you're not treated unfairly.

In the Bible, this is what a kinsman-redeemer does. They are part of the family who can rescue members of their family who are in big trouble, like buying back land that had to be sold when someone was really poor or helping a widow who needs someone to support her. It's like having a family hero who's always ready to make sure everyone in the family is safe and okay!

The Strength of Loyalty

Ruth's story is a powerful affirmation of how loyalty can change destinies. Her faithfulness in staying with Naomi, despite her personal losses and the uncertainty of her future, illustrates the powerful impact of loyalty on those around us.

Hope during Hard Times

Ruth's story is filled with the theme of hope. Even in her darkest hours, her actions were guided by a hopeful outlook toward the future, demonstrating that perseverance through adversity can lead to unexpected and rewarding paths.

The Beauty of God-orchestrated Love Stories

The union of Ruth and Boaz is not just a love story but a beautiful picture that highlights how God can turn sorrow into joy, scarcity into abundance, and uncertainty into blessing. Their story underscores the belief that God is intimately involved in the details of our lives, weaving our stories into His grander plan.

Fun Family Activity

Loyalty Bracelet: Using string and beads, make bracelets representing loyalty, reflecting Ruth's unwavering loyalty to Naomi. At the same time you are making your bracelet think about how you can show loyalty to friends and family.

Making it Personal

Reflective Questions

1. **What about you?**: Imagine you're facing significant life changes after moving to a new city for your parent's new job. You feel alone and uncertain about the future, much like Ruth must have felt in Bethlehem. How would you navigate this new chapter? Would you retreat into isolation or reach out, forming new bonds and embracing new opportunities despite the challenges?

2. **Loyalty and Devotion**: Ruth chose to stay with Naomi even though it meant leaving her home and facing an uncertain future. Can you think of a time when you decided to help or stand by someone, even if it was difficult? How did it make you feel?

3. **Embracing New Opportunities**: Ruth left Moab to live in Bethlehem and embraced new traditions and people. How can we be open to new opportunities and experiences, even when unfamiliar or challenging?

4. **Generosity and Kindness**: Boaz showed kindness and generosity to Ruth by allowing her to gather grain freely in his fields. What are some ways that we can be gen-

erous and kind to people in our own lives, particularly those who are new or different? How can you be helpful to someone new to your neighborhood or school?

5. **Faith and Blessings**: Ruth's faithfulness to Naomi and God eventually led to unexpected blessings. How does this story help us understand that patience and kindness can lead to positive outcomes even if we don't see them immediately?

Reflecting on Ruth's journey, consider her bravery in embracing a new life and her proactive efforts to care for Naomi and integrate into a new community. Like Ruth, you can choose to face new environments with courage and openness, beginning new relationships and finding your place in new settings. Her story encourages us to embrace new beginnings with hope and faith, trusting that our paths, when walked with integrity and love, can lead to profound fulfillment and unexpected blessings.

Esther - The Courageous Queen (Esther Ch. 1-10)

"Who knows if perhaps you were made queen for just such a time as this?" Esther 4:14b NLT

Rising to Royalty

Esther's story, set in the beautiful but dangerous courts of King Xerxes, king of Persia, unfolds like a dramatic tale of intrigue, courage, and providence. Born as Hadassah and raised by her cousin Mordecai, Esther's ascent to queenhood is not merely a beautiful story but one of strategic courage and divine intervention that would lead to the salvation of the Jewish people in exile.

Introduction to Esther and Mordecai

Esther's early life was marked by displacement and orphanhood, having lost both parents at a young age. Raised by her cousin Mordecai, a minor official in the Persian government, Esther was nurtured quietly in her Jewish faith and culture, beneath the radar of broader societal notice in the sprawling empire.

Esther's Selection as Queen

When King Xerxes sought a new queen after deposing Queen Vashti for her defiance, Esther was gathered with many other young women in a royal contest of beauty and grace. Her charm and intelligence caught the eye of the king, and she found favor above all other maidens. Esther, guided by Mordecai's wisdom, kept her Jewish identity hidden, navigating the very different life in the palace with great skill.

Mordecai's Advice to Esther

Throughout her early days in the palace, Mordecai continued to advise Esther, communicating with her through messages. He counseled her to conceal her Jewish identity, a strategic decision that would later play a crucial role in her efforts to save her people.

Discovery of Haman's Plot

Haman, the king's ambitious advisor, devised a plot to eliminate the Jews throughout the empire due to his personal vendetta against Mordecai, who refused to bow to him. The decree, sealed by the king's ring and delivered across the land, set a date for this plan to eliminate all Jews, throwing the community into despair.

Esther's Brave Approach to the King

Knowing the risk of approaching the king unsummoned—a move punishable by death—Esther displayed remarkable bravery. She called for a fast among her people and prepared herself spiritually and mentally before making her move. Dressed in her royal garments, she stood in the inner court of the king's palace, winning his favor and an audience. During a carefully arranged banquet, she revealed her Jewish identity and Haman's awful plan to the king.

The Triumph of the Jews

The revelation shocked King Xerxes and led to Haman's downfall; he was executed on the gallows he had prepared for Mordecai. The king then granted Mordecai high office and allowed him and Esther to write another decree, enabling the Jews to defend themselves effectively against their enemies. This swift reversal of fortune not only saved the Jews but elevated Mordecai and Esther's statuses within the empire.

Courage in the Face of Adversity

Esther's story is a powerful lesson in courage and the ability to face overwhelming danger with grace and wisdom. Her decision to approach the king, fully aware of the potential consequences, highlights the strength it takes to confront evil and protect others, even at great personal risk.

Standing Up for What is Right

Esther's moral strength in standing up for her people against Haman's plot is a timeless reminder of the power of righteousness and justice. Her actions demonstrate the impact one individual can have when they choose to stand against wrongdoing, no matter the power dynamics at play. Knowing that her people fasted and prayed with her gave her even more confidence to stand up for what was right.

The Power of Faith and Prayer

Before taking any action, Esther sought the support of her community in prayer and fasting. This special reliance on spiritual preparation shows the importance of faith and divine guidance when facing critical decisions. It emphasizes the belief that with God's help, we can navigate even the most difficult situations.

Fun Family Activity

Banquet Planning Game: Organize a "banquet" with your family, where kids can decide what foods they would serve if they were planning a feast like Esther. Discuss why Esther chose to reveal her request at a banquet and how meals can be an important time for sharing and decision-making.

Making it Personal

Reflective Questions

1. **What about you?** Imagine you are aware of a plan that could harm many people in your community, and you are one of the few who knows who to call for help that can prevent it. You face significant risks in exposing this, and the pressure can feel overwhelming. How would you handle this situation? Would you take the safer path to avoid personal risk, or would you stand up for what is right and confront the issue head-on to protect others?

2. **Understanding Courage and Risk**: Esther took a big risk by going to the king without being called. Can you

think of a time when you had to be brave to help someone else, even if it meant you might get into trouble?

3. **Importance of Clever Planning**: Esther was very clever in how she revealed her people's danger to the king. Why do you think she invited the king and Haman to two banquets instead of just telling the king her request the first time she saw him?

4. **Standing Up for Others**: Esther used her position to save her people. Why is it important to stand up for others? Can you think of ways you might stand up for someone at school or in your community?

5. **The Role of Identity**: Esther initially hid her Jewish identity but later revealed it to save her people. Why do you think knowing who we are is important? How can being true to ourselves make a difference in how we act?

Drawing inspiration from Esther's bravery, think about the importance of standing up for what is right, even when it's difficult. Consider the value of seeking counsel and support, not just from those around you but also through personal reflection and prayer. Esther's story encourages us to be brave and prepare ourselves thoughtfully for the challenges we decide to tackle. Like Esther, your actions, guided by courage and wisdom, can make a significant difference in the lives of many, echoing the timeless lesson that one person's brave decision can alter the course of history.

Hannah - The Prayerful Mother (1Samuel Ch 1:1 - 2:21)

Heartfelt Desires

Hannah's story, as recounted in the First Book of Samuel, is a powerful story of longing, faith, and divine intervention. Living in a time when not being able to have a baby when you get married was often viewed as a personal failure or divine disfavor, Hannah's journey from deep sorrow to profound joy through the birth of her son Samuel not only reflects individual triumph but also marks a pivotal moment in the history of Israel.

Hannah's Barrenness and Sorrow

Hannah was one of two wives of Elkanah. Unlike Peninnah, the other wife who had children, Hannah was barren. This condition brought her considerable grief, made worse by Peninnah's provoking taunts and societal pressure. Each year, during their pilgrimage to the Shiloh temple, Hannah's pain would surface with particular intensity, highlighting her desire for motherhood and her feeling of incompleteness in a culture that prized the ability to build a big family.

Elkanah's Comforting Love

Despite her barrenness, Elkanah's love for Hannah was evident and profound. He offered her a double portion of the sacrifices at Shiloh, signaling his favored affection towards her. His attempt to console her, asking, "Am I not more to you than ten sons?" speaks volumes about their relationship. However, his consolation could not fully ease her distress, underscoring the deep personal longing for her own child that Hannah experienced.

The Taunts of Peninnah

Peninnah's taunts added to Hannah's misery, serving as a constant reminder of her barrenness. This domestic rivalry aggravated Hannah's emotional pain, deepening her prayers and cries for a child. The familial strife in these interactions provides a background against which Hannah's faith and character are dramatically highlighted.

A Promise to God

Hannah's Prayer at the Temple

Overwhelmed by her grief, Hannah poured out her soul to God at the temple in Shiloh, weeping bitterly and making a solemn vow: if God gave her a son, she would dedicate him to the

Lord's service all the days of his life. Her fervent, silent prayer was so intense that Eli, the priest, initially mistook her for being drunk. Upon understanding her genuine distress and devotion, Eli blessed her, praying that God would grant her petition.

Eli's Blessing and Assurance

Eli's blessing gave Hannah renewed hope. His words, "Go in peace, and the God of Israel grant your petition that you have made to him," affirmed her faith, allowing her to return home with a lighter heart. This change marked a pivotal moment in Hannah's life, as her demeanor shifted from sorrow to serene trust in God's providence.

Birth of Samuel

God answered Hannah's prayers, and she gave birth to Samuel, whose name means "asked of God." True to her vow, she brought Samuel to Shiloh after weaning him, dedicating him to the Lord's service under Eli. This act of fulfilling her vow not only demonstrated her heart to honor God but also set Samuel on the path to becoming one of Israel's greatest prophets.

Power of Fervent Prayer

Hannah's story exemplifies the power of fervent prayer. Her earnest cries to God in prayer and the intensity of her commitment to God highlight how true faith and heartfelt prayer can lead to divine responses, transforming personal despair into joy and societal contribution.

Dedication and Faithfulness to God

Hannah's unwavering commitment to fulfill her vow, even when it meant giving up her beloved son, illustrates her faithfulness. This dedication is a testament to her character and demonstrates the virtues of loyalty and trust in God's greater plan.

The Joy of Answered Prayers

The fulfillment of Hannah's prayer brought not only personal satisfaction but also joy to her family and blessings to Israel through Samuel's leadership. Her story teaches that the answers to our prayers can have far-reaching effects beyond our own lives, impacting our communities and future generations. Her faithfulness was met with the blessing of Eli when he said "May the Lord bless you with other children to take the place of this one she gave to the Lord." The Lord blessed Hannah, and she had three more sons and two daughters.

Fun Family Activity

Making A Prayer Journal: Work as a family to make your own prayer journals. Gather up notebooks, stickers, markers, and other decorative items. As you each create your journals, think about things you might pray for, just like Hannah prayed for a child. Parents may pray to be debt-free or for a new car. Kids might pray for faith-filled friends or for God's help in making better decisions when temptations come. Remember to go back and read over those prayers and give thanks to God for answering them. Write it down when a prayer was answered, as it will encourage your faith when you look back later.

Making it Personal

Reflective Questions

1. **What about you?:** Imagine you're facing a significant challenge or deep-seated desire in your life, something you've longed for but have not yet achieved. Perhaps it's a desire to be on the school sports team, a personal improvement, or a relationship restoration. How do you approach this desire? Do you feel tempted to give up, or do you seek new ways to pursue your goal?

2. **Understanding Patience and Perseverance**: Hannah waited for many years before her prayers were answered. Can you think of something you had to wait a long time for? How did you feel when you waited, and what was it like when your waiting was over?

3. **The Power of Prayer**: Hannah's story shows us how powerful prayer can be. Why do you think prayer is important? Have you ever felt that a prayer helped you or someone else?

4. **Keeping Promises**: Hannah made a promise to God, and she kept it by taking Samuel to the temple when he was still very young. Why is it important to keep promises? Can you think of a promise you have made and how you kept it?

5. **Expressions of Gratitude**: After receiving what she prayed for, Hannah expressed her gratitude through prayer. Why is it important to be thankful? What are

some ways you can show gratitude in your own life?

Reflecting on Hannah's story, consider how you might use prayer or meditation to find strength and clarity. Hannah's transformation from despair to peace through prayer can inspire you to maintain hope and continue working towards your goals, no matter how distant they seem. Her example encourages persistence and faithfulness, reminding us that while the timing and nature of our desires' fulfillment may not be as we initially envision, the journey toward them can be deeply enriching and ultimately rewarding.

Deborah - The Leading Lady (Judges Ch 4-5)

"So we can confidently say, 'The Lord is my helper; I will not fear; what can man do to me?'" Hebrews 13:6 NLT

A Judge and Prophetess

Deborah's story, captured in the Book of Judges, chapters 4 and 5, presents a dynamic portrait of leadership, courage, and divine inspiration. As a prophetess and the only female judge mentioned in the Bible, Deborah stands out as a very important figure in Israelite history, guiding her people through a period of military and spiritual crisis.

Introduction to Deborah's Leadership

In an era when Israel grappled with internal chaos and external threats, Deborah emerged as a pillar of strength and guidance. She held court under the Palm of Deborah, between Ramah and Bethel in the hill country of Ephraim, where the Israelites came to her for judgment. Her role was judicial and spiritual, as she communicated God's will to the people and provided counsel based on divine wisdom from God.

The State of Israel During Her Time

The Book of Judges depicts a cycle of the children of God abandoning their faith and their walk with God, oppression, repentance, and deliverance in Israel, with Deborah's leadership occurring at a time when the Israelites had been subdued by Jabin, king of Canaan. The oppression under Jabin's commander, Sisera, who cruelly enforced Jabin's dominance with a force of 900 iron chariots, had lasted for twenty years, leading to Deborah's call to action.

Deborah's Wisdom and Counsel

Deborah's leadership was characterized by her wisdom and ability to inspire confidence and action among her people. She was respected for her fairness and revered for her connection to God, qualities that made her judgments trusted and followed. Her prophetic abilities were evident in her foresight and strategic command in the face of looming battles.

Call to Barak

Deborah's strategic wisdom was displayed when she summoned Barak, the son of Abinoam from Kedesh in Naphtali, and instructed him to take ten thousand men to Mount Tabor to face Sisera's army. She prophesied a victory that was unusual in its strategy and execution, demonstrating her confidence in God backing the army.

The Battle Against Sisera

The battle plan involved drawing Sisera's chariots to the River Kishon, where the terrain would put them at a disadvantage with their heavy chariots after heavy rains caused the river to flood—another aspect of Deborah's divine insight. Despite Barak's insistence that Deborah accompany him, her presence on the battlefield was symbolic, serving both as a spiritual guide and a tactical leader.

Jael's Decisive Action

The narrative reaches its high point with the unexpected heroism of Jael, the wife of Heber the Kenite, who delivered the final blow to Sisera, thus fulfilling Deborah's prophecy that a woman would claim the honor of victory over Jabin's army. Jael's killing of Sisera by driving a tent peg through his skull while he slept in her tent is one of the most dramatic moments in the biblical account, highlighting the unpredictable ways in which God's deliverance can manifest.

Leadership with Wisdom

Deborah's story underscores the importance of wise and decisive leadership. Her ability to lead in multiple capacities—spiritual, judicial, and military—demonstrates that effective leadership often requires a multifaceted approach, balancing insight with action.

Trusting in God's Plan

Her unwavering faith in God's plan, even in the face of formidable challenges, provides a powerful example for all leaders.

Deborah's trust was not passive; it actively shaped her strategies and reassured those she led.

Empowering Others to Act

Deborah's interactions with Barak reveal her skill in empowering others. By sharing the divine vision and encouraging Barak to lead the troops, she fostered leadership in others, contributing to a legacy of courage and action beyond her own direct involvement.

Fun Family Activity

Create a Leadership Shield: Use materials such as cardboard, markers, paint, and decorations to create a "Leadership Shield." Think about images that symbolize the qualities you believe are important for a leader, inspired by Deborah's example of wisdom, courage, and guidance. Things like doves or olive branches can be used for peace—eagles for courage and wisdom, and maybe a dog for guidance.

Making it Personal

Reflective Questions

1. **What about you?:** Imagine you are a leader in a group project facing significant challenges that seem too hard to overcome. Your team is discouraged, and the goal appears increasingly out of reach. How would you inspire your team to continue working towards the goal? Would you take a step back, or would you seek innovative ways to motivate and lead? Would you stop and

pray and ask God to help you succeed?

2. **Qualities of Leadership**: Deborah was a leader who people trusted to make fair decisions and guide them in difficult times. What do you think makes a good leader? Can you think of when you had to lead others and how you acted? Have you had to follow the leadership of one of your peers? Did their leadership inspire you to give your all to the task?

3. **Importance of Good Advice**: Deborah gave Barak advice that led to a victory. Why is it important to listen to good advice? Have you ever received advice that helped you make a better decision?

4. **Role of Women in Society**: Deborah was a rare example of a female leader in biblical times. What does her story tell us about the roles women can play in society? How does seeing women in strong roles affect the goals and future ambitions of girls and boys today?

5. **The Power of Faith in Leadership**: Deborah's faith in God was central to her leadership. How can your faith be a strength for someone who is leading others? Can you think of a situation where having faith made a difference in what someone was able to achieve?

Reflecting on Deborah's story, like Deborah, you can combine wisdom with decisive action, perhaps by re-evaluating strategies or by offering reassurance and support to your team members. Her example teaches us the importance of faith in your vision and the power of encouraging those around you to rise to their own potential. Through such leadership, you can help transform challenges into victories, much like Deborah did for Israel.

Abigail - The Peacemaker (1 Samuel 25)

"But the wisdom that is from above is first pure; then peaceable, gentle, willing to yield, full of mercy and good fruits, without partiality and without hypocrisy." James 3:17 NKJV

A Difficult Marriage

Abigail's story, as told in the First Book of Samuel, is a striking story of diplomacy, wisdom, and decisive action in the face of impending violence. Living in a time of tribal conflicts and rough justice, Abigail emerges as a figure of remarkable intelligence and grace, averting a crisis through her swift and thoughtful intervention.

Introduction to Abigail and Nabal

Abigail was married to Nabal, a wealthy but stingy and foolish man known for his harshness and selfishness. This story sets the stage by contrasting Abigail's intelligence and good understanding with Nabal's grumpy nature, creating immediate tension in their household. This tension forms the backdrop to a significant encounter that tests Abigail's diplomatic skills and courage.

Nabal's Folly with David's Men

David, who would later become king of Israel, and his men had been providing unofficial protection to Nabal's shepherds and livestock. During the sheep-shearing festival, a time of feasting and generosity, David sent messengers to Nabal seeking provisions as compensation for their protection. Nabal's response was negative and insulting, dismissing David's men rudely and questioning David's legitimacy. This response provoked David's wrath, and he vowed to destroy Nabal and all his household by morning.

Abigail's Discernment

Upon hearing of her husband's reckless actions and David's plans for retaliation, Abigail quickly assessed the situation. Understanding the disastrous consequences that were sure to follow due to her husband's folly, she took quick action without consulting Nabal, knowing that his judgment could not be trusted in this critical situation.

Abigail's Gift to David

Abigail acted swiftly to counteract the threat of violence. She gathered a significant gift of food—bread, wine, sheep, grain, raisins, and figs—and loaded them on donkeys. Then, without informing Nabal, she went to meet David, who was already on his way with armed men.

Her Plea for Peace

Meeting David in a mountain pass, Abigail quickly dismounted and bowed before him, taking full responsibility for Nabal's insult and pleading for forgiveness. Her plea was eloquent, urging David to consider his planned vengeance's moral and serious outcome. She appealed to his better judgment, reminding him of God's plans for his future reign and the stain that needless bloodshed could leave on his conscience.

David's Gratitude and Nabal's Fate

Moved by Abigail's wisdom and argument, David acknowledged her intervention as God-sent and called off the attack, thanking her for preventing him from committing a great evil. When Abigail returned home, she found Nabal holding a banquet and drunk. The next morning, when she told him what had transpired, he had a stroke and died ten days later. Following Nabal's death, David, recognizing Abigail's qualities, sent for her, and she became his wife.

The Value of Discernment

Abigail's ability to assess the situation accurately and anticipate the consequences of her husband's actions shows us the critical value of discernment in crisis management. Her story teaches that understanding the dynamics at play and acting wisely can prevent disaster.

Seeking Peace Over Conflict

Abigail's initiative to seek peace over vengeance illustrates the power of diplomacy and non-violence. Her intervention not only saved lives but also maintained her integrity and the integrity of those around her.

The Rewards of Righteousness

Abigail's righteousness and her proactive nature in seeking peace brought her safety, respect from David, and a new role as the wife of the future king. Her story highlights how righteousness and active peacemaking are rewarded, often leading to unforeseen opportunities and blessings.

Fun Family Activity

Peace Treaty Craft: Create your own "peace treaty." Write down rules for handling disagreements or arguments inspired by how Abigail prevented violence through her wise intervention. You can decorate your treaty and even make gift bracelets as a special offering to remind you of the peace treaty.

Making it Personal

Reflective Questions

1. **What about you?:** Imagine you are part of an organization or community group where a misunderstanding between the two top members threatens to escalate into a serious fight. You see a potential for significant trouble if the situation is not handled carefully. How would you intervene? Would you take the initiative to mediate or would you wait for others to resolve the issue?

2. **Wisdom in Action**: Abigail acted quickly and wisely to prevent a disaster. Can you think of a time when you or someone you know had to act quickly to solve

a problem? What did you learn from that experience about making decisions under pressure?

3. **The Power of Words**: Abigail used her words to calm David's anger and prevent violence. Why do you think her words were so powerful? How can we use our words to resolve conflicts?

4. **Making Peace**: Abigail made peace between her household and David without fighting. Why is it sometimes better to make peace than to win a fight? Can you think of a situation where you could make peace like Abigail?

5. **Courage to Act**: It took courage for Abigail to go against her husband's wishes and meet David with gifts. What does this tell us about doing the right thing, even when it's hard or when others might disagree or get mad at you?

Drawing on Abigail's example, consider the benefits of proactive peacemaking. Think about how you could effectively communicate with each party, offer a balanced perspective, and propose a fair resolution. Like Abigail, demonstrating wisdom and courage in the face of conflict can resolve tensions and enhance your leadership and peacemaking skills. This approach builds a more harmonious environment and can prevent the far-reaching consequences of unresolved disputes.

Rahab - The Faithful Harlot (Joshua 2, 6:23-25)

"And let us not grow weary while doing good, for in due season we will reap if we do not lose heart." Galatians 6:9

A Questionable Reputation

Rahab's story, found in the Book of Joshua, is a compelling tale of redemption and courage set against the backdrop of the Israelite conquest of Canaan. A resident of Jericho, Rahab was known as a harlot, which was not a good reputation. Yet, her actions during a critical moment in biblical history highlight her profound faith and wisdom, marking her as one of the most unexpected heroes of the Bible.

Introduction to Rahab's Life

Rahab lived in the fortified city of Jericho, which was on high alert due to the impending threat posed by the Israelites, who had been sweeping through Canaan. Her home was situated on the city wall, placing her in a strategic position to encounter those who would normally go unnoticed by the city's leadership.

The Israelite Spies in Jericho

As Joshua prepared to take the city, he sent two spies to assess the situation. These spies found their way to Rahab's house, likely because it was a place where strangers could come and go without being suspicious. This meeting would prove pivotal not only for the fate of the spies but also for Rahab and her family.

Rahab's Aid to the Spies

Recognizing the power of Israel's God and the certainty of Jericho's fall, Rahab made a courageous decision to hide the spies from the city's authorities, who came searching for them. She acknowledged their God as "the LORD your God, He is God in heaven above and on earth beneath" (Joshua 2:11), declaring her faith in their appointed mission. In return for her protection, she sought a guarantee of safety for herself and her family.

Rahab's Request for Protection

Rahab's negotiation with the spies resulted in a solemn oath. She was to mark her house with a scarlet cord in the window through which she let the spies escape. This cord would signal to the invading Israelite forces to spare all within her house.

The Scarlet Cord

The scarlet cord symbolized her agreement with the spies and her faith in the God of Israel. It became a beacon of her commitment and trust, visible to all who would observe the victory over the city. When Joshua commanded the army to completely destroy everything as an offering to the Lord, he also commanded them that Rahab and her family in her house were to be spared (Joshua 6:17).

Fall of Jericho and Rahab's Salvation

When Jericho fell, Rahab and her family were spared as promised, demonstrating the faithfulness of God to those who trust in Him. Her house, marked by the scarlet cord, stood as a testament to her faith amidst the ruins of Jericho. Following this, Rahab and her family were assimilated into the Israelite community, and she would go on to become an ancestor of King David and, ultimately, of Jesus Christ, according to the genealogy in the Gospel of Matthew.

God's Love for All, Regardless of Past

Rahab's story is a powerful example of divine grace that extends beyond social standings and past transgressions. Her faith and actions underscore the biblical theme that redemption is available to all who seek God earnestly, regardless of their background.

Faith in the Unseen

Despite her circumstances, Rahab chose to place her faith in a God she had only heard of through the stories of the Israelites. Her faith in the unseen, based on the reports of God's mighty deeds, highlights a profound spiritual insight and courage. She lived in a city filled with people who didn't believe in God, yet she had a special faith that God honored when she trusted Him to protect and keep her safe.

The Impact of Wise Decisions

Rahab's wise decision to shelter the spies and seek their protection altered her destiny and that of her family. Her story illustrates how strategic and thoughtful choices, guided by recognition and respect for God, can lead to preservation and honor.

Fun Family Activity

Spy Adventure Game: Create a spy mission game where you and your family or friends have to navigate through a series of obstacles to reach a designated safe zone, similar to how the spies had to escape Jericho. Use pillows, boxes, blankets, and other household items to create a fun and challenging course.

Making it Personal

Reflective Questions

1. **What about you?:** Imagine you are at a crossroads in your life where you must choose between the familiar, although difficult, paths of your past and an uncertain future that promises a better but unguaranteed outcome. This decision might involve changing schools, moving to a new city, or leaving a negative but familiar situation behind. How would you navigate this choice? Would you have the courage to step into the unknown because you believe it's the right thing to do, or would you cling to the familiar out of fear?

2. **Understanding Courage**: Rahab showed great courage by hiding the spies and helping them escape. Can you think of a time when you had to be brave to

help someone else? What did you do, and how did you feel afterward?

3. **The Importance of Choices**: Rahab made a significant choice to help the spies despite the risk to herself and her family. Why do you think she decided to help them? What does this teach us about making decisions?

4. **Faith in Difficult Times**: Rahab put her trust in the God of Israel after hearing about His mighty deeds. Why do you think Rahab believed in God's power? How can her faith inspire us in times of difficulty?

5. **Redemption and New Beginnings**: Rahab's actions saved her family and changed her life path, leading her to become an ancestor of King David and Jesus. What does this tell us about how making good choices can lead to new beginnings, even in difficult situations?

Reflecting on Rahab's decision to protect the spies despite the personal risk, consider the importance of making choices that align with your deeper values and beliefs. Like Rahab, who chose to align herself with a greater power she recognized as true and just, you can choose to pursue paths that reflect your desires for a better, more fulfilling life. Her story encourages us to act boldly and wisely, trusting that our faith in what is right, though unseen, can lead to profound transformations and blessings.

Mary - The Mother of Jesus (Luke 1:26-55, Luke 2:1-20, Luke 2:34-35)

"Blessed is she who believed, for there will be a fulfillment of those things which were told her from the Lord ." Luke 1:45 NKJV

A Divine Calling

Mary, the mother of Jesus, holds a distinguished place in Christian tradition as an emblem of obedience, faith, and grace. Her life story, punctuated by moments of profound joy and deep sorrow, unfolds within the pages of the Gospels as a testament to her pivotal role in the history of salvation.

The Angel Gabriel's Announcement

Mary's journey began in the small town of Nazareth, where she lived a life of humility and piety. Engaged to Joseph, a carpenter, her ordinary world was transformed when the angel Gabriel appeared to her. Gabriel's greeting, "Hail, full of grace, the Lord is with thee," was both an announcement and a blessing. He revealed to Mary a divine plan unlike any other—she was chosen to bear the Son of God. This revelation was met with astonishment but also with a poised acceptance that reflected her deep faith.

Mary's Humble Acceptance

Despite the potential for societal disgrace and personal misunderstanding, Mary responded with profound humility and obedience: "Behold the handmaid of the Lord; be it unto me according to thy word." This response highlights her unconditional trust in God's plan and her willingness to embrace a role that would change the course of history. Her acceptance was not passive but an active affirmation of her faith and commitment to God's will.

Visit to Elizabeth

Following the angel's visit, Mary traveled to visit her cousin Elizabeth, who was also miraculously pregnant with John the Baptist. Elizabeth's greeting, "Blessed art thou among women, and blessed is the fruit of thy womb," affirmed the angel's message. The encounter between these two women is a moment of mutual joy and prophetic fulfillment as Mary proclaimed the Magnificat, a song of praise for God's mercy and faithfulness.

Journey to Bethlehem

The story progresses with Mary and Joseph's journey to Bethlehem, complying with a census decree from Caesar Augustus. Despite the hardships of travel in her advanced pregnancy, Mary remained steadfast. Her faith and resilience were again tested upon their arrival, as they found no traditional lodging, with Mary ultimately giving birth in a humble stable.

Birth of Jesus

The birth of Jesus in such modest circumstances—laid in a manger surrounded by animals—contrasts sharply with His divine nature and the magnitude of His mission. This setting underscores themes of humility and accessibility, illustrating that the Savior of the world came not with grandeur but with simplicity.

The Shepherds and Magi's Visit

The significance of Jesus' birth was marked by visits from shepherds, who were informed by angels, and later, Magi from the East, guided by a star. These visits fulfill Old Testament prophecies and signify Jesus' universal significance—as a messiah not only for the Jews but for all humanity. Mary's reactions to these events, particularly her quiet contemplation of the shepherds' words, reflect her deep thoughtfulness and role as a reflective witness to the unfolding events.

Obedience to God's Call

Mary's life exemplifies complete obedience to God. Despite the uncertainties and risks involved, her unwavering acceptance of God's plan teaches believers the importance of trust and submission to God's will. It is important to remember we are all given free will to choose; however, submitting to God's perfect will for your life brings blessings beyond our understanding.

Trust in Uncertain Times

Throughout her life, Mary encountered situations that tested her faith and required her to trust God's providence. Her ability to maintain faith under pressure, from Jesus' birth to His crucifixion, shows us her profound spiritual strength found only in God.

The Honor of Serving God's Purpose

Mary was uniquely honored to be the mother of Jesus, participating directly in God's plan for salvation. Her role highlights the dignity and grace of serving God, regardless of the personal cost or challenge involved.

Fun Family Activity

Magnificat Song: Read Luke 1:46-55 NLT, where Mary sings her song of Praise to God. Write your own songs of praise, similar to Mary's Magnificat, reflecting on the things you are thankful for in your life. This activity can help you connect personally with Mary's expression of gratitude and trust in God. Remember, everyone's song is as different and unique as they are. In everything, we are to give thanks and praise to God.

Making it Personal

Reflective Questions

1. **What about you?:** Imagine facing a situation where doing the right thing might lead to misunderstanding, judgment, or significant personal sacrifice. It may be a choice about standing up for what is right at work or in

school, or it may involve an important life decision that others may not understand or support. How would you respond to this challenge? Would you proceed with caution, or like Mary, would you move forward with conviction despite potential repercussions?

2. **Faith in God's Plan**: Mary accepted God's plan for her with faith, even though it was unexpected and came with challenges. Can you think of a time when something unexpected happened to you? How did you react, and what can you learn from Mary's example?

3. **Courage and Humility**: Mary humbly accepted her role in God's plan despite the potential for social stigma and personal danger. What do Mary's courage and humility teach us about handling difficult situations in our own lives?

4. **Role of a Mother**: Mary played a crucial role in Jesus' life, from birth to his crucifixion. How do you think her support influenced Jesus? How does this reflect the importance of a mother's role in a family?

5. **Spiritual Reflection**: Mary pondered many things in her heart after the shepherds visited and after finding Jesus in the temple. Why is it important to reflect on our experiences, especially those that involve our faith? How can we follow Mary's example in our daily lives?

Drawing inspiration from Mary's story, consider the value of steadfastness and integrity in your own life. Like Mary, embracing a path of righteousness, guided by faith and a commitment to doing what is right, can be daunting yet profoundly rewarding. Her life encourages us to face our challenges with grace and courage, trusting that our roles, however small they may seem, are part of a larger, divine mosaic.

Mary and Martha - The Sisters of Devotion (Luke 10:38-42, John 11:1-44)

"But one thing is needed, and Mary has chosen that good part, which will not be taken away from her." Luke 10:42 NKJV

Introduction to Mary and Martha

In the quaint village of Bethany, just a short journey from the bustling streets of Jerusalem, lived two sisters, Mary and Martha, along with their brother Lazarus. These siblings are most remembered for their close family ties and deep friendship with Jesus, which is highlighted through several powerful encounters in the New Testament.

Mary and Martha often hosted Jesus at their home, providing a rare glimpse into personal relationships during His ministry. Martha is typically portrayed as pragmatic and hospitable, always busy with the busyness of serving and managing the household. In contrast, Mary is depicted as thoughtful and emotional, often found at Jesus' feet, listening intently to His words. These differences in demeanor and approach to life set the stage for lessons about the balance between duty and spirituality.

Significant Encounters with Jesus

One of the most telling incidents occurred during one of Jesus' visits to their home. As Martha busied herself with the preparations, Mary chose to sit by Jesus, absorbing His teachings. Frustrated by her sister's lack of help, Martha asked Jesus if He cared that she had been left to do all the work alone. Jesus' response was gentle yet clear, "Martha, Martha, you are anxious and troubled about many things, but one thing is necessary. Mary has chosen the good portion, which will not be taken away from her" (Luke 10:41-42). This interaction highlights the importance of prioritizing spiritual nourishment and the value of being present.

The story deepens with the death of their brother, Lazarus. When Jesus arrives in Bethany after Lazarus has died, both sisters express their grief but also their steadfast faith. Martha affirms her belief in Jesus' power and in the resurrection. At the same time, Mary's emotional approach moves Jesus deeply, leading up to one of His most dramatic miracles—raising Lazarus from the dead. This powerful event demonstrates the sisters' faith and Jesus' deep love for this family.

Balancing Duty and Devotion

The lives of Mary and Martha teach a crucial lesson about the balance needed between active service and personal devotion. Martha's dedication to service is commendable and essential in any community, reflecting a faith expressed through action. However, Mary's choice to focus on Jesus' words reminds us of the need for spiritual growth and the importance of listening to God's voice in our lives.

Faith in Trials

The event of Lazarus' death and resurrection highlights another dimension of their characters—unwavering faith in the face of despair. Both sisters show great faith, although in different ways. Martha approaches Jesus with a statement of faith even before Lazarus is raised, while Mary's tears stir Jesus' spirit. Their reactions teach that faith can be manifested in active proclamation as well as in sincere emotion.

Personal Relationship with Jesus

Both sisters had a personal and deep relationship with Jesus, which allowed them to express their devotion in ways that suited their personalities. This diversity in relationships with Christ exemplifies that there is no single correct way to love and serve God, but rather, each individual's unique relationship with Him is to be cherished and nurtured.

Fun Family Activity

Reflection and Action Journals: Start a dual-section journal with one part dedicated to actions (serving others like Martha) and the other to reflections (listening and learning like Mary).

This activity can help you think about implementing both aspects in your daily life.

Making it Personal

Reflective Questions

1. **What about you?:** Imagine you're a student involved in numerous clubs and activities, finding yourself overwhelmed and struggling to find time for quiet reflection or spiritual growth. It's easy to feel like Martha, constantly on the move, managing tasks and responsibilities. But how can you incorporate moments of peace and reflection into this busy life?

2. **Scheduling Time for Jesus:** Think about your current schedule. Could you dedicate moments to quiet reflection early in the morning or before bed? Could you, like Mary, find opportunities to sit down and absorb wisdom, maybe through reading or meditation?

3. **Balancing Service and Devotion**: Mary and Martha showed two different ways of expressing their care for Jesus. Martha was busy serving, while Mary chose to listen to Jesus speak. Why do you think both actions are important? How can we balance doing and listening in our own lives?

4. **Understanding Priorities**: Jesus said Mary chose the

"better part" by listening to him. What do you think Jesus meant by that? Can there be a time when listening or learning is more important than doing?

5. **Learning from Criticism**: When Jesus gently corrected Martha, she had to consider about her priorities. How can we respond positively to gentle correction or advice, especially when it comes to balancing our responsibilities?

6. **Role of Women**: Mary and Martha interacted with Jesus in significant and meaningful ways. What do their stories teach us about the roles and contributions of women in family and spiritual settings?

Taking inspiration from both sisters, try to balance your active participation in life with moments of rest and reflection in the Word of God. Martha learned the value of pausing to appreciate the presence of Jesus, while Mary showed the importance of engagement when she joined the others in mourning Lazarus. By finding a balance, you enhance your spiritual well-being and maintain a more sustainable pace in your daily life. This approach to living—embracing both action and reflection—can help you navigate life's challenges with grace and resilience, much like Mary and Martha in their unique walks with Jesus.

Priscilla - The Devoted Disciple (Acts 18:1-26, Romans 16:3-4, 1 Corinthians 16:19)

"Greet Priscilla and Aquila, my fellow workers in Christ Jesus, who risked their own necks for my life, to whom not only I give thanks, but also all the churches of the Gentiles." Romans 16:3-4 NKJV

Introduction to Priscilla and Aquila

Priscilla, often mentioned alongside her husband Aquila, emerges in the New Testament as an important figure in the early Christian church. Her story, primarily recounted in the Acts of the Apostles and the Epistles of Paul, highlights the role of women as early church leaders and the impact of partnering ministry in spreading the Christian faith.

Priscilla and Aquila first appear in the Book of Acts as Jewish tentmakers who, like many others, were expelled from Rome during the reign of Emperor Claudius. They settled in Corinth, where they met Paul, who shared their trade. This initial connection through tentmaking quickly deepened into a significant spiritual partnership as Priscilla and Aquila embraced Paul's mission and became his close partners in ministry.

Meeting Paul and the Bond Formed

The bond between Paul, Priscilla, and Aquila was founded on mutual respect and shared faith. They worked together in Corinth, not only practicing their trade but also engaging deeply in the work of evangelism. Paul's stay with them for eighteen months signifies the depth of their relationship and their commitment to the early church's growth.

Ministry in Corinth

In Corinth, Priscilla and Aquila were instrumental in nurturing the newly forming Christian community. Their home became a meeting place for believers, illustrating the practice of house churches in early Christianity. This setting allowed for intimate teaching and fellowship, crucial for building the community's faith and unity.

Teaching Apollos

One of the most notable episodes involving Priscilla occurs with Apollos, an eloquent speaker and educated man from Alexandria, well-versed in the Scriptures. Apollos was fervent in spirit and spoke boldly in the synagogue, but he only knew the baptism of John. Recognizing his potential and his incomplete understanding, Priscilla and Aquila explained "the way of God more accurately." This act of mentoring enriched Apollos's ministry and underscored Priscilla's role as a teacher in her own right.

Church in their Home

The couple's home continued to serve as a hub for Christian activity not only in Corinth but later in Ephesus and possibly even back in Rome. Their hospitality and leadership in these house churches facilitated the spread of the gospel and strengthened the early Christian communities.

Contribution to Paul's Letters

While Priscilla is not directly credited with writing any of the Pauline letters, her influence is recognized. Paul often sends greetings to Priscilla and Aquila in his epistles, highlighting their importance in his ministry and the early Christian community. Their mention in multiple letters suggests that their ministry was widely recognized and deeply valued across the early church networks.

Importance of Discipleship

Priscilla's life exemplifies the importance of discipleship in Christianity. Her efforts in educating others, especially Apollos, highlight how knowledge and understanding of the faith are crucial for its growth and deepening personal faith.

Working Together in Faith

The partnership between Priscilla and Aquila shows the power of unity in ministry. Their mutual support and shared commitment to the gospel demonstrate how working together can increase the impact of individual efforts. They would be considered a power couple today as their faith and commitment influenced those they encountered.

Dedication to God's Work

Priscilla's story is a testament to her dedication to spreading the gospel. Her life reflects a deep commitment to God's work, showcasing her as a model of early Christian discipleship and leadership.

Fun Family Activity

Tent-Making Craft: Since Priscilla and Aquila were tent-makers, create a mini tent using popsicle sticks, fabric or paper, string, glue, and maybe some Play-Doh. This craft can help you understand the daily life and trade of Priscilla and Aquila and how it played a part in their role in the early Christian community. Think about ancient travel and living conditions, particularly how practical skills like tent-making could serve both economic and evangelical purposes.

Making it Personal

Reflective Questions

1. **What about you?**: Imagine you are part of a community project or organization facing significant challenges. You have the skills and knowledge to help but are hesitant because it requires a considerable commitment of time and resources. How would you decide whether to step forward? Would you consider the potential impact of your involvement, or would the cost to your personal life hold you back?

2. **Importance of Teaching and Learning**: Priscilla and Aquila took Apollos and explained the way of God more accurately. Why do you think it is important to teach others? Can you think of a time when you learned something important from someone else?

3. **Working Together**: How did Priscilla and Aquila demonstrate the importance of working together as a married couple and with others in their community? What can we learn from their collaboration about how to work well with others?

4. **Hospitality in Ministry**: Priscilla and Aquila often opened their home for church meetings. Why do you think hospitality is important in building a community? How can you be hospitable to others around you?

5. **Discipleship and Mentorship**: Priscilla and Aquila were mentors to Apollos, helping him grow in his understanding and ability to teach others. Why is mentorship important in our lives? Who are the mentors in your life, and what have they taught you?

Considering Priscilla's example, consider how your skills and knowledge could serve others and further a cause you care about. Despite the personal risks and costs, Priscilla and Aquila's commitment to teaching and building community resulted in a lasting legacy within the Christian faith. Like them, you can make a significant difference through dedication and active participation in your community or field, contributing to positive change and exemplifying leadership and commitment.

Embracing the Legacy of Greatness

"She is clothed with strength and dignity, and she laughs without fear of the future. When she speaks, her words are wise, and she gives instructions with kindness. She carefully watches everything in her household and suffers nothing from laziness. Her children stand and bless her. Her husband praises her: "There are many virtuous and capable women in the world, but you surpass them all!" Charm is deceptive, and beauty does not last; but a woman who fears the LORD will be greatly praised. Reward her for all she has done. Let her deeds publicly declare her praise." Proverbs 31: 25-31

Recap of the Adventures Explored

As we close the pages of "Adventures in Scriptures for Kids: Exploring the Great Women of the Bible," we reflect on the incredible journeys of the women we've met along the way. Each story, filled with challenges and triumphs, has taught us about the historical and spiritual landscapes of the times and offered timeless lessons applicable to our lives today.

From the courageous actions of Esther, who saved her people, to the steadfast faith of Hannah, who prayed with all her heart for a child, each woman's story has been a unique adventure. We've traveled from the gardens of Eden with Eve to the tents of the wilderness with Sarah and from the courts of Persia with Esther to the humble home of Mary in Nazareth. Each one brought us face-to-face with heroism, wisdom, perseverance, and an unwavering trust in God.

Reflection on the Lessons Learned

- **Eve** taught us about consequences and the importance of making wise choices.

- **Sarah** demonstrated the virtues of patience and faith even when promises seemed impossible.

- **Ruth** exemplified loyalty and kindness and how these qualities can lead to unexpected blessings.

- **Esther** illustrated the power of courage and advocacy, reminding us that we can be a force for good in the face of great danger.

- **Hannah** revealed the power of prayer and commitment to God's will, teaching us that faith can bring miraculous joy.

- **Deborah** highlighted the importance of leadership and the strength to guide others with wisdom, seeking God first.

- **Abigail** demonstrated that wisdom and courage in the face of conflict can resolve tensions and enhance your leadership and peacemaking skills.

- **Rahab** showed us that our past does not define our future and that bravery and faith can save lives.

- **Mary** underscored obedience and trust in God's plan, showing us the grace of accepting our roles in God's larger story.

- **Mary and Martha** showed the need to balance active service and personal devotion.

- **Priscilla** demonstrated the importance of discipleship and partnership in spreading and nurturing faith.

Encouragement to Live Out the Values and Virtues Observed

Now, it's your turn to take these stories to heart. Whether you're faced with a tough decision, like Eve, or an opportunity to help others, like Priscilla, remember that the virtues these women embodied are timeless. They show us that bravery, wisdom, loyalty, and faith are as important today as they were thousands of years ago.

We encourage you to think about how you can apply these lessons in your own life:

- **Be Courageous:** Stand up for what is right, even when it's difficult.

- **Be Wise:** Seek knowledge and understanding before acting.

- **Be Loyal:** Support those you care about, in both good times and bad.

- **Be Faithful:** Trust in your journey and believe that you are part of a bigger plan.

As you grow and face your own challenges, let the stories of these incredible women inspire you to live a life filled with faith, hope, and love. Remember, no matter where you are, you can make a difference. You, too, can be a leader, a peacemaker, a protector, or a teacher. Just like the great women of the Bible, you have the potential to create a legacy of faith and courage that will inspire those around you.

Thank you for joining us on these adventures. Carry these stories in your heart, and let them guide you as you make your mark in the world, continuing the legacy of greatness.

Adventures in Scripture for Kids: Exploring The Life of Jesus

Lorie Eubank

Getting to Know Jesus

Welcome, young adventurers, to a journey through time, story, and spirit in "Adventures in Scripture for Kids: Exploring The Life of Jesus." This book is your passport to understanding one of history's most remarkable figures—Jesus of Nazareth. But who is Jesus, and why does his story continue to inspire millions around the globe? Let's set out on this exploration together to understand the life and teachings of a man whose legacy lights the path of kindness, wisdom, and faith.

Why Jesus Matters

Imagine a person whose words are so powerful that they've been shared all around the globe for over two thousand years! That's Jesus. But why do His life and words matter so much, especially to kids like you? Here are a couple of reasons:

- **Universal Teachings**: Jesus spoke about love, kindness, forgiveness, and how to be a true friend. These ideas are like golden rules that make the world a better place, no matter where you are or what language you speak.

- **Walking in Our Shoes**: Jesus is special because He was both God and man. He lived like us, felt happy and sad like us, and even faced challenges like us. But He showed us the best way to live without ever doing wrong. It's like having the ultimate role model who truly understands what it's like to be human.

- **Being Christ-like**: To be a Christian means to follow Jesus's example, to be 'Christ-like'. It's about trying to spread kindness, stand up for what's right, and help others, just like Jesus did.

How to Use This Book

This book is like your personal map to treasure. The treasure? Wisdom, courage, and a heart full of love. Here's how to make your journey amazing:

- **Ask Questions**: Ever wonder why the sky is blue or why dogs bark? Questions are the beginning of great discoveries. Don't be shy to ask anything about what you read here. Questions make your adventure even more exciting!

- **Think and Reflect**: At the end of each chapter, there will be questions to help stimulate your mind and establish in your heart the lessons we can learn from Jesus. Take a moment to think about it. How would you feel if you were there? What would you have done? Reflection helps you connect with the great stories you'll read.

- **Talk About It**: Share what you learn with your parents, caregivers, or friends. Talking about it makes the adventure more fun, and you'll learn even more from the conversations that follow.

What to Expect

Your adventure through this book will be filled with stories, teachings, and fun activities. Here's a sneak peek:

- **The Life of Jesus**: From His birth in a humble manger to His incredible miracles and His teachings about love and kindness. You'll walk through the key moments of His life.

- **Core Teachings**: Learn about the parables Jesus told to teach people about important life lessons. These stories are packed with meaning and will get you thinking.

So, grab your adventurer's hat (imaginary ones are great too!) and let's set off on this remarkable journey through the life of Jesus. It's going to be an adventure filled with learning, laughter, and lots of love. Welcome aboard!

The Birth of Jesus

"For with God nothing will be impossible. Then Mary said, "Behold the maidservant of the Lord! Let it be to me according to your word." And the angel departed from her." Luke 1:37-38 NKJV

The Angel Visits Mary

Mary, a young woman living in Nazareth, led a quiet and humble life. Engaged to Joseph, a carpenter, she could not have anticipated the encounter with an angel that would change her life and the world forever. One day, the Angel Gabriel appeared to Mary, greeting her with words of great favor. "Greetings, you who are highly favored! The Lord is with you," Gabriel announced. Confused and troubled, Mary listened as Gabriel explained that she would conceive and give birth to a son, whom she was to name Jesus. He would be great and called the Son of the Most High.

Mary's response was one of humble acceptance. "Behold the maidservant of the Lord!" she answered. "Let it be to me according to your word." This moment of absolute faith and obedience set the stage for the miraculous events that were to follow.

Joseph's Dream

Joseph, upon learning of Mary's pregnancy, was initially filled with doubt and concern. As a righteous man, he did not want to expose Mary to public disgrace, and he planned to divorce her quietly. However, an angel of the Lord appeared to him in a dream, reassuring him that the child conceived in Mary was from the Holy Spirit. The angel instructed Joseph to take Mary as his wife and to name the child Jesus, for he would save his people from their sins.

Awakening from the dream, Joseph displayed remarkable faith and determination. He took Mary as his wife, embracing the plan God placed before him and protecting her from potential shame.

The Journey to Bethlehem

During this time, a decree from Caesar Augustus required everyone to return to their ancestral towns for a census. For Mary and Joseph, this meant a difficult journey from Nazareth to Bethlehem. The journey, approximately 90 miles, was difficult, especially for Mary, who was in the late stages of her pregnancy. Despite the hardships, they pressed on, driven by their faith and the necessity of fulfilling the decree.

Upon arriving in Bethlehem, they found the town bustling with people who had also come for the census. With no room available at the inn, Mary and Joseph took refuge in a humble stable. It was there, in the simplicity and quiet of that setting, that Jesus, the Savior of the world, was born.

Angelic Announcements

On the night of Jesus' birth, shepherds were watching over their flocks in the fields nearby. Suddenly, an angel of the Lord appeared to them, and the glory of the Lord shone around them. The shepherds were terrified, but the angel reassured them, saying, "Do not be afraid. I bring you good news that will cause great joy for all the people. Today in the town of David, a Savior has been born to you; he is the Messiah, the Lord."

The angel provided a sign: the baby would be found wrapped in cloths and lying in a manger. As the angelic host praised God, the shepherds hurried to Bethlehem to see the miraculous event for themselves. They found Mary, Joseph, and the baby Jesus, just as the angel had described. Overwhelmed with joy, the shepherds spread the news of what they had witnessed, glorifying and praising God.

Gifts of the Magi

Far to the east, wise men, known as Magi, observed a new star rising in the sky. Interpreting it as the sign of the birth of a great king, they embarked on a long journey to find and honor him. Guided by the star, they eventually arrived in Bethlehem and found the child with his mother, Mary. The Magi bowed down and worshipped him, presenting gifts of great significance: gold, representing Jesus' kingship; frankincense, symbolizing his priestly role; and myrrh, foreshadowing his suffering and death.

Protecting the Baby Jesus

King Herod, hearing of the birth of a new king from the Magi, felt threatened and sought to kill the infant Jesus. Warned in a dream of Herod's intentions, Joseph took immediate action to protect his family. He fled to Egypt with Mary and Jesus, where they remained until Herod's death. This journey to Egypt fulfilled the prophecy: "Out of Egypt, I called my son."

After Herod's death, an angel appeared to Joseph again, instructing him to return to the land of Israel. However, learning that Herod's son was reigning in Judea, Joseph was warned by God in a dream to settle in the town of Nazareth, thus fulfilling the prophecy that Jesus would be called a Nazarene.

Humility and Simplicity

The birth of Jesus in a stable, surrounded by animals, and visited by lowly shepherds is the perfect picture of humility and simplicity. Despite being the Son of God, Jesus entered the world in the most unassuming circumstances, teaching us that true greatness lies in humility.

Importance of Faith

The unwavering faith of Mary and Joseph in the face of obedience to God and societal challenges highlights the importance of trusting in God's plan. Their faithfulness serves as an enduring example for all believers.

God's Plan and Providence

The events surrounding Jesus' birth, from the fulfillment of prophecies to the protection from Herod's wrath, demonstrate God's providence and meticulous plan. Every detail of Jesus' birth was orchestrated according to God's will, reinforcing the message that God's plans are perfect and purposeful.

Making it Personal -Reflective Questions

1. How can I show humility in my own life?

2. In what ways can I strengthen my faith and trust in God's plan?

3. How do I respond to unexpected challenges and God's guidance?

4. What gifts can I offer to Jesus in my daily life?

The story of the birth of Jesus is rich with God's intervention, humble beginnings, and lessons from obedience. From the angelic announcements to the journey of the Magi, each event underscores the miraculous nature of Jesus' arrival and the fulfillment of God's promises. Reflecting on these events encourages us to embrace humility, deepen our faith, and trust in God's providence. The Nativity story continues to inspire and remind us of the enduring impact of Jesus' birth on humanity.

Young Jesus

"Then He went down with them and came to Nazareth, and was subject to them, But His mother kept all these things in her heart. And Jesus increased in wisdom and stature and in favor with God and men." Luke 2:51-52

Daily Life and Culture

Nazareth, a small town in the region of Galilee, was the humble setting for Jesus' childhood. Life in Nazareth was simple and centered around family, community, and religious practices. The people of Nazareth worked in fields and vineyards, and the town was marked by its modest homes and close-knit community.

Jewish customs and traditions played a central role in daily life. The Sabbath was observed with rest and worship, and festivals such as Passover, Sukkot, and Hanukkah were celebrated with great reverence. Synagogue attendance for prayer and learning was a regular part of life, contributing to a strong sense of spiritual and communal identity.

Jesus and His Family

Jesus grew up in a devout Jewish family. His mother, Mary, and his earthly father, Joseph, were dedicated to raising him according to Jewish laws and traditions. Jesus had several siblings, and family life was characterized by mutual support and shared responsibilities. Mary and Joseph provided a nurturing environment where Jesus learned about faith, work, and community.

As the oldest son, Jesus would have taken on responsibilities to help support his family. This included participating in household chores and learning the trade of carpentry from Joseph. Family life also would include the observance of religious practices and celebrations, instilling in Jesus and his siblings a deep connection to his faith and heritage.

The Carpenter's Son

Known as the carpenter's son, Jesus learned the skills of carpentry from Joseph. Carpentry in that era was not limited to woodwork; it often included working with stone and building essential structures for the community. This trade required patience, precision, and hard work, qualities that Jesus exhibited throughout his life.

Through his work as a carpenter, Jesus developed a strong work ethic and a sense of craftsmanship. This background in manual labor also connected him to the everyday lives of the people he later ministered to, allowing him to relate to their struggles and needs.

Lost and Found

When Jesus was twelve years old, Mary and Joseph took him to Jerusalem for the Passover festival, a special religious event that drew Jews from all over the region. After the festival, as they were returning home, Mary and Joseph realized that Jesus was not with them. They searched anxiously among their relatives and friends but could not find him.

Returning to Jerusalem, they found Jesus in the temple courts after three days. This incident, often referred to as "The Boy Jesus Amazes the Scholars," highlights Jesus' deep connection to his heavenly Father and his early sense of purpose.

Astounding the Scholars

When Mary and Joseph found Jesus in the temple, he was sitting among the teachers, listening to them and asking questions. The scholars and teachers were amazed at his understanding and his answers. Despite his young age, Jesus displayed remarkable wisdom and insight, which left a lasting impression on those who heard him.

This event hinted at Jesus' future role as a teacher and rabbi. It demonstrated his connection to godly wisdom and his commitment to learning, engaging, and sharing the religious teachings passed down through the generations.

Honoring One's Parents

When Mary and Joseph expressed their concern and confusion about his absence, Jesus responded, "Why did you seek me? Did you not know that I must be about My Father's business?" Though they did not fully understand his words, Jesus returned to Nazareth with them and was obedient to them.

This highlights the balance Jesus maintained between his God-given mission and his earthly responsibilities. It shows his respect and honor for his parents while also acknowledging his unique relationship with God the Father.

Spirit, Mind, and Body

As Jesus grew, he developed in all aspects of his being: physically, mentally, and spiritually. He experienced the normal growth and challenges of childhood and adolescence, yet he also grew in wisdom and favor with God and man.

Jesus' overall development prepared him for his future ministry. His physical strength, mental sharpness, and spiritual depth were all integral to his mission on earth.

Learning from Elders

In Nazareth, Jesus had the opportunity to learn from the elders and religious leaders of his community. He absorbed the teachings of the Torah and participated in synagogue services, where he engaged with the scriptures and learned about his faith.

This period of learning and growth was crucial in shaping Jesus' understanding of his mission. The wisdom and knowledge he gained from his elders contributed to his ability to teach and guide others later in life. Even though He had all knowledge as the Son of God, he listened to the elders teach and grew in perspective as both God and man.

Preparing for the Journey Ahead

During his formative years, Jesus was being prepared for the journey ahead. Though he lived a relatively quiet and ordinary life, these years were filled with preparation for his public ministry. He was developing the character, skills, and wisdom necessary to fulfill his divine purpose.

Jesus' time in Nazareth was a period of about 30 years of preparation and growth, laying the foundation for the transformative work he would later undertake once He began His Ministry.

Making it Personal – Reflective Questions

1. How can I incorporate the values of humility and hard work into my daily activities, just as Jesus did during his childhood in Nazareth?

2. In what ways can I show respect and honor to my family and elders, following Jesus' example of obedience to Mary and Joseph?

3. How can I seek wisdom and grow in my faith through prayer and learning, like Jesus did when he engaged with the teachers in the temple?

4. What steps can I take to prepare myself for the future and the plans God has for me, drawing inspiration from Jesus' early years of preparation for his ministry?

The early years of Jesus' life in Nazareth were marked by simplicity, faith, and preparation. From his daily life and work as a carpenter to his profound experience at the temple, these years were foundational in shaping his character and mission. Jesus' growth in wisdom, stature, and favor with God and man highlights the importance of overall development and preparation. Reflecting on Jesus' childhood inspires us to embrace humility, seek wisdom, honor our families, and prepare for the purposes God has for us.

The Beginning of His Ministry

"And John tried to prevent Him, saying, "I need to be baptized by You, and You are coming to me?" But Jesus answered and said to him, "Permit it to be so now, for thus it is fitting for us to fulfill all righteousness." Then he allowed it." Matthew 3:14-15 NKJV

Meeting John the Baptist

As Jesus approached the beginning of his public ministry, he sought out John the Baptist, his relative and the prophetic voice calling for repentance in the wilderness. John, known for his disciplined lifestyle and powerful preaching, was baptizing people in the Jordan River, urging them to prepare for the coming of the Messiah. When Jesus came to John to be baptized, John initially resisted, feeling unworthy to baptize the one he knew was the Lamb of God. However, Jesus insisted, saying, *"Permit it to be so now, for thus it is fitting for us to fulfill all righteousness."*

The Significance of Baptism

Jesus' baptism marked the official start of his ministry and symbolized his identification with humanity's sin and need for repentance. Though sinless himself, Jesus underwent baptism to set an example and to demonstrate his connection with those he came to save. This act also highlighted the importance of baptism as a public declaration of faith and commitment to God's will.

The Holy Spirit Descends

As Jesus emerged from the water, a remarkable event occurred. The heavens opened, and the Holy Spirit descended upon him in the form of a dove. A voice from heaven declared, "This is My beloved Son, in whom I am well pleased." This divine affirmation confirmed Jesus' identity as the Son of God and anointed him with the Holy Spirit's power, equipping him for the mission ahead.

40 Days and Nights

Immediately following his baptism, Jesus was led by the Spirit into the wilderness to be tempted by the devil. For forty days and nights, Jesus fasted, enduring physical hunger and spiritual testing. This period of solitude and deprivation was a time of preparation and strengthening, as Jesus faced the challenges that would test his obedience and resolve.

Overcoming Temptation

During this time, the devil tempted Jesus with three powerful enticements: turning stones into bread to satisfy his hunger, jumping from the pinnacle of the temple to test God's protection, and gaining all the kingdoms of the world in exchange for worshiping the devil. In each instance, Jesus resisted, refusing to misuse his holy power or to deviate from his mission. His responses to the temptations demonstrated his unwavering commitment to God's will and his rejection of self-serving shortcuts.

The Power of Scripture

In confronting each temptation, Jesus wielded the power of Scripture. He countered the devil's offers with verses from the Hebrew Scriptures, affirming his reliance on God's word and authority. "It is written," Jesus declared, emphasizing that true strength and victory come from adherence to God's truth. This reliance on Scripture provided a model for believers to follow when facing their own spiritual battles. Just like Jesus, you can find a scripture to stand on when you are struggling in an area of temptation or weakness.

First Disciples -Fishers of Men

After emerging victorious from the wilderness, Jesus began to call his first disciples. Walking along the Sea of Galilee, he encountered Simon Peter and his brother Andrew, who were fishermen. Jesus said to them, "Follow me, and I will make you fishers of men." Immediately, they left their nets and followed him. Matthew 4:19-20 This invitation to become "fishers of men" signified a new purpose and mission, as they would now be gathering people into God's kingdom.

Leaving Everything Behind

The call to discipleship required a radical commitment. James and John, the sons of Zebedee, also left their boat and their father to follow Jesus. These early disciples demonstrated a willingness to leave behind their livelihoods, families, and comforts to pursue a higher calling. Their decision to follow Jesus marked a significant shift in their lives and set the stage for the transformative work they would participate in.

Building a Team for God

Jesus' selection of his first disciples was the beginning of building a team for God's mission. These ordinary men, from various backgrounds and professions, were chosen to learn from Jesus, share in his ministry, and eventually carry on his work after his ascension. Their journey with Jesus would involve training, witnessing miracles, and experiencing profound teachings that would equip them to spread the gospel to the ends of the earth.

Making it Personal – Reflective Questions

1. How can I demonstrate my commitment to God's will in my daily life?

2. In what ways can I rely on Scripture to overcome challenges and temptations? Hint: 1 Corinthians 10:13: "No temptation has overtaken you except such as is common to man; but God is faithful, who will not allow you to be tempted beyond what you are able, but with the temptation will also make a way of escape, that you may be able to bear it.

3. What am I willing to leave behind to follow Jesus more closely? When you are younger, you won't be leaving your family behind, but maybe there are oth-

er things that consume your time, like video games or TV/Movies, that you can choose to spend time following Jesus through the Bible.

4. How can I contribute to building and supporting a community of faith? Is there a Sunday school class you can attend? Can you start a Bible study at home with family and friends?

The beginning of Jesus' ministry was marked by significant events that set the foundation for his work and message. His baptism by John, the victorious overcoming of temptation in the wilderness, and the calling of his first disciples all highlighted his purpose-filled mission and unwavering commitment to God's will. These early moments in Jesus' ministry serve as powerful examples for believers, encouraging them to embrace their faith, rely on Scripture, and commit to following Jesus with dedication and purpose. Reflecting on these events invites us to deepen our relationship with God and to actively participate in his redemptive work in the world.

Teach Us To Pray

At that time Jesus prayed this prayer: "O Father, Lord of heaven and earth, thank you for hiding these things from those who think themselves wise and clever, and for revealing them to the childlike. Yes, Father, it pleased you to do it this way!" Matthew 11:25-26 NLT

The Importance of Prayer – Prayer as Communication with God

Prayer is the fundamental way believers communicate with God. It is a direct line to express gratitude, seek guidance, ask for help, and build a deeper relationship with the Creator. Through prayer, individuals can share their innermost thoughts, fears, and hopes, knowing that God listens and responds according to His will. It is an intimate act that connects the human spirit with God, developing spiritual growth and comfort.

Historical and Cultural Context of Prayer in Jesus' Time

In Jesus' time, prayer was a central part of Jewish religious life. It was customary to pray at specific times of the day, and synagogues served as places for communal prayer and worship. Prayers were recited during meals, in the morning and evening, and on special occasions and festivals. This cultural context shaped Jesus' own practices and teachings on prayer. Growing up in a culture where prayer was a significant part of your day, it is only fitting that it becomes a part of who you are.

Personal and Communal Aspects of Prayer

Prayer has both personal and communal dimensions. Individually, it allows believers to seek personal guidance and strength. Communally, it unites believers, building a sense of unity and shared faith. In Jesus' ministry, he emphasized the importance of both private prayer, as seen in his retreat to solitary places to pray, and communal prayer, as demonstrated in his teaching of the Lord's Prayer to his disciples. Both aspects of prayer are vital for building up our faith and strengthening our connection to God the Father.

The Lord's Prayer: A Model for All (Matthew 6:9-13 NKJV)

One of Jesus' most significant teachings on prayer is the Lord's Prayer, which serves as a comprehensive guide for all believers.

Our Father in heaven, hallowed be your name – It begins with acknowledging God's holiness and sovereignty

Your kingdom come, Your will be done on earth as it is in heaven. – expresses a desire for God's will to be done over our own will

Give us today our daily bread. – and includes petitions for daily needs

Forgive us our debts, as we forgive our debtors – forgiveness for ourselves and others who sinned against us.

And lead us not into temptation, but deliver us from the evil one – a request for guidance to avoid temptation and protection from evil

For Yours is the kingdom and the power and the glory forever. Amen – This is an acknowledgment of His kingdom and power and His glory in your life.

This prayer encapsulates the essence of a faithful and humble heart in communion with God.

The Parable of the Persistent Widow

In the Parable of the Persistent Widow (Luke 18:1-8), Jesus teaches about the importance of persistence in prayer. The story features a widow who repeatedly seeks justice from an unjust judge, who eventually grants her request because of her persistence. Jesus uses this parable to encourage believers to pray continually and not lose heart, trusting that God, unlike the unjust judge, is righteous and compassionate and will respond to their prayers.

Perseverance and patience are essential elements of effective prayer. Jesus' parable of the persistent widow teaches that persistent prayer demonstrates unwavering faith and dependence on God. Believers are encouraged to continue praying, even when answers are not immediate, trusting in God's timing and wisdom.

The Parable of the Pharisee and the Tax Collector

In the Parable of the Pharisee and the Tax Collector (Luke 18:9-14), Jesus contrasts two attitudes in prayer. The Pharisee prays with pride, boasting of his righteousness, while the tax collector prays with humility, acknowledging his sinfulness and asking for mercy. Jesus teaches that it is the humble and contrite heart that God honors, emphasizing the importance of humility and sincerity in prayer.

Humility and sincerity are crucial in prayer. Approaching God with a humble heart, acknowledging one's own limitations and need for God's grace, opens the way for genuine communion with Him. Sincere prayer is honest and transparent, free from acting or hypocrisy, as exemplified by the tax collector in Jesus' parable. We must acknowledge the sin or wrongdoing in our life and recognize our need for God's help in making the change necessary to leave the sin behind.

Elements of Effective Prayer -Faith and Trust in God

Effective prayer requires faith and trust in God. Believers must have confidence that God hears their prayers and that He will respond according to His perfect will. This trust is rooted in the understanding of God's character as loving, just, and faithful. Jesus often highlighted the necessity of faith in prayer, assuring his followers that their faith could move mountains.

In Mark 1:40-41, the leper said to Jesus, "If you are willing, You can make me clean." Jesus responded with, "I am willing, be cleansed." The Bible tells us that Jesus is the same yesterday, today, and forever. Hebrews 13:8. You can have faith knowing that if Jesus did it before for someone else, he will do it again for you.

Developing a Personal Prayer Routine

Developing a consistent personal prayer routine helps deepen one's relationship with God. Setting aside regular times each day for prayer, whether in the morning, evening, or throughout the day, creates a habit of seeking God's presence and guidance. This routine can include reading scripture, meditating on God's word, presenting personal requests, and giving thanks for prayers answered.

Praying in Different Life Situations

Prayer is adaptable to all life situations, whether in moments of joy, sorrow, uncertainty, or decision-making. Jesus demonstrated this by praying in various circumstances, from moments of solitude to times of distress, such as in the Garden of Gethsemane. As believers, we are encouraged to bring every aspect of our lives before God, trusting in His care and provision. In Luke 18:27 NKJV, Jesus said, "The things which are impossible with men are possible with God."

To paraphrase what Jesus said in Matthew 6:25-34, Jesus tells us not to worry, if God cares about the birds, meeting all of their needs, how much more valuable to God are you? If God can clothe the grass with the beautiful lilies, how much better will He clothe you? He went on to close this teaching with this in verses 33-34, "But seek first the kingdom of God and His righteousness, and all these things shall be added to you. Therefore do not worry about tomorrow, for tomorrow will worry about its own things. Sufficient for the day is its own trouble."

Take everything to God in prayer for He cares about all that concerns you.

The Power of Prayer in Community

Community prayer unites believers and strengthens their faith. Praying together in small groups, worship services, or prayer meetings builds a sense of unity and collective dependence on God. Jesus promised that where two or three gather in His name, He is present, highlighting the power and importance of communal prayer. We are even reminded in Hebrews 10:25 not to forsake the assembling together. In verse 24, it says that as we consider one another, we stir up love and good works. As we follow this command we are honoring and glorifying God. And this truly pleases our heavenly Father.

Making it Personal – Reflective Questions

1. How can I incorporate prayer into my daily routine more effectively?

2. In what areas of my life do I need to trust God more fully through prayer?

3. How can I approach God with greater humility and sincerity in my prayers?

4. How can I participate in and contribute to the prayer life of my community?

Jesus' teachings on prayer provide a practical guide for believers. By understanding the importance of prayer, embracing the elements of effective prayer, and applying Jesus' teachings in daily life, believers can deepen their relationship with God and experience the transformative power of prayer. Reflecting on these principles encourages us to develop a personal and communal prayer life that aligns with God's will and brings about spiritual growth and blessing.

The Miracles of Jesus

"And they went out and preached everywhere, the Lord working with them and confirming the word through the accompanying signs. Amen" Mark 16:20 NKJV

One of the most frequently recorded miracles of Jesus is his healing of the sick. Throughout the Gospels, Jesus is shown to heal a wide variety of ailments and diseases, demonstrating his compassion and divine power. Examples include healing the woman with the issue of blood, curing lepers, and restoring the paralyzed. Each healing miracle not only alleviated physical suffering but also brought spiritual renewal and social restoration to those who were sometimes considered outcasts due to their illnesses.

Heals the Blind (John 9:1-12)

Among Jesus's miracles is the restoration of sight to the blind. In one notable instance, Jesus healed a man who had been blind from birth by making mud with his saliva, applying it to the man's eyes, and instructing him to wash in the Pool of Siloam. This miracle not only gave physical sight but also served as a powerful metaphor for spiritual enlightenment, illustrating Jesus as the Light of the World who brings true vision to those in darkness.

When they saw the blind man, they assumed that either he or his parents sinned, causing the blindness. But Jesus said neither sinned (vs. 3) but that the works of God should be revealed in him. He goes on to say in verses 4-5, "I must work the works of Him who sent Me while it is day, the night is coming when no one can work. As long as I am in the world, I am the light of the world."

Night refers to darkness, where it is impossible to work without light. When we accept Jesus as our Savior, we carry the Light of the world in us. When we share our faith, we share the Light with others, bringing them out of the dark and healing their spiritual blindness.

Raising the Dead

Perhaps the most awe-inspiring of Jesus' healing miracles are those in which he raises individuals from the dead. The accounts of raising Jairus' daughter, the widow's son at Nain, and Lazarus after four days in the tomb demonstrate Jesus' authority over life and death. These miracles foreshadow his own resurrection and affirm his power to grant eternal life, offering hope and comfort to those who believe in him.

In John 11, the details of Lazarus's death and resurrection from the dead are told. After being told his friend was sick, Jesus waited before going to him. In verses 9-10, he tells the disciples again that if anyone walks in the day, he does not stumble because he sees the light of the world. But if he walks in the night, he stumbles, because the light is not in him. He tells them that Lazarus is dead, yet He is glad for their sake (the disciples) that He was not there that they may believe.

When they arrive at Bethany, Lazarus has been dead for four days. Martha comes out to meet Him and declares her faith in Jesus's ability and that whatever Jesus asks God, God will give Him. And Jesus tells her that her brother will rise. Jesus could have come sooner to heal him before he died, but he said it was better that he didn't so they would believe. With Lazarus being dead for four days, it would require a miracle no one had ever seen for him to be raised from the dead.

When Jesus told them to take away the stone, Martha said there would be a stench, but Jesus replied, "Did I not say to you that if you would believe, you would see the glory of God?" And he commanded with a loud voice, "Lazarus, come forth!" And Lazarus came out wrapped in the graveclothes. Jesus told them, "loose him, and let him go." This was a reflection that he was no longer bound by death physically or spiritually. And in all of this, God was glorified. And many who were there and saw what Jesus did believed in Him.

Calming the Storm Luke 8:22-25

One evening, as Jesus and his disciples were crossing the Sea of Galilee, a furious storm arose, threatening to capsize their boat. While the disciples panicked, Jesus slept peacefully. When they woke him, pleading for help, Jesus rebuked the wind and waves, and immediately the storm ceased and there was calm. He only asked them, "Where is your faith?" This miracle not only demonstrated his mastery over the natural elements but also revealed His God-given authority and the peace he brings in the midst of chaos.

Feeding the 5,000

Matthew 14:13-21, Mark 6:30-44, Luke 9:10-17, John 6:1-14

In a remote area, a large crowd gathered to hear Jesus teach. When it was late, the disciples told Jesus to send the people away so they could get food. Jesus and the disciples had no food to feed the people, yet Jesus told the disciples to give them something to eat. They found a young boy with five barley loaves of bread and two fish (John 6:9). Jesus gave thanks and distributed the food to the crowd. Miraculously, all 5,000 men, plus women and children, ate and were satisfied, with twelve baskets of leftovers collected. This miracle of multiplication shows Jesus' compassion for physical needs and his ability to provide abundantly, reinforcing his identity as the Bread of Life who satisfies spiritual hunger.

Walking on Water Matthew 14:22-33

During another crossing of the Sea of Galilee, Jesus' disciples found themselves struggling against a strong wind. Jesus approached them, walking on the water. Terrified, the disciples thought he was a ghost, but Jesus reassured them, "Take courage! It is I. Don't be afraid." Peter, seeking confirmation, asked to walk on the water towards Jesus. As Peter stepped out of the boat and walked, however when he took his eyes off of Jesus, he became fearful and began to sink, but Jesus immediately reached out and saved him. This miracle illustrated Jesus' power over nature and the importance of faith and trust in him.

Lessons from the Miracles – Compassion and Empathy

Jesus' miracles were motivated by deep compassion and empathy for those in need. His willingness to heal, provide, and intervene in dire circumstances demonstrated God's love and care for humanity. These acts of compassion challenge believers to embody similar love and kindness in their own lives, reaching out to help others in tangible ways. Asking yourself what would Jesus do in this situation helps you to do and be more like Jesus when you respond based on what you have read about him.

Faith and Doubt

The miracles of Jesus often highlighted the tension between faith and doubt. Many miracles were performed in response to expressions of faith, as seen in the healing of the centurion's servant and the woman with the issue of blood. Conversely, instances like Peter sinking while walking on water underscore the consequences of doubt. Jesus' miracles encourage believers to cultivate unwavering faith and trust in God's power and goodness.

Divine Nature and Power

Jesus's miracles unmistakably point to his divine nature and authority. By healing the sick, controlling nature, and raising the dead, Jesus revealed his identity as the Son of God with power over all creation. These miracles serve as signs that authenticate his message and mission, inviting believers to recognize and worship him as their Lord and Savior.

Making it Personal – Reflective Questions

1. How can I demonstrate compassion and empathy in my daily interactions?

2. In what areas of my life do I need to cultivate greater faith and trust in God?

3. How do the miracles of Jesus deepen my understanding of his divine nature and power?

4. What steps can I take to bring hope and healing to those around me?

The miracles of Jesus offer profound insights into his character and mission. Through healing the sick, controlling nature, and raising the dead, Jesus demonstrated his compassion, highlighted the importance of faith, and revealed his divine authority. Reflecting on these miracles encourages believers to deepen their faith, embody Christ-like compassion, and trust in the power of God to work in and through their lives. By applying the lessons from Jesus' miracles, believers can experience and share the transformative power of God's love.

The Teachings of Jesus

"And Jesus went about all Galilee, teaching in their synagogues, preaching the gospel of the kingdom, and healing all kinds of sickness and all kinds of disease among the people." Matthew 4:23

The Beatitudes

The Sermon on the Mount begins with the Beatitudes, a series of blessings that describe the attitudes and characteristics of those who are truly blessed by God. Jesus declared, "Blessed are the poor in spirit, for theirs is the kingdom of heaven. Blessed are those who mourn, for they will be comforted. Blessed are the meek, for they will inherit the earth." These statements by Jesus highlight values such as humility, mercy, and purity of heart, challenging conventional views of happiness and success. The Beatitudes present a radical vision of God's kingdom, where the disregarded and oppressed can find hope and promise.

Go the Second Mile

In Matthew 5:38-42, Jesus teaches the principle of "Go the Second Mile," challenging the conventional wisdom of retaliation and justice. He instructs, "You have heard that it was said, 'Eye for eye, and tooth for tooth.' But I tell you, do not resist an evil person. If anyone slaps you on the right cheek, turn to them the other cheek also. And if anyone wants to sue you and take your shirt, hand over your coat as well. If anyone forces you to go one mile, go with them two miles." This teaching calls for radical generosity and non-retaliation, urging believers to respond to wrongs with grace and kindness rather than seeking revenge. By going beyond what is required or expected, followers of Jesus demonstrate a profound love and commitment to peace, embodying the selfless nature of Christ.

Teachings on Love, Anger, and Forgiveness

Jesus' teachings on love, anger, and forgiveness are central to the Sermon on the Mount. He instructed his followers to love their enemies and pray for those who persecute them, demonstrating a love that transcends human inclination and reflects God's unconditional love. Jesus also addressed the destructive power of anger, equating it with murder in the eyes of God, and called for reconciliation and peacemaking. Additionally, he emphasized the importance of forgiveness, teaching that just as God forgives our sins, we must also forgive others.

Core Principles and Values – The Greatest Commandment

When asked about the greatest commandment in the Law, Jesus summarized the entirety of the Law and the Prophets with two commandments: "Love the Lord your God with all your heart and with all your soul and with all your mind," and "Love your neighbor as yourself." These commandments encapsulate the core of Jesus' teachings, highlighting the priority of love in a relationship with God and in interactions with others.

Love Your Enemies

One of Jesus' most challenging teachings is the call to love one's enemies. In a society where retaliation and retribution were common, Jesus' command to love, bless, and pray for enemies was revolutionary. This principle underscores the transformative power of love and the call to reflect God's perfect love, which extends even to those who oppose and harm us. What some refer to as the golden rule, "Therefore, whatever you want me to do to you, do also to them" (Matthew 7:12), is a summary of Jesus' ethical teaching. This principle, found in the Sermon on the Mount, encourages proactive kindness and empathy, building a spirit of mutual respect and consideration. It calls believers to treat others with the same compassion and fairness they desire for themselves.

Charity and Almsgiving

Jesus emphasized the importance of charity and almsgiving, teaching that acts of kindness and generosity should be done discreetly and sincerely, without seeking public recognition. He highlighted the spiritual value of giving to those in need, encouraging believers to store treasures in heaven rather than seeking earthly rewards.

Honesty and Integrity

In his teachings, Jesus stressed the importance of honesty and integrity. He instructed his followers to let their "yes" be "yes," and their "no" be "no," emphasizing the need for straightforward and truthful communication. Jesus condemned hypocrisy and urged his disciples to live authentically, with their actions aligning with their professed beliefs.

Humility and Servanthood

Jesus modeled and taught humility and servanthood, challenging societal norms that valued status and power. He taught that true greatness is found in serving others, saying, "Whoever wants to become great among you must be your servant." Jesus demonstrated this principle by washing his disciples' feet and ultimately laying down his life for humanity.

Living Out the Teachings – Practical Applications in Daily Life

Living out Jesus' teachings involves integrating his principles into everyday life. This includes practicing love and forgiveness, showing compassion and generosity, and maintaining honesty and integrity in all dealings. Believers are called to embody the values of the kingdom of God in their relationships, work, and community involvement.

Examples from the Early Church

The early church provides numerous examples of how Jesus' teachings were lived out. The believers shared their possessions, cared for the needy, and devoted themselves to prayer and the apostles' teaching. Their communal life reflected the principles of love, unity, and service that Jesus taught, and their witness had a profound impact on the surrounding society.

Modern-Day Relevance and Practice

Jesus' teachings remain relevant today, offering guidance for ethical and moral living in a complex world. Believers are called to apply these principles in contemporary contexts, such as promoting social justice, practicing environmental stewardship, and advocating for peace and reconciliation. The timeless wisdom of Jesus' teachings continues to inspire and challenge individuals and communities to reflect God's love and justice in the world.

Making it Personal – Reflective Questions

1. How can I make the principles of the Beatitudes a part of my daily life?

2. In what ways can I deepen my prayer life and align it with the Lord's Prayer?

3. In what areas of my life do I need to practice love and forgiveness, even towards those who may have wronged me?

4. What steps can I take to live out the core principles and values taught by Jesus in my interactions with others?

The teachings of Jesus offer powerful insights into living a life that reflects God's love and righteousness. From the Sermon on the Mount to his instructions and core principles, Jesus' words challenge and inspire believers to live with compassion, integrity, and humility. By applying these teachings in daily life, believers can contribute to a more just and loving world, living the transformative power of the gospel. Reflecting on these teachings encourages personal growth and a deeper commitment to following Jesus' example in every aspect of our lives.

The Parables of Jesus

He answered and said to them, "Because it has been given to you to know the mysteries of the kingdom of heaven, but to them it has not been given." Matthew 13:11

What is a Parable?

A parable is a simple story used to illustrate a moral or spiritual lesson, often told by Jesus to convey deeper truths about the kingdom of God. Unlike straightforward teaching, parables engage the listener's imagination and emotions, making complex concepts more relatable and memorable. Jesus used everyday scenarios and characters familiar to his audience, such as farmers, shepherds, and laborers, to communicate profound spiritual truths in an accessible way.

Understanding the Context

Understanding the context of parables is important for grasping their full meaning. Jesus' audience lived in an agrarian or agricultural society, so many parables feature agricultural themes and practices. Additionally, the listeners' cultural and religious backgrounds influenced how they interpreted these stories. Recognizing the historical and social setting helps modern readers appreciate the original impact of the parables and their relevance to contemporary life.

Engaging the Listener

Parables were designed to engage listeners, prompting them to reflect and discover the underlying message. Jesus often concluded his parables with a challenge or a thought-provoking statement, encouraging his audience to ponder the deeper significance. This method not only made the teachings memorable but also invited personal reflection and self-examination.

The Prodigal Son

The Parable of the Prodigal Son (Luke 15:11-32) tells the story of a young man who demands his inheritance, leaves home, and squanders his wealth in reckless living. When he finds himself broke and feeding pigs, he decides to return to his father and seek forgiveness. His father, filled with compassion, runs to meet him, forgives him, and celebrates his return. This parable illustrates themes of repentance, forgiveness, and the boundless love of God the Father.

Luke 15:11-24 NKJV "Then He said: "A certain man had two sons. And the younger of them said to his father, 'Father, give me the portion of goods that falls to me.' So he divided to them his livelihood. And not many days after, the younger son gathered all together, journeyed to a far country, and there wasted his possessions with prodigal living. But when he had spent all, there arose a severe famine in that land, and he began to be in want. Then he went and joined himself to a citizen of that country, and he sent him into his fields to feed swine. And he would gladly have filled his stomach with the pods that the swine ate, and no one gave him anything. But when he came to himself, he said, 'How many of my father's hired servants have bread enough and to spare, and I perish with hunger! I will arise and go to my father, and will say to him, "Father, I have sinned against heaven and before you, and I am no longer worthy to be called your son. Make me like one of your hired servants."'

"And he arose and came to his father. But when he was still a great way off, his father saw him and had compassion and ran and fell on his neck and kissed him. And the son said to him, 'Father, I have sinned against heaven and in your sight and am no longer worthy to be called your son.' But the father said to his servants, 'Bring out the best robe and put it on him and put a ring on his hand and sandals on his feet. And bring the fatted calf here and kill it, and let us eat and be merry; for this, my son was dead and is alive again; he was lost and is found.' And they began to be merry."

The Good Samaritan

The Parable of the Good Samaritan (Luke 10:25-37) describes a man who is beaten and left for dead on the roadside. Several people pass by without helping, but a Samaritan, considered an outsider and enemy by the Jews, stops to assist. He cares for the injured man and ensures his recovery. This parable highlights the importance of loving one's neighbor and showing mercy, regardless of social or ethnic boundaries.

Luke 10:25-37 NKJV And behold, a certain lawyer stood up and tested Him, saying, "Teacher, what shall I do to inherit eternal life?" He said to him, "What is written in the law? What is your reading of it?" So he answered and said, "'You shall love the Lord your God with all your heart, with all your soul, with all your strength, and with all your mind,' and 'your neighbor as yourself.'" And He said to him, "You have answered rightly; do this and you will live." But he, wanting to justify himself, said to Jesus, "And who is my neighbor?" Then Jesus answered and said: "A certain man went down from Jerusalem to Jericho, and fell among thieves, who stripped him of his clothing, wounded him, and departed, leaving him half dead.

Now by chance a certain priest came down that road. And when he saw him, he passed by on the other side. Likewise a Levite, when he arrived at the place, came and looked, and passed by on the other side. But a certain Samaritan, as he journeyed, came where he was. And when he saw him, he had compassion. So he went to him and bandaged his wounds, pouring on oil and wine; and he set him on his own animal, brought him to an inn, and took care of him. On the next day, when he departed, he took out two denarii, gave them to the innkeeper, and said to him, 'Take care of him; and whatever more you spend, when I come again, I will repay you.' So which of these three do you think was neighbor to him who fell among the thieves?" And he said, "He who showed mercy on him." Then Jesus said to him, "Go and do likewise."

The Sower

In the Parable of the Sower (Matthew 13:1-23), Jesus describes a farmer who sows seeds on different types of soil. Some seeds fall on the path and are eaten by birds, others on rocky ground where they wither, some among thorns that choke them, and some on good soil where they produce a bountiful harvest. This parable illustrates the different responses to the message of the kingdom of God, emphasizing the importance of a receptive and faithful heart.

Matthew 13:3-9 NKJV Then He spoke many things to them in parables, saying: "Behold, a sower went out to sow. And as he sowed, some seed fell by the wayside; and the birds came and devoured them. Some fell on stony places, where they did not have much earth; and they immediately sprang up because they had no depth of earth. But when the sun was up they were scorched, and because they had no root they withered away. And some fell among thorns, and the thorns sprang up and choked them. But others fell on good ground and yielded a crop: some a hundredfold, some sixty, some thirty. He who has ears to hear, let him hear!"

Unpacking the Messages – Repentance and Forgiveness

Many parables, such as the Prodigal Son, emphasize the themes of repentance and forgiveness. These stories reveal God's willingness to forgive those who turn back to Him with a humble heart. They underscore the transformative power of repentance and the joy that accompanies reconciliation with God.

Loving Your Neighbor

The parable of the Good Samaritan teaches that love and compassion should extend to all people, regardless of social divisions. It challenges listeners to show mercy and kindness, reflecting God's love in their interactions with others. This parable calls for an active, inclusive love that transcends prejudices and barriers.

Seeds of Faith

The Parable of the Sower highlights the varying responses to the gospel message. It encourages self-examination and the cultivation of a receptive heart, ready to embrace and nurture God's word. This parable teaches that faith requires depth, perseverance, and an openness to God's transformative work.

Making it Personal – Reflective Questions

1. In what ways can I show forgiveness and seek reconciliation in my relationships?

2. How can I demonstrate love and compassion to those who are different from me?

3. What steps can I take to prepare my heart to receive, embrace, and truly live out God's word?

4. How do the parables of Jesus challenge and inspire me in my daily life?

The parables of Jesus are timeless stories used to convey profound spiritual truths through simple, relatable narratives. They challenge listeners to reflect on their own lives, attitudes, and relationships, encouraging growth in faith and love. By unpacking the messages of repentance, forgiveness, love for one's neighbor, and the importance of a receptive heart, the parables offer valuable lessons for living out the principles of the kingdom of God. Reflecting on these parables and applying their teachings can lead to a deeper, more transformative relationship with God and others.

Last Days and The Crucifixion

"On the last day, that great day of the feast, Jesus stood and cried out, saying, "If anyone thirsts, let him come to Me and drink. He who believes in Me, as the Scripture has said, out of his heart will flow rivers of living water." John 7:37-38

Breaking Bread

The Last Supper was a significant event where Jesus shared a final meal with his disciples before his crucifixion. During this meal, Jesus took bread, gave thanks, broke it, and gave it to his disciples, saying, "This is my body given for you; do this in remembrance of me." He then took a cup, gave thanks, and offered it to them, saying, "This cup is the new covenant in my blood, which is poured out for you." This act of breaking bread and sharing the cup established a new covenant and symbolized Jesus' impending sacrifice for the salvation of humanity.

Predicting Betrayal

During the Last Supper, Jesus made a startling prediction that one of his disciples would betray him. This revelation caused great distress among the disciples, who began to question who among them would commit such a deed. Jesus identified Judas Iscariot as the betrayer, fulfilling the prophecy and setting the stage for the events that would lead to his arrest and crucifixion. This moment highlighted the betrayal and the fulfillment of God's redemptive plan through Jesus' suffering.

Teaching about Communion

During the Last Supper, Jesus shared an important lesson with his disciples about something called communion. He knew that he was about to give his life for our sins, and he wanted to help his disciples—and all of us—understand the great love and sacrifice he was about to make.

Jesus took some bread, broke it, and gave it to his disciples, saying, "This is my body." He wanted them to remember that his body would soon be hurt and bruised for us. The Bible tells us in Isaiah 53:5 and 1 Peter 2:24 that when Jesus was beaten, it was to bring us healing and peace.

Then, Jesus took a cup of wine and told them, "This is my blood." The wine was a symbol of his blood, which he would shed on the cross to wash away our sins and bring us forgiveness. By doing this, Jesus opened the door for us to be truly forgiven and to have a close relationship with God.

Jesus asked his disciples to keep practicing this special meal, called communion, so that every time they broke bread and drank from the cup, they would remember the incredible price he paid out of love for us. Today, when we take communion, it's a way of connecting with Jesus, remembering his sacrifice, and celebrating the forgiveness and healing he offers to all who believe in him

Arrest in Gethsemane – The Trial

After the Last Supper, Jesus and his disciples went to the Garden of Gethsemane to pray. Jesus, knowing what was to come, prayed fervently, seeking strength and submitting to God's will. It was here that Judas Iscariot arrived with a group of soldiers and officials sent by the chief priests and Pharisees. Judas identified Jesus with a kiss, leading to his arrest. Despite the chaos and the disciples' initial attempt to defend him, Jesus surrendered peacefully, demonstrating his obedience to God's plan.

Before the Sanhedrin

Following his arrest, Jesus was taken to the house of the high priest and brought before the Sanhedrin, the Jewish council. There, he faced false accusations and was subjected to an unjust trial. The Sanhedrin sought to find grounds to condemn him to death, but their testimonies were inconsistent. When asked directly if he was the Messiah, the Son of God, Jesus affirmed his identity, which the council deemed blasphemous. This led to their decision to hand him over to the Roman authorities for execution.

Pontius Pilate's Role

Jesus was then brought before Pontius Pilate, the Roman governor, as the Jewish leaders lacked the authority to execute him. Pilate questioned Jesus and found no basis for a charge deserving of death. However, under pressure from the crowd and the Jewish leaders, who demanded Jesus' crucifixion, Pilate attempted to appease them by offering to release a prisoner, as was the custom during Passover. The crowd chose Barabbas, a known criminal, over Jesus. Reluctantly, Pilate handed Jesus over to be crucified, symbolically washing his hands to absolve himself of responsibility.

Carrying the Cross

As Jesus was led away to be crucified, he carried his own cross. But because he had been severely beaten, the weight of the cross became too much for him to bear alone. Seeing his struggle, the soldiers forced a man named Simon of Cyrene to help carry the cross. Simon's act of carrying the cross for Jesus symbolizes how we can help carry the burdens of others in their time of need. Just as Simon carried the cross for Jesus in his moment of weakness, Jesus carried the much heavier burden of our sins on himself. By taking our sins upon him, Jesus allowed his blood to redeem us, bringing us forgiveness and the hope of eternal life. This journey to Golgotha, marked by suffering and humiliation, powerfully demonstrates Jesus' unwavering commitment to saving us, even at the cost of his own life.

The Crucifixion

At Golgotha, Jesus was nailed to the cross, a method of ex-ecution reserved for the most heinous criminals. Despite the excruciating pain and the mocking of the onlookers, Jesus prayed for his persecutors, saying, "Father, forgive them, for they do not know what they are doing." He was crucified between two criminals, one of whom recognized Jesus' innocence and asked to be remembered in his kingdom. Jesus assured him, "Today, you will be with me in paradise." This act of grace amidst suffering highlighted the profound depth of Jesus' love and mercy.

"It is Finished"

As Jesus hung on the cross, he endured hours of agony. In his final moments, he declared, "It is finished," signifying the completion of his mission to atone for the sins of humanity. With these words, Jesus surrendered his spirit and died. The earth shook, the temple curtain was torn in two from top to bottom, and darkness fell over the land. These supernatural events underscored the significance of Jesus' death and the fulfillment of God's redemptive plan through his sacrifice.

Making it Personal – Reflective Questions

1. How does Jesus' willingness to sacrifice himself for humanity impact my understanding of God's love?

2. How can I show forgiveness and grace, even in difficult situations?

3. How can I participate in and appreciate the practice of communion in my faith community?

4. What steps can I take to live out the humility and obedience exemplified by Jesus during his trial and crucifixion?

The last days and crucifixion of Jesus are central to the Christian faith, embodying the themes of sacrifice, redemption, and divine love. From the Last Supper and the prediction of betrayal to the trial before Pilate and the ultimate act of crucifixion, each event reveals Jesus' unwavering commitment to God's redemptive plan. His death on the cross marked the fulfillment of prophecy and the establishment of a new covenant between God and humanity. Reflecting on these events challenges believers to embrace the depth of God's love, practice forgiveness even when it is hard, and live out the teachings of Jesus in our daily lives.

The Resurrection and Ascension

"Why do you seek the living among the dead? He is not here, but is risen! Remember how He spoke to you when He was still in Galilee," Luke 24:5-6

The Empty Tomb – The Stone is Rolled Away

On the third day after Jesus' crucifixion, early in the morning, some women, including Mary Magdalene, went to the tomb where Jesus had been laid to anoint his body with spices. To their astonishment, they found the large stone that had sealed the tomb rolled away. The tomb was empty, and Jesus' body was nowhere to be found. This event marked the beginning of the most significant event in the Christian faith—the resurrection of Jesus Christ.

Mary Magdalene's Discovery

Mary Magdalene, bewildered and distraught, ran to inform the disciples Peter and John and all who were with them. Then Peter and John rushed to the tomb and confirmed that it was empty, seeing the linen cloths that had wrapped Jesus' body lying there. Mary remained at the tomb, weeping. Two angels appeared to her, asking why she was crying. She responded that they had taken her Lord away. Turning around, she saw Jesus standing there but did not recognize him until he spoke her name. Overwhelmed with joy, Mary Magdalene ran to tell the disciples, "I have seen the Lord!"

Jesus Appears to the Disciples

That evening, Jesus appeared to his disciples as they were gathered behind locked doors, fearful of the Jewish authorities. He greeted them with peace and showed them his hands and side, proving that he was indeed the risen Lord. The disciples were overjoyed, and Jesus breathed on them, saying, "Receive the Holy Spirit." His appearance transformed their fear into faith and prepared them for the mission ahead.

Doubting Thomas

One of the disciples, Thomas, was not present when Jesus appeared to the others. When told of Jesus' resurrection, he expressed doubt, declaring that he would not believe unless he saw and touched Jesus' wounds. After eight days, Jesus appeared again and invited Thomas to touch his wounds. Thomas, overcome with belief, exclaimed, "My Lord and my God!" Jesus responded, "Because you have seen me, you have believed; blessed are those who have not seen and yet have believed." This encounter emphasizes the importance of faith and the reality of Jesus' resurrection.

Breakfast on the Beach

After his resurrection, Jesus appeared to his disciples by the Sea of Tiberias. The disciples had been fishing all night without catching anything. As dawn broke, Jesus stood on the shore, though they didn't recognize him at first. He called out to them and told them to cast their net on the right side of the boat. When they did, they caught so many fish that they could hardly haul in the net. Realizing it was Jesus, Peter, who had previously denied knowing Jesus three times, was overwhelmed with emotion. He jumped into the water to reach Jesus as quickly as possible.

When they all gathered on the shore, Jesus had prepared breakfast for them and shared a meal with them. After the meal, Jesus took the opportunity to restore Peter, who was likely still burdened with guilt for his earlier denial. Just as Peter had denied him three times, Jesus asked Peter three times, "Do you love me?" Each time Peter affirmed his love, Jesus responded by giving him a task: "Feed my sheep." Through this, Jesus not only forgave Peter but also reaffirmed his role in leading and caring for others, showing that despite our mistakes, we can be restored and given a purpose in God's plan.

The Great Commission

Before his ascension, Jesus gathered his disciples and gave them the Great Commission. He instructed them to go and make disciples of all nations, baptizing them and teaching them to obey all his commands. Jesus assured them of his presence, saying, "Surely I am with you always, to the very end of the age." Matthew 28:20 This commission empowered the disciples to spread the gospel and established the foundation for the global Christian mission.

Ascending to Heaven -The Final Blessing

Jesus led his disciples to the vicinity of Bethany, where he lifted his hands and blessed them. This final blessing was a gesture of his ongoing love and assurance of God's favor upon them. It also signified the completion of his earthly ministry and the beginning of their mission to continue his work.

As Jesus was blessing his disciples, he was taken up into heaven. The disciples watched in awe as he ascended until a cloud hid him from their sight. Two angels appeared, assuring them that Jesus would return in the same way he had ascended. This event confirmed Jesus' divine nature and his place at the right hand of God, promising his eventual return. Acts 1:9-11

Waiting for His Return

After Jesus' ascension, the disciples returned to Jerusalem with great joy. They gathered together in prayer and anticipation, awaiting the coming of the Holy Spirit as Jesus had promised. This period of waiting was marked by faith and expectation as they prepared to carry out the mission entrusted to them.

Making it Personal – Reflective Questions

1. How does the resurrection of Jesus impact my understanding of life and death?

2. How can I strengthen my faith, especially when faced with doubt like Thomas?

3. How can I live out the Great Commission in my daily life and interactions with others?

4. What steps can I take to remain hopeful and faithful as I await Jesus' return?

The resurrection and ascension of Jesus Christ are foundational events in the Christian faith, confirming his victory over death and his divine authority. From the discovery of the empty tomb to his appearances to the disciples and his ascension into heaven, these events affirm the reality of the resurrection and the promise of eternal life. Jesus' teachings and final instructions challenge believers to live out their faith with conviction, spreading the message of hope and salvation. Reflecting on these events encourages a deeper commitment to follow Jesus and share his love with the world.

To Know Him is to Love Him

Recap of the Journey

Throughout this book, we have explored the profound and transformative journey of Jesus Christ, from his miraculous birth to his ascension into heaven. We began by looking at the humble circumstances of his birth in Bethlehem, followed by his formative years in Nazareth, where he grew in wisdom and stature. We looked at the beginning of his ministry, marked by his baptism, temptation in the wilderness, and the calling of his first disciples.

Jesus' teachings, captured in the Sermon on the Mount, his core principles of love and forgiveness, and his ethical instructions, have provided us with timeless guidance. His parables and miracles demonstrated his compassion, divine power, and the call to faith. We also reflected on his last days, including the Last Supper, his trial, and crucifixion, culminating in his victorious resurrection and ascension.

Through these events and teachings, we have learned valuable lessons about humility, obedience, faith, love, and the power of God's grace. We have seen how Jesus' life was a perfect example of living in alignment with God's will, offering us a model to emulate in our own lives.

Lessons Learned

The journey of exploring Jesus' life teaches us several key lessons:

1. **Faith and Trust in God**: Jesus' unwavering faith, from his baptism to his crucifixion, shows us the importance of trusting God's plan, even in difficult times.

2. **Compassion and Empathy**: His miracles and teachings emphasize the need for compassion and empathy towards others, encouraging us to act with kindness and love.

3. **Humility and Service**: Jesus' humble birth, life, and his ultimate sacrifice highlight the value of humility and serving others selflessly.

4. **Forgiveness and Reconciliation**: His teachings and actions, especially on the cross, underscore the power of forgiveness and the necessity of reconciling with others.

These lessons are not just historical insights but practical guidelines for our moral and spiritual growth, helping us to live more Christ-like lives.

Applying Jesus' Teachings Today – Acts of Kindness

One of the simplest ways to live like Jesus is through acts of kindness. Whether it's helping a friend in need, sharing with those who have less, or simply offering a kind word, these small actions reflect Jesus' love and compassion. Kids can practice kindness daily by being considerate and helpful to their family, friends, and even strangers when it is safe.

Being Respectful and Loving

Jesus taught us to love our neighbors as ourselves and to treat others with respect. This means listening to others, valuing their opinions, and showing respect to everyone, regardless of differences. Kids can apply this by being respectful to their parents, teachers, and peers and by standing up against bullying and unfair treatment.

Future Bible Studies

The journey through Jesus' life is just the beginning of exploring the rich and profound teachings of the Bible. I encourage you to continue reading and studying the scriptures, both individually and with others. Each passage holds deeper insights and lessons that can guide you in your faith journey.

Prayers and Reflection

Prayer is a powerful way to connect with God and reflect on His teachings. I encourage you to make prayer a regular part of your life, seeking God's guidance, expressing gratitude, and asking for strength to live according to His will. Reflecting on

Jesus's life through prayer can deepen your understanding and commitment to following Him.

Final Thoughts

As we conclude this exploration of Jesus' life, remember that the journey of faith is ongoing. Each day is an opportunity to grow closer to God, to live out the teachings of Jesus, and to make a positive impact in the world. By embracing the lessons we have learned and applying them in our daily lives, we can reflect the light of Christ and inspire others to do the same.

May you continue to seek God's wisdom, live with compassion and love, and grow in your faith. The Bible is a treasure trove of knowledge, guidance, and inspiration—keep exploring, praying, and reflecting, and may your journey with Jesus be filled with blessings and spiritual growth.

A Prayer of Salvation

As we conclude our journey through the life of Jesus, it's important to reflect on the love and sacrifice that Jesus made for each one of us. If you haven't yet invited Jesus into your heart to be your Lord and Savior, now is a perfect time to do so. Jesus loves you deeply and wants to have a close relationship with you. He has already paid the price for your sins, and all you need to do is accept his gift of salvation.

Let's pray together:

Prayer of Salvation:

"Dear Jesus,

I know that I have made mistakes and sinned against You. I believe that You died on the cross to take away my sins and that You rose from the dead to give me new life. I ask You to come into my heart and be my Lord and Savior. Please forgive me for all my sins and help me to live for You from this day forward. I give my life to You and trust You with my future. Thank You for Your love, forgiveness, and the promise of eternal life. Amen."

If you prayed this prayer and truly meant it, you have just made the most important decision of your life. Jesus is now in your heart, and you are a part of God's family!

What to Do Next:

1. **Tell Someone:** It's important to share your decision with others. Let your family, friends, or someone you trust know that you have accepted Jesus as your Savior. This is a big step, and sharing it helps strengthen your commitment.

2. **Baptism:** If you are part of a church, talk to your pastor or church leaders about getting baptized. Baptism is a way to publicly show your faith and commitment to Jesus. It's a powerful symbol of dying to your old life and being raised to new life in Christ.

3. **Stay Connected:** Continue to explore the Bible and learn more about Jesus. Stay connected with your church and other believers who can encourage and support you in your faith journey.

Congratulations on your decision to follow Jesus! Remember, He is always with you, and His love for you will never change. Keep seeking Him, growing in your faith, and sharing His love with others. Your journey with Jesus has only just begun, and it's filled with hope, joy, and purpose.

ACTS Prayer Model

Adoration – Glorify God with Praises for Who He is

Confession – Confessing our sins and asking for forgiveness

Thanksgiving – Give thanks for what God is doing in your life

Supplication – Make the request for God's help

What Does the Prayer Look Like

Adoration

God, you are so wonderful. You created me and everything I see around me in heaven and earth.

Confession

Forgive me for _My Sins_. I know it didn't please you and I need your help to change.

Thanksgiving

Thank you for helping me to make it right through Your mercy and grace. Thank you for guiding and directing my steps in everything I do.

Supplication

Help me today to make the right choices. Help me to stay close to You and sensitive to Your leading.

Praying to God is simple; it is like talking to your best friend. Just like you tell your best friend how good they did on something and how much you appreciate them, that is like adoration. It is a great way to open a conversation. If you did something that hurt their feelings, wouldn't you want to apologize to make things right with them? Being thankful and having an attitude of gratitude makes the atmosphere pleasant. And when you have a good relationship with your friend, it always seems a little easier to ask them for help when you need it. It is the same with God.

Adventures in Scriptures

Other Books in the Series

If you enjoyed and found inspiration reading Exploring The Life of Jesus, you won't want to miss the other captivating volumes in our series. Each book takes a deeper look into key biblical themes and virtues, offering a treasure trove of wisdom and guidance for your spiritual journey. From "Exploring the Fruit of the Spirit" to the uplifting lessons in "Exploring the Parable Teachings of Jesus," our series is designed to nurture your soul, strengthen your faith, and light your path. Let's set out on this continuing adventure to discover more about love, grace, and the transformative power of faith. Let each page turned be a step closer to a deeper understanding and a fuller heart. Join us as we explore the riches of God's word and the endless beauty it holds for our lives.

1. Exploring the Fruit of the Spirit

2. Exploring The Full Armor of God

3. Exploring the Parable Teachings of Jesus

4. Exploring the Great Men of the Bible

5. Exploring the Great Women of the Bible

6. Exploring the Life of Jesus

We hope "Exploring the Life of Jesus" has been a source of inspiration and growth on your spiritual journey. If this book has touched your heart, illuminated your path, or brought new insights into your life, we'd be honored if you would share your experience. Please take a moment to leave a review. Your feedback not only supports our work but also guides others in their quest for spiritual enrichment. Share how "Exploring The Life of Jesus" has blessed you with a better understanding of who Jesus is and what he did in his life and ministry, so that it may inspire others on this journey of faith. Leave your review today and help spread the seeds of faith and knowledge. Thank you for being a part of our community and for your invaluable contribution to this shared journey.

References

- ACTS Prayer Model https://himpublications.com/blog/acts-prayer-model/

Biblical References Notices

NKJV

Scripture taken from the New King James Version®. Copyright © 1982 by Thomas Nelson. Used <u>by</u> permission. All rights reserved. All Scripture quotations

NIV

Scripture quotations marked (NIV) are taken from the Holy Bible, New International Version®, NIV®. Copyright © 1973, 1978, 1984, 2011 by Biblica, Inc.™ Used by permission of Zondervan. All rights reserved worldwide. www.zondervan.comThe "NIV" and "New International Version" are trademarks registered in the United States Patent and Trademark Office by Biblica, Inc.™

NLT

Scripture quotations marked (NLT) are taken from the Holy Bible, New Living Translation, copyright ©1996, 2004, 2015 by Tyndale House Foundation. Used by permission of Tyndale House Publishers, Carol Stream, Illinois 60188. All rights reserved.

9 798348 542474